Louise Margaret Granahan

Children's Books that Nurture the Spirit

CHOOSING AND USING THE BEST

Northstone

Editors: Dianne Greenslade and Michael Schwartzentruber
Cover and interior design: Margaret Kyle

Cover artwork: *Story Tree* by Ansgar Holmberg, CSJ.
Copyright © Ansgar Holmberg, CSJ. Used with permission.

All quotations from the Bible are from the *New Revised Standard Version*, copyright © 1989 by the Division of Christian Education of the National Council of Churches of Christ in the United States of America, and are used by permission. All rights reserved.

Northstone Publishing acknowledges the financial support of the Government of Canada through the Book Publishing Industry Development Program for its publishing activities.

Northstone Publishing is an imprint of Wood Lake Books Inc., an employee-owned company, and is committed to caring for the environment and all creation. Northstone recycles and reuses and encourages readers to do the same. Resources are printed on recycled paper and more environmentally friendly groundwood papers (newsprint), whenever possible. The trees used are replaced through donations to the Scoutrees For Canada Program. A portion of all profit is donated to charitable organizations.

National Library of Canada Cataloguing in Publication Data
Granahan, Louise Margaret, 1964 –
Children's books that nurture the spirit: choosing and using the best / Louise Margaret Granahan
Includes bibliographical references and index.
ISBN 1-896836-51-8
1. Children's literature – Bibliography. 2. Children – Books and reading. 3. Best books –
Children's literature. 4. Christian literature for children – Bibliography. I. Title.
Z1037.G73 2003   011.62   C2003-910000-6

Published by Northstone Publishing,
an imprint of Wood Lake Books Inc.
Kelowna, British Columbia, Canada
www.joinhands.com

Printing 10 9 8 7 6 5 4 3 2 1

Printed in Canada at
Transcontinental Printing

Of making many books, there is no end...
ECCLESIASTES 12:12B

Acknowledgments

Many thanks to Dianne Greenslade, my editor, and Mike Schwartzentruber, my editor at Wood Lake Books/Northstone, for their support and good humor. I would like to thank the Bellefair community for their support and a quiet place to work. The Reverend Doctor Karen A. Hamilton shared with me her knowledge and expertise about the Time with the Children, and Carol Matas taught me about the importance of Holocaust literature. I would also like to thank Crystal Stuckenbrock, Mary Gilkinson, Sue McNay, and Alexandra Caverly Lowery for their support. Special thanks to Melanie Darroch, my former colleague at Roden Public School, who shared her sons' VeggieTales videos and books with me.

I dedicate this book to my students from
Roden Junior Public School
Secord School
Victoria Park School

Contents

1

Introduction

Train children in the right way,
and when old, they will not stray.

PROVERBS 22:6

My child, give me your heart,
and let your eyes observe my ways.

PROVERBS 23:26

I rarely take the subway in Toronto, but when I do, I usually embarrass myself. You see, I have two problems, and they both relate to children's books. I spend far too much money on children's books, and when I am riding the subway home from a downtown book shopping trip, I often like to read my purchases. If the sight of a well-dressed, professional woman in her 30s reading picture books on a subway doesn't bring strange looks, then our society is truly jaded.

My other subway reading problem is one shared by many teachers. I have been an elementary school teacher in Toronto's inner city for 13 years now. I'm sure that at least six of those years have been spent reading to my students. When I get on the subway and take a trashy novel out of my bag, I must constantly resist the urge to hold it in my right hand at shoulder level, craning my neck to read it so everyone can see the pictures.

So I usually ride my bike, or walk or drive where I need to go, and I can tell you that reading while doing those things is not any easier than taking the subway! What this all comes down to is that I have a passion for children's books. I love reading to my students and sharing with them the worlds of possibility that exist in books. I love the artwork that is so accessible in books, and the words that sing their beauty.

The world of Christian children's literature is opening up, and more books of excellent quality are being produced than ever before. There is a growing awareness of the need for children to have books that express their faith and spirituality, as well as the need for parents, teachers, and other caregivers to share their values and beliefs through literature. Christian children's books are becoming more available and accessible, even through public libraries and mainstream bookstores.

I have read every book I have reviewed for this resource. I have watched every video. I have also watched and read many more that did not warrant inclusion in this book. That does not mean that every book I present is worth buying, reading, or using, but it does mean that each book could be used for certain purposes, depending on the situation, setting, and audience.

In reviewing this literature, I am very aware that I am also seeing through my own personal and cultural contexts. I may have preferences depending on my personal tastes and ideas about what is good and bad. For instance, I generally dislike oil paintings used in children's books because of their heavy feel. I love anything glittery, especially the gold decorations such as those found in Brian Wildsmith's paintings. Because I am so aware of the need for increased use of inclusive language in all settings, I am drawn to literature, especially poetry that uses inclusive language. I dislike triumphalist statements about God or about the necessity for certain beliefs to the exclusion of others. My preferences will certainly influence my reviews, and even though I have tried to stay as objective as possible, I cannot escape my upbringing and current context.

Purpose of the Book

The purpose of this book is to introduce people to quality children's literature for faith development. It is intended to be a resource to help parents, ministers, teachers, grandparents, camp counselors, Christian education directors, and others select literature and understand more about how these books can be used in their various settings. Each chapter also provides ideas for ways to use the literature with children.

My goal is to show the wide variety of books that is available in a number of different genres, and to act as a resource to support Christian education programs. In doing this, I hope to promote children's literature for faith development, and increase its use in churches, schools and homes.

What Is Children's Literature
for Faith Development?

*Good or great literature is most effective in its recognition of the reader's
response in the task of making intelligible those values which give meaning to
life or by which our lives can acquire a story, a sense of constancy, continuity
and unity comprehending more than we immediately desire or deserve.*

(JASPER, 1989, P. 63)

[Ed. note: full citations listed within references at end of chapter.]

Children's literature for faith development covers literature of all types
(books, magazines, videos, film, music, and computer programs) which
supports children on their own spiritual journeys. It may be used to inform,
entertain, empower, educate, enlighten, influence, encourage critical
thinking and questioning, and provide children with a vision of themselves
and others as the children of a loving God. Literature alone cannot achieve
all these goals, but can be an effective teaching and learning tool as well as
an extremely enjoyable and worthwhile experience. This literature comes
from not only Christian sources but represents a number of faith traditions,
including Jewish, Sikh, Muslim, Hindu, and Native spirituality.

This literature is varied, and reflects the variety of beliefs and expressions
of those beliefs. In that expression, it must be noted that the literature
produced reflects the belief system in which it exists. We are all a product of
our culture, faith, race, education, and current circumstances. We are defined
by this context, and this definition will extend into the literature which is
produced by and for us.

The term "literature" is not necessarily used as a value judgment, or as
a means to compare or classify books. Literature here refers to all books,
regardless of merit or lack thereof. There is no time limit on literature. Too
often, literature has been seen as books that have withstood the test of time.
This is particularly immaterial for children's literature. By the time children
have outgrown a book, its staying power has no relevance. There are, of
course, books which continue through many reprints, and are shared and
passed down through the generations, but these are rare.

The purpose of *Children's Books that Nurture the Spirit* is to allow
children to make personal connections. Through story, children are able to
make sense of their world. Jesus taught in parables to enable people to
connect his teaching with their own lives. By connecting with story, children

are able to engage with the lessons being presented in positive and enjoyable ways, allowing readers of various ages to approach the literature at their own levels. Books also provide a wonderful way for people to share their faith in God.

I am not suggesting that these books be the only ones in a child's collection. A balanced collection of books is necessary in personal collections as well as library, classroom, or Sunday school collections. To tip this balance runs the risk of sending messages of exclusion and self-centeredness. Books that are always didactic and preachy can be resented. Every child should have access to a wide variety of books – books which are Christian, mainstream, from many traditions, fiction, non-fiction, poetry, activity based, computer and Internet-linked, old favorites, and new treasures. A balance of materials enables the child to see the world and all its integral parts (family, friends, community, church, school, country) in the literature.

Children develop in many ways – physically, intellectually, socially, spiritually. In each of these modes of development, children need to be nurtured by loving guides who may be parents, teachers, ministers, and friends. The development of a child's faith can be nurtured through family devotions, bedtime prayers, discussions, and the example of positive role models, just to name a few. Story is another way to foster and support a child's faith development. Children can become more familiar with stories they have heard in Sunday school or through reading the Bible. They can find role models in the positive characters in the literature, and can feel empathy for others when they see a different point of view presented.

Why Is This Book Needed?

This book will open the reader to the variety of books that is available on a number of different topics. It will provide leaders with ideas for using the literature and extending the stories. This book will also help people make their own judgments about what to look for in literature by presenting the many wonderful, positive traits of children's literature as well as alerting the reader to cautions about certain topics or language which may be offensive, challenging, or may warrant further discussion.

By grouping the literature into text sets, those using this resource will be able to compare and contrast books on specific topics. This will help people choose books appropriate to the age levels of the children, and will provide information about other aspects of the books such as language or illustration that may attract or deter the reader from using any particular work. The text sets will also cross-reference to other categories where appropriate (e.g., a book on creation may also fit with poetry).

Children's Books that Nurture the Spirit mainly looks at biblically based literature, as in the retellings of beloved Bible stories. It will also look at books that cover issues of social justice such as the environment, interfaith books which present stories from many faith traditions, and inclusive literature which values all of God's children. Other books included look at theological issues such as prayer and the nature of God.

Reading Christian Children's Literature

The way to read Christian children's literature depends on the audience and the setting. There are a number of different ways to read, whether it is in the home, at school, or in church. The reading may have a purpose which is dictated by a leader or agreed on by a group, or it may be entirely self-directed.

First, there is pleasure reading. Many of the books I have reviewed can be read for pure personal enjoyment. Efferent, or informative, reading is done for a specific purpose, such as researching a topic or to gather information about a topic for personal interest. Shared reading can also be pleasure reading or can be used to glean information for response. Reading aloud can and should take place at home, at church, or in the classroom. This happens when an adult reads to the children, as opposed to oral reading, where the children read to a teacher for purposes of assessment. In guided reading, a number of children follow a text, led by the teacher, where the responses are either assigned or agreed on by the group itself.

Fostering a love for reading while fostering a love for God is possible when there is quality literature available; time set aside for reading and time made for sharing; and an atmosphere created to allow for questioning, criticism, and celebration. You cannot force children to share your loves and values, but you can provide them with a positive atmosphere which will allow these to flourish.

David Doake point out in his book *Reading Begins at Birth*, that children who are read to from a very early age usually become readers themselves. He compares this to children who learn to walk and talk when they are developmentally ready. So, too, for reading. We speak to a child even though they may not be able to respond in a way we can understand, but all the while their brains are busy processing the language and making the necessary connections to eventually produce speech. We can read to children before they are able to read themselves, and they will eventually imitate our actions.

Children are also able to understand what is being read to them before they can read the material themselves. There is usually a gap between understanding and the necessary decoding and synthesization ability in reading. That means that you can read a child a book that may be above their reading level, but the child may still be able to understand the concepts presented. Children who are just learning to read can often sit for a chapter book that a parent reads parts of before bedtime if the book is interesting and understandable for the child. The opposite can also be true. A child can love the sound of the language and not be able to understand a poem's metaphors.

The Bible and Christian children's literature are full of concepts that children are not ready for. Again, I stress the need to choose carefully, to know your audience, and to monitor reactions and responses. Many biblical stories are full of horrible actions, prejudice, and injustice. Even though there may be a positive ending, the way in which the evil is depicted can be disturbing.

Responding to Literature

If children are to connect with literature in authentic ways, then they need to respond to it in ways that are truly meaningful to them. How many of us have been forced to write dry, dull book reports as assignments, which ultimately have had little lasting importance or personal significance?

Talk is one of the best ways to respond to literature, but it is important that a proper atmosphere be fostered to allow this talk to flow freely and without judgment. If a child feels that you are looking for certain answers, then they will tailor their responses to fit those expectations. However, if the atmosphere invites a child to "tell us" rather than "tell me," then the responses will be real and inarguable, because they come from the child's personal experience with the literature.

At my school board, students are able to join a book review conference on the board's internal website. Through this conference, the students talk to each other about books they are reading and share information and personal reviews. This offers a wonderful way to get kids to talk to each other about books. It is important, however, to have a moderator for conferences such as this to keep track of and remove any inappropriate messages.

Children or teachers could write book reviews and place them in the church or school newsletter. This is especially good if there is an accessible library of these books for others to borrow. Very young children could dictate their reviews or use a checklist. Drawing may also provide a way for a child to communicate a response to a book before being able to write, or as an alternative response.

I present open-ended ideas in each chapter and leave room for adaptation depending on the size of the group (even if it is a parent and child), the ages of the children, the experience level and knowledge of the children, and the setting of the group. Most important is the ability of the leader to see when something is working and when something is not, and not being afraid to adapt and move on when needed, or to extend and revisit when desired. The comfort level of each leader is extremely important when carrying out the activities. A leader must be absolutely at ease with each activity or it will not go well. There is no harm trying things out before doing them with the children to see if the activity will work.

Response is not always necessary for every reading act. If response is always expected, then reading can be seen as a chore. There must be time set aside in every setting for pleasure reading which allows the reader to simply engage with the book on a personal level with no further expectations.

Cautions

A number of issues should be considered when choosing children's literature. Books that look good on the surface may have hidden messages, either in the text or in the illustrations. Just because a book is found in a Christian bookstore or has a title that sounds Christian, does not mean that the book has been carefully selected or edited.

You are the best judge of the literature, and reading it is the only way to know what it contains. I hope that my reviews will help, but there is no doubt that some people will disagree with my reviews. Follow your heart. Choose books that speak to you. If a book makes you uncomfortable for any reason, move on. You have plenty of books to choose from, so there is no sense settling for anything less than the best.

Just as there are a variety of beliefs and practices within Christianity, there is also a wide variety of books which present those beliefs. Not every "Christian" book will suit each reader. Some books that present a more liberal interpretation of the Bible may not sit well with more fundamentalist believers. In the same vein, books that present a very traditional view of family life and gender roles may not sit well with progressive congregations. There is no right or wrong – just different interpretations and expressions. As Christians, we must value and respect the many ways people find God's truths.

Beware of books that state the message too obviously and overtly. Children resent being preached at. If, however, the points are made through story and example using quality text and illustration such as in *Old Turtle* by Douglas Wood, children can revisit that book at different points in their development and still find truth that they can relate to. These books often appeal to adults, too.

I remember the first time I read a book during the children's time in worship. It was a long weekend, and a sudden summer storm had kept all but 20 people from the service. I was asked if I would still read, even though there were only three children present. I agreed, albeit reluctantly. When I had finished, I walked to the back of the church. I passed a frail gentleman in his 90s. He looked up with his sparkling eyes and smiled at me. As I melted into tears, I knew at that moment the potential timelessness of "children's" literature, which, at its best, transcends all boundaries of age, gender, race, faith, culture, and status.

Looking at Selection

We may select children's literature based on a number of factors: recommendations of others, reading book reviews, previous experience with other books by the same author or illustrator, the theme we are teaching, as well as the look of the cover or illustrations. Availability is also a large factor – whether the books are found in libraries, bookstores, classrooms, or homes. We select books based on the connections we make with them, but until we interact with a book personally, we should not make critical decisions about its merit or worth.

A number of studies have been done on the selection of literature in general. Here are some factors that influence how children choose books (adapted from Maxwell, 1978; Ross, 1979; and Wendelin and Zinck, 1983).

1. a friend's recommendation
2. length of the book
3. print size
4. cover
5. title
6. titles of the chapters
7. first page
8. ease of reading
9. setting
10. character of same age and gender
11. familiarity with the book
12. preference for paperbacks or hardcovers
13. awards
14. action
15. teacher recommendation
16. movies and television
17. books by familiar authors/ illustrators
18. book jacket descriptions of the book
19. thickness
20. picture on the cover
21. number and quality of illustrations

Reutzel and Gali (1997) found that there was a recognizable pattern which children followed when selecting books. They found that children chose books based on the physical characteristics of the books. They also found that there were limitations such as the number of books that could be signed out of a library, time limits, and personal self-concept restrictions that influenced selection. Librarians, teachers, and bookstore owners should note that when books were shelved at or below the child's eye level, it was more likely that these books would be chosen.

My Personal Top Ten Christian Children's Books

1. *Old Turtle*
2. *Love Is...*
3. *To Everything There Is a Season*
4. *In God's Name*
5. *Jesus* (Wildsmith)
6. *Shalom, Salaam, Peace*
7. *Let There Be Light*
8. *Let My People Go*
9. *The Narnia Chronicles*
10. *The Diary of Anne Frank*

Bibliotherapy: Children's Literature as Medicine

Children cannot be sensitized to the existence of people who are not like them by merely being told to like others...Through reading, we briefly share in the lives and feelings of the characters rather than dealing only with the facts.

(BIEGER, 1996, P. 308)

There is no shortage of books that deal with difficult issues. AIDS/HIV, death (especially of grandparents), anorexia and bulimia, racism, sexism, homophobia, drug use, alcohol abuse, peer pressure, divorce, abuse, moving to another house, fears, etc. These books fall under the category of bibliotherapy – books that try to resolve or deal with relevant issues in children's lives. The problem with this type of literature is that a book cannot be expected to teach, soothe, or bring empathy on its own. These books, unlike any other category of literature, require the guidance of a caring adult; in particular, an adult who is a constant in the life of the child, not a guest reader who will then leave the subject. A child needs to feel that he or she can go to the person presenting this type of literature with questions or concerns, and it is important to know that these may not arise immediately.

I do not want to imply that books cannot have soothing or healing qualities. Many books can be wonderfully healing, and can speak directly to our souls; however, we must not rely on books to solve difficult problems on their own.

One of the instant warning signs I look for is the author's credentials on the front of the book. If I see a book written by Dr. So-and-So, Ph.D., I know it is usually a bibliotherapeutic book. It is okay if they have their credentials listed in their biography on the back cover, but not on the front! That usually shows that their credentials are being used to sell the book, rather than having the book stand on its own merit.

Curt Dudley-Marling describes his experiences using folk tales from around the world with a Grade 3 class in an honest critique of what went wrong with his good intentions. In his attempt to provide a mirror for the cultures represented in his class, he found that the students did not always appreciate his intentions and efforts, and did not want to be singled out and identified as being different. He also realized there was a problem of portrayal, and that a child from a privileged background may not necessarily identify with a poor child from the same country, saying "...it was unreasonable for me to have assumed that a piece of literature could speak to the culture and experience of all people from a particular continent, region, or country" (Dudley-Marling, 1997, p. 127).

Dudley-Marling found that using such literature as "medicine" was also unsuccessful because it singled students out and some resented him for doing so. In particular, the use of stories about other religions "may have been an unwelcome intrusion into students' personal lives that also had the effect of marking some students as 'different'" (1997, p. 130). His idea was not to avoid using books that reflect the cultures of our students. Instead, he proposed allowing students access to books in which they find accurate representations of themselves, not what we as teachers or outsiders from their cultures think they should see. As Mascha Rudman has pointed out, "When a book is assigned as medicine, the chances of its being accepted are slim" (Rudman, 1984, p. 3).

Bibliotherapeutic books, while attempting to fulfill a specific role, often lack the literary quality that makes books attractive to readers. The attempt to provide a moral or lesson can overshadow the plot, characters, and quality of illustration (Bishop, 1992). Louise Rosenblatt explores the dilemma of meeting the needs of the student to develop relationships, grow as an individual, become part of the larger world, and open himself or herself to possibilities. According to Rosenblatt, there is a fine line between the importance of literature as a tool to meet social, psychological and ethical needs, and the danger of losing the aesthetic appreciation of literature when it is used for didactic purposes. She cautions, "Wise teachers have opposed any tendency to make of literature a mere handmaiden of the social studies or a body of documents illustrating moral points" (Rosenblatt, 1976, p. 4). Rosenblatt (1978) describes the difference between efferent reading and aesthetic reading, and states that what is important with efferent reading is the "residue" of information, solutions to problems, and plans for further actions that will be carried out as a result of the reading. Rosenblatt does not propose a middle ground for a text that can have efferent qualities while still remaining aesthetically beautiful. This middle ground is the domain into which quality literature should fall.

Violet Harris discusses the importance of the use of African American children's literature in classes where there are no black children. The importance of allowing the students to interact with the literature opens them to perspectives they may never otherwise encounter. However, she also states that using the literature this way must be done willingly, and that teachers "cannot be harangued into doing so" (Harris, 1991, p. 42).

The same is true of reading books about different faiths when there are no children in the class or home of that faith. By opening children to what may or may not be around them, they can gain knowledge about others, and hopefully, be better prepared when they encounter people with different faith backgrounds.

Ultimately, it is the important interactions – interaction with the text, with fellow readers, and with parents and teachers – that determine the usefulness of any book.

Time with the Children

I have visited many churches to observe the Time with the Children, and in most instances, I have found it disappointing. In general, the minister is not well prepared for this time, and speaks above the children's heads. It is often a time for the adults rather than the children. The children's "cute" answers become the fuel for the adults' entertainment. Gimmicks are remembered; not the point of the lesson.

The Time with the Children is a difficult part of the service. The leader is faced with children of different ages and backgrounds. There may be new children with no church experience, and others who have attended church since birth. Some hear Bible stories in the home, but others do not. So how do we present a short lesson that is effective for a varied audience?

To look at the Time with the Children, I interviewed the Reverend Doctor Karen Hamilton, who, at the time, was the minister at St. James-

Bond United Church in Toronto, Ontario. During my observations, I was impressed with Karen's ability to speak with the children in a way that was respectful and honored them as an important part of the congregation. Karen used children's literature effectively, and during this time, she acted as a role model for teachers, caregivers, parents, and grandparents who would share literature and stories with children.

1. **What do you try to achieve in the Time with the Children?**

   KH: I want the children to hear and feel the story, not just the facts, but to also experience it. I want them to learn about our faith and traditions, and to construct a relationship with God. It is important, too, to build a relationship with the children, and have them feel comfortable in the space and with me. They should have fun during this time of learning.

   Many people talk about engaging the kids and getting them to talk during the Time with the Children. They say we should not give them the answers, and must smile at every bit of wisdom. But that does not work all that well, and may not be always faithful to the passing on of our Christian stories and traditions. Also, the children are not on the microphone and the congregation cannot hear what they say. Kids should not be made a show of or put on the spot individually. It is better to watch the kids, and cut the conversation off and move on if needed. I often like to have the children moving or singing.

2. **Why do you use Christian children's literature and Bible stories during the Time with the Children? What are the drawbacks?**

   KH: If the reality of faith is a part of children's lives from the beginning, they have a firmer foundation for life. If I see a story, and it is a good one, then I will use it. I often use Bible stories. The issue with Bible stories can be what to do with gaps in the story or unknowns. Do you tell it literally as it stands, or do you build on it and fill in the gaps? I have mixed feelings about this, as there is intentionality in the biblical stories. I will fill in the gaps and will add to the story, with fear and trepidation, but I rarely take away from a story. There is danger in taking away, but in adding you also lurk on the edge of destroying what the authors and editors wanted you to gain from the story. We also should never underestimate our children. They can handle difficult stories.

3. **Which books have you found to be most effective?**

   KH: *But God Remembered; Shalom, Salaam, Peace; Three Wise Women.*

4. **Why do you tell stories rather than read them?**

KH: At times I am torn between reading and telling the stories because the children are more engaged when I tell a story. I often make a deliberate decision not to read it, even when the text and pictures are lovely. Reading a story often feels exclusive. The congregation cannot see the pictures, and it can be difficult to ensure that all of the kids can see them.

I do not like many of the resources for the Time with the Children that I have seen. Most of them are preachy and boring. If you are going to make a point about a moral, it should be simple and direct. Should we moralize? I like the stories that have a moral but it must be clearly laid out. We need to know exactly what the point is. Maybe we have been too vague. People have said similar things about sermons, and I have become much more directional in sermons. It is good if the congregation can walk away with something concrete to do in response to what is said, like writing a letter. Telling them to "be kind" is too vague. We must be more specific. It is difficult to find the line between telling the moral and being preachy. Simplicity is a key.

5. **When you tell a story from a children's book, how do you prepare it?**

KH: I read the story about three times, and construct a frame for it in my mind. I read it underlining important events or phrases in my mind, trying to see the pattern and thus be able to tell it in a poetic way. I look at where phrases are repeated.

During the storytelling, if I see that a child is losing attention, I will focus on something specific or increase the pace or volume to bring that child back into the story. It is also important to focus on new children, and to be conscious of ones on the side and include them.

If you are not good at telling a story, then it is fine to read it, but I think most people can learn how to tell a story. Is is important to practice the timing and the pace. You should also work on good voice control, projection, volume, and voice dynamics.

6. **How do you feel the Time with the Children affects the adults in the congregation?**

KH: People will often respond to a story and say it was "amazing" or "touching." I can see they're listening. People in this congregation really like interactive stories. They like to participate too and there is no problem getting the adults engaged. Some topics allow that to happen and some do not. It is important, however, not to do that too often or it gets stale.

I like to do unexpected things, like to emphasize unexpected words to just liven up the text. You pay attention when you hear something in a different way, and if it is not what you are expecting.

7. **What advice would you have for other ministers with regards to the Time with the Children?**
    KH: Do not be boring!

- Know the children's names.
- Enjoy the children.
- Do not use notes.
- Use props.
- Keep talking and distract them and the congregation if things don't go right – like the day the popcorn machine took far too long to produce the popcorn!
- Engage the kids. This time is about building relationships and sharing experiences.
- Be lively.
- Care about the kids.
- Make jokes.
- Love the kids.

How Will This Book Help the Reader?

Many books have been written to support people who use children's literature (see Bibliography at end of chapter). Few of these books, however, deal with literature about religion or spirituality. A quality resource is needed to provide teachers, Christian education directors, ministers, and others with ways to select and use books that will support their programs; and for parents who are looking for quality children's literature that will be positive and will reflect the values they are hoping to share with their children.

It is important to recognize the role that the reader plays in the interactions with the text (Rosenblatt, 1976). To each reading, readers bring their own personal experiences, knowledge, emotions, beliefs, interests, curiosities, thoughts, ideas, prejudices, misunderstandings, and problems. Each reader may have their own interpretation of a text, and therefore, will have a different outcome of experience with the textual transaction and interaction.

How to Use This Resource

The main purpose of this book is to introduce people to quality children's literature for faith development by reviewing literature that is currently and readily available. Each chapter contains one "text set" – a group of books related by genre, topic, author, illustrator, etc. For example, "God and the

Environment" is one text set which contains a number of books on this topic for children of different ages. Each chapter also contains an introduction with suggestions for ways to use the literature, as well as complete bibliographical information with a synopsis and review.

This information will help the readers choose books to use with their children. The ideas will enable the reader to find ways to extend the reading and make connections with it by following suggestions for activities and discussion topics. Not every idea will work in each setting. The ideas are meant as tools to connect the literature in meaningful ways to the lives and experiences of the readers by allowing the children to bring their own ideas and understanding to the reading. You will probably come up with your own ideas, too. I hope you will send me your ideas, so they can be shared in future editions.

Review Contents

Each book review has a number of features. The usual bibliographical information also has the ISBN (the International Standard Book Number) – a number assigned to each book, which makes it possible for bookstores to order books easily. You can also use the ISBN to look up books in most library catalogues. Each book also has a synopsis of the story and a short review. If the book has won any major awards such as the Caldecott or Newbery Medals, they are listed with the year in which it was won. A few books use inclusive language, which attempts to use a balance of male and female pronouns and/or imagery for God, as well as including a variety of people in different and often non-traditional roles. I have tried to point out these books because of the need for more books that are open to alternative views of God and our roles in creation.

Age levels are recommended for each book. These are only recommendations, as each child's development is different, and each child may develop at different rates in certain areas of his or her development, whether it is spiritual, intellectual, emotional, physical, experiential, etc. The key is to know your children and to judge the suitability of the books by the children's needs and readiness. I have not placed an upper age limit on books, because I believe that some books can appeal to many age levels and that even very simple books can be used to open discussion with older children and adults.

References

Bieger, E. (1996). "Promoting multicultural education through a literature-based approach." *The Reading Teacher*, vol 49 no 4.

Bishop, R. (1992). "Multicultural literature for children: Making informed choices." *Teaching Multicultural Literature in Grades K-8*. Norwood, MA: Christopher-Gordon Publishers.

Bright, R., McMullin, L. and Platt, D. (1998). *From your child's teacher: Helping your child learn to read, write and speak*. Stettler, AB: FP Hendriks Publishing, Ltd.

Doake, D. (1988). *Reading Begins at Birth*. Richmond Hill: Scholastic.

Dudley-Marling, C. (1997). "'I'm not from Pakistan': Multicultural literature and the problem of representation." *The New Advocate*, vol 10 no 2.

Harris, V. (1991). "Multicultural curriculum: African American children's literature." *Young Children*, January.

Hunt, G. (1989). *Honey for a Child's Heart*. Grand Rapids: Zondervan Publishing House.

Jasper, D. (1989). *The Study of Literature And Religion*. London: Macmillan Press.

Maxwell, P. (1978). "Getting books into those empty hands." *The Reading Teacher*, vol 31, pp 397–399.

Reutzel, D. and Gali, K. (1997). "The art of children's book selection: A labyrinth unexplored." *Reading Psychology*, vol 18 no 2.

Rosenblatt, L. (1978). *The Reader, the Text, the Poem*. Carbondale: Southern Illinois University Press.

Rosenblatt, L. (1976). *Literature as Exploration*. New York: Modern Language Association of America.

Ross, R. (1979). "The young critic." *Ripples*. vol 5, pp 5–7.

Rudman, M. (1984). *Children's Literature – An Issues Approach*. White Plains, NY: Heath.

Sweet, L. (1997). *God in the Classroom: The Controversial Issue of Religion in Canada's Schools*. Toronto: McClelland and Stewart, Inc.

Taylor, D. and Strickland, D. (1986). *Family Storybook Reading*. New York: Scholastic.

Thomas, V. and Miller, B. (1986). *Children's Literature for All God's Children.* Atlanta: John Knox Press.

Wendelin, K. and Zinck, R. (1983). "How students make book choices." *Reading Horizons*, vol 23 no 2.

Bibliography of Books that Review Children's Literature

Booth, D., Swartz, L., and Zola, M. (1987). *Choosing Children's Books.* Markham: Pembroke.

The Canadian Children's Book Centre (1996). *Too Good to Miss II: Classic Canadian Children's Books.* Toronto.

The Canadian Children's Book Centre (1994). *Writing Stories, Making Pictures.* Toronto.

Cianciolo, P. (1990). *Picture Books for Children.* Chicago: American Library Association.

Donavin, D. (1992). *Best of the Best for Children.* New York: Random House.

Egoff, S. and Saltman, J. (1990). *The New Republic of Childhood: A Practical Guide to Canadian Children's Literature in English.* Toronto: Oxford University Press.

Egoff, S., Stubbs, G., Ashley, R., and Sutton, W. (1996). *Only Connect: Readings on Children's Literature.* Toronto: Oxford University Press.

Freeman, J. (1990). *Books Kids Will Sit Still For: The Complete Read-Aloud Guide.* New York: R. R. Bowker.

Gillespie, J. and Gilbert, C. (1985). *Best Books for Children: Preschool through the Middle Grades.* New York: R. R. Bowker.

Green, J. (1996). *Our Choice 1996/97.* Toronto: The Canadian Children's Book Centre.

Greenwood, B. (1994). *The Canscaip Companion: A Biographical Record of Canadian Children's Authors, Illustrators, and Performers.* Markham: Pembroke.

Hauser, P. and Nelson, G. (1988). *Books for the Gifted Child.* New York: R. R. Bowker.

Hearne, B. (1981). *Choosing Books for Children: A Commonsense Guide.* New York: Delacorte.

Hopkins, L. (1969). *Books Are by People*. New York: Citation Press.

Jensen, J. and Roser, N. (1993*). Adventuring with Books: A Booklist for Pre-K–Grade 6*. Urbana: National Council of Teachers of English.

Jobe, R. and Hart, P. (1991). *Canadian Connections: Experiencing Literature with Children*. Markham: Pembroke.

Kezwer, P. (1995). *Worlds of Wonder – Resources for Multicultural Children's Literature*. Toronto: Pippin.

Kovacs, D. and Preller, J. (1991). *Meet the Authors and Illustrators: 60 Creators of Favorite Children's Books Talk about Their Work*. Richmond Hill: Scholastic.

Landsberg, M. (1988). *Michele Landsberg's Guide to Children's Books*. Markham: Penguin.

Marantz, S. and K. (1994). *Multicultural Picture Books: Art for Understanding Others*. Worthington: Linworth Publishing.

Norton, D. (1987). *Through the Eyes of a Child – An Introduction to Children's Literature*. Columbus: Merrill Publishing.

Noyes, S., Pearson, N., and McCallum, J. (1994). *Writing Stories, Making Pictures: Biographies of 150 Canadian Children's Authors and Illustrators*. Toronto: The Canadian Children's Book Centre.

Odean, K. (1997). *Great Books for Girls*. New York: Ballantine Books.

Rasinski, T. and Gillespie, C. (1992). *Sensitive Issues – An Annotated Guide to Children's Literature, K-6*. Phoenix: Oryx Press.

Roberts, P., Cecil, N. and Alexander, S. (1993). *Gender Positive! A Teachers' and Librarians' Guide to Nonstereotyped Children's Literature, K-8*. Jefferson, NC: McFarland & Company.

Stoll, D. (1994). *Magazines for Kids and Teens: A Resource for Parents, Teachers, Librarians and Kids!* Newark: International Reading Association.

Trelease, J. (1985). *The Read-Aloud Handbook*. New York: Penguin.

Waterston, E. (1992). *Children's Literature in Canada*. New York: Twayne Publishers.

Zippan, F. and Atkinson, D. (1993). *Check It Out! The Essential, Indispensable Guide to Children's Video*. Richmond Hill: Scholastic.

2

Art & Literature
Picture Books & Videos

So too is every artisan and master artisan
who labors by night as well as by day;
those who cut the signets of seals,
each is diligent in making a great variety;
they set their heart on painting a lifelike image,
and they are careful to finish their work.

SIRACH 38:27

Definition of Art as It Applies to
Christian Children's Literature

Art in Christian children's literature forms an integral part of a picture book. It can stand alone to tell a story without words, or it can enhance and deepen the text. Art can draw a person into the book and help them engage and interact with the text. Of course, art can also deter from the text and present views which work against the story, setting a different tone entirely.

As J. Daniel Brown points out, art can be a language of its own. "As language, a particular art expression can have its own accent, speak its own idioms and colloquialisms, and have varying degrees of success at communicating" (1997, p. 122). I agree with his statement, but would offer that the opposite is also true – that language can also be art, creating images of beauty and wonder through words alone. "Clearly, the very nature of words makes literary art, in particular poetry, especially apt for expressing the 'metaphysical' dimension of existence." (Viladesau, 1999, p. 158).

It is possible to see in the art of Christian children's literature an incredibly wide range of artistic forms, media, and techniques. Classical paintings used as illustration, intricate paper sculpture, soft watercolors, powerful oils and acrylics, pop-ups, cartoons, photography, collage, pastels, clay or Plasticine, paste papers, marbling, embroidery, charcoal, cutwork, tapestry, found materials, pencil sketches, children's own artwork, woodcuts, quiltwork, and other media have all been successfully used to illustrate Christian children's literature. There is truly something for everyone.

The Function of Art in Christian Children's Books

The importance of art and illustration in children's books cannot be underestimated. For the youngest child and the pre-reader, art connects them to the story. Children can see before they can speak, and visual images surround us all. Artwork can transport us into the story and stir our imaginations. It can challenge our assumptions and strengthen our resolve. It can educate and influence. It can remind us of personal experiences or introduce us to new ones. It can evoke pleasure, pain, and every other possible emotion.

Yet children's literature is often overlooked. Its influence and importance is rarely evident in secondary literary criticism and theory. How sad that Christian children's art is seen by art theorists as unworthy of mention. These theorists do not seem to realize that children's books are a way of exposing art, and in this case, Christian art, to a broad audience. Art in children's books is reproduced at an astounding rate. It influences a large number of readers, yet there is no mention of it as a genre unto itself.

When I fall in love with a children's book, it is almost always one with beautiful artwork. I am rarely attracted to a book on the basis of the story alone. For me, a good children's book must have a balance of beauty and story. I will buy a book with exquisite pictures, but a great story without the illustrations to back it up is sadly missing a piece of itself.

A favorite book is one that can be reread many times, as any parent will know. There is no harm in rereading beloved books, and children can find comfort in familiar books or characters. Children who are pre-readers will memorize the book shortly, and anyone who has missed a word, passage, or page will be quickly reminded. Early readers will learn to follow along and will pick out words they recognize. Independent readers will return to their own special choices and share them with others.

Some of my personal favorites are *Old Turtle, Sacred Places, Love Is, In God's Name,* and *The River and The Rain.* Each is as different as the next, but in each, I see something new every time I pick up the book. These books have a timeless quality about them, and a beauty I find difficult to describe.

Standards of Beauty

But beauty does not have to hold to exacting cultural standards. Characters can be beautiful and still have flaws and peculiarities. The North American standard of beauty, so abhorrently influenced by unattainable media and model icons, is not shared by all cultures or all people within North America. Beauty in illustration can show the idiosyncrasies of individuality without bowing to the pressure to conform to standards that cannot be realized by most people. Beauty in illustration should show a variety of sizes, shapes, color, features, and relationships. Beauty can just have an intriguing quality that cannot and need not be explained.

Issues in Artwork

There are some issues to be aware of in the artwork of Christian children's literature. As much or more is said in the artwork of a book as in the written text itself. Illustrations can convey unspoken messages, or can extend the text, giving nuance and detail that are not evident in the story. Sometimes, the illustrator is telling their own story which can be quite separate from the text. Illustrations can make a story come alive, but can also hinder the reader's ability to connect with the story in a meaningful and authentic way. Illustration can even contain a subtext or a parallel story, such as the border illustrations in *Something for Nothing* by Phoebe Gilman, that is not found in the written text.

Some critical questions must be asked when looking at the artwork of any children's book:

1. Are the portrayals of people accurate?
2. Does the artwork portray the rich diversity of society?
3. Does the artwork match the text in tone and quality?
4. Is the artwork too mature for the reader?
5. Are violent scenes handled with sensitivity?
6. Is the artwork stereotypical or even racist?
7. Is the artwork physically attractive?

8. Are cartoon-like drawings an excuse for inaccuracy, and do they lead to stereotypical characters?

9. Does the illustrator come from the culture represented?

10. Should we accept poor text just because the artwork is outstanding?

Accuracy

Accuracy in the portrayal of historical characters is extremely important. Too often in the history of art have we seen religious images that reflect the culture of the artist, but not the culture being portrayed. We must also consider the importance of such things as accuracy of time and setting, cultural practices, gender interactions, and clothing.

In many Christian children's books, Jesus is portrayed as a white man. What disservice are we doing to our children if we refuse to acknowledge the heritage of Jesus as a Middle Eastern Jew? While we do not know exactly what he looked like, we can imagine that he was bearded (from his Jewish culture) and olive or dark skinned (from his Middle Eastern background). So why do so many children's books insist on portraying Jesus as a white man? Does this allow children to relate to Jesus in a more personal way? Or do we not want to acknowledge the Jewish heritage of the early church?

The context of the illustration is also very important. If the book is meant to be an historically accurate book, check to see if the items illustrated are authentic to the time period and culture. *Lydia*, by Marty Rhodes Figley, is a fictionalized tale of the first Christian convert. It is a lovely story, but is not biblically accurate. The illustrations, by Anita Riggio, show many items which do not fit with the time and setting of the story. When we present books to children, we must take care to explain if it is only loosely based on a biblical story, and we should separate such stories from accurate retellings which are true to the biblical telling.

It must be noted that we do not always know the faith of the illustrator. While it is usually evident if the author is writing from a faith perspective, when it comes to the illustrator, unless it is made clear in the biography, it can be hard to determine whether the illustrator shares the beliefs and values put forward in the text.

Richard Harries does not feel that this is a problem. "From an artistic point of view that does not affect the spirituality of the work produced" (Harries, 1993, p. 114). He goes on to state that what is really important is "a fundamental seriousness, fierce artistic integrity" (1993, p. 114). I disagree with Harries, and feel that the faith of the illustrator makes up a vital part of the work. Of course, if a Christian publisher has published the book, they may have insisted on employing Christian artists, and discerning this will be less problematic.

Diversity

Another issue with portrayal is the depiction of people in society. If the book is modern, and not historically or culturally specific, then the illustrations should reflect the diversity of modern society. This could mean the diversity of race, faiths, physical and mental abilities, gender, family structures, worship styles, wealth, status, and schooling. Books should be reviewed carefully to see if the portrayals match the values of the readers. Consumers do not need to purchase materials that go against their personal beliefs, whether those beliefs are fundamental or liberal. People can let publishers know what they like or dislike about books. Voting with our wallets is one of the most powerful ways to send a clear message.

To portray a wide variety of peoples requires a sensitivity and attention to detail. An artist portraying people outside of the artist's own culture must do so with great care. Consultation with people from the culture being portrayed is essential, especially for portraying cultural nuances and avoiding stereotypes.

One book which achieves this successfully is *To Every Thing There Is a Season: Verses from Ecclesiastes*, illustrated by Leo and Diane Dillon. In this book, the Dillons illustrate a passage from Ecclesiastes 3 using a variety of illustration styles from different time periods through history and from different cultures. Included with the book is a section in which the Dillons explain the contents and techniques of each illustration. It is clear in this example, the Dillons have researched the images they are representing, and it culminates in a book which is outstanding in its richness and beauty.

Of course, the other negative possibility of portrayal is the danger of tokenism. It is difficult to say exactly where a book falls into this category, because it is such a subjective notion – often a gut reaction to an illustration. I do not know how to avoid such tokenism, and even wonder if it is better to have tokenism than not to portray people from parallel cultures at all. At least with tokenism, people can see themselves reflected. It is a delicate balance that must be struck if acceptance of all peoples is to be promoted.

Some of the best books that portray a variety of peoples without tokenism are those by Patricia Polacco (see, for example, *Chicken Sunday* or *Pink and Say*). In her books, which are often based on autobiographical events, Polacco shows people of different faiths and races interacting together in genuine and believable ways. Her books show an authenticity of relationship, and do not cross the line of using interracial or interfaith relationships for overtly didactic purposes. Polacco's art illustrates real people in authentic situations.

Maturity Level

Some of the artwork seems not meant for the child at all, but rather for more mature tastes. I often wonder if the illustrator did not understand children, or if the book is really meant for an older audience. An example of this is *Genesis* by Ed Young. The extremely dark and foreboding images give a real sense of the juxtaposition of chaos and creation. But are these images ones to which a child would be attracted or would appreciate?

There are few books which transcend all boundaries of age and race. Some books allow readers of all levels and maturities to approach the text and illustration at their own stage. These books hold within them the ability to allow each reader to engage at their own ability without any part of the book being forsaken. An example of this, in my opinion, is *Old Turtle* by Douglas Wood.

When choosing books for children, we must ask if the illustrations are appealing to us as adults, or if the intended audience is the child. There has been a recent surge in books such as *The Life of Jesus in Masterpieces of Art* by Mary Pope Osborne which portray the life of biblical characters using classical paintings as the illustrations. It can be very interesting to use these paintings to do a comparison study and look at how the characters have been portrayed by different artists through the years – to see how the artists' cultures and contexts are being reflected in the paintings.

Violence

The Bible is a violent book. Many of the passages are not for the squeamish. Many of the stories in which the heroes of the Bible triumph also have victims – from individuals, to armies, to nations. Stories such as David and Goliath, the crossing of the Red Sea, Joshua at Jericho, and even the beloved Noah's Ark all have victims. What about the death of Jesus, the cornerstone of the Christian faith? Even if the emphasis is on the Resurrection, you cannot avoid the fact that Jesus was murdered, although "died" sounds much more acceptable.

When children's books depict these stories, the way in which the violence is portrayed is important. Modern liberal thinking makes it difficult for us to glory in the victimization of people because of their race or beliefs; yet in the Bible, and in particular in the Old Testament, such assumptions were made frequently. God was called on to triumph over enemies and to be with the Israelites in battle. Do we really want to glorify this approach, or should it be sanitized? How can we show the historical reality of such thinking without implying that it is acceptable in our own time and place?

Any book that shows the reality of violence must be carefully vetted to see if the depictions are too overt or if they may be disturbing to the reader.

Sex

This is always a thorny issue. As with violence, the Bible is full of sex, too, most of which takes place outside the acceptable limits of marriage. Sex is rarely portrayed in children's literature, but one exception is in books that explain the ten commandments. How does one explain adultery to a child? Usually, children's books replace this with, "You shall be true to your wife or husband," or something similar.

We should also be aware of the portrayals of the human body. Are the characters portrayed as representative of the culture/age of the story? Are people drawn with realism in mind? Is everyone stick-thin or with large breasts? We are sexual beings, and we must not deny this gift, but we must also portray a wide range of body shapes and sizes in both genders.

Media

As video and DVDs become more accessible for a wider range of people, there has been a mirroring effect in children's book publishing. Any bookstore has a plethora of books based on films and television shows. This is also true of Christian children's literature. Film and video characters such as the characters from the VeggieTales series and DreamWorks' *Prince of Egypt* are now showing up in book form.

Consumers must be careful when it comes to choosing these books. Check the quality of the illustrations and text. Often, the book is a poorer version of the film. Yes, the film can be better than the book! You also need to ask yourself if the book is merely a marketing tool for the video, or the other way around.

Stereotypes

Stereotyping in illustration (and anywhere else) is unacceptable. There are ways to avoid cultural stereotyping. Illustrators should be from the culture they are portraying, or should at least be familiar with the culture through personal interaction and research. Consultants from the cultures in question should be used whenever possible.

There are some things consumers can do to see if the author and illustrator have taken care with their work. Check the book jacket for biographical notes on the author and illustrator. Read the introduction to the book if there is one. Read the dedication. Find out more about the author and illustrators on the Internet. Often, it is impossible to know if the author and illustrator have done their homework, but consumers of the literature should do theirs.

Some of the worst books for stereotyping are those with cartoon-like illustrations. They often either have people with identical features (but sometimes with color), or characters with exaggerated features. Nuances are not possible in cartoons, so you will rarely see people from a culture with varying skin tones or features. Books with cartoon illustrations are often very cheaply produced and are usually easily accessible to a wide range of people because of their low cost.

Some stereotypes can be subtle and very easy to overlook. For example, are all African children in a book portrayed as poor and shoeless? Are people from certain cultures portrayed with better clothes and more outward signs of wealth? Are Native peoples grouped together rather than identifying different nations individually? Are cultures portrayed as having only one look or belief, without variation?

Ways To Use the Literature

Illustration can be used as a starting point for a number of different activities with children. Here are just a few examples of how you could use the illustrations in children's books to extend and enhance a story:

- Children can take a number of different books on the same story, Noah's Ark, for instance, and compare how different illustrators interpret the story. You may ask the children to bring in a copy of the story they have at home.

- The portrayal of biblical characters can be compared by looking at illustrators from different cultures, faiths, and time periods. Remember that a number of the characters in the Bible are also in the Qur'an.

- Choose a character from the Bible and look up paintings of that character on the Internet (with adult supervision). Use these paintings to illustrate the story of that character's life. You may find both classical and modern interpretations of the characters.

- Children can take a book like *In God's House*, by Robert Coles, in which the young contributors are the artists, and create their own book by collecting contributions from their friends/classmates.

- The style of a specific artist can be examined and used as a guide for children's artwork. An example of this is *Two by Two*, by Barbara Reid, who uses Plasticine for her vibrant designs. This could easily be accomplished by children with wonderful results. Take a sturdy board and apply a thin layer of Plasticine for the background. Build up your illustration with more Plasticine. Use different tools like forks, toothpicks, toothbrushes, and rollers to create different effects.

- Illustrations from a favorite book could be interpreted into set designs (with adult help) and used to retell a story.

- Illustrations could be used to explain customs and practices of different cultures or religions, such as in *The Always Prayer Shawl*, by Sheldon Oberman.

- Children can dress up as their favorite characters from a book or story. Some churches do this as an alternative to Halloween.

- Take a significant detail from an illustration and re-create it. This helps the child focus on detail, and can simplify a busy illustration.

- Re-create an illustration using a completely different medium to see what other effects you can make.

- Make illustrations for a strictly text-based novel. Create illustrations to go along with the text, or create your own inspired illustrations as a response to the text.

- The role of different people in society can be seen through illustration. This can cover a wide range: from the way Jesus is portrayed when speaking to women in different books, right through to how modern stories show women and their changing roles.

- History can be examined through illustration. Children can learn about events and styles of art through the years as it is re-created in children's books.

- Read the story without the written text by using the illustrations to make up your own story.

- Investigate different types of media found in books. Some books use pastel, pencil, oils, acrylics, or fabric. How many different media can you find and identify? Are there some books that use more than one medium?

- Take a wordless picture book, such as *Noah's Ark* by Peter Spier and act it out or retell the story from the illustrations.

- Take the text of a favorite story and create your own illustrations.
- Ask the child for their own response to the illustrations, and allow the child to be critical and honest in those responses. You might ask:

  - Do you like the illustrations?

  - How do they make you feel?

  - What do they make you wonder about?

  - What have you learned from them?

  - What do you still want to find out about?

  - What do you disagree with?

  - What do the illustrations remind you of?

  - What would you do differently?

  - What is your favorite part of the illustrations?

  - Have you read any other books that are illustrated like this?

- Most importantly, children can explore their own inspirations gained from illustrations. In order to foster this, it is important to have on hand a wide variety of materials and media to allow children to explore freely. Children learn through art, and they express themselves through their own creativity, without criticism. Children who cannot yet write may be able to tell stories (which can then be written by an adult or older child) that emerge from their artwork. Celebrating the creative work of a child is the most important thing a parent or teacher can do.

References

Brown, J. D. (1997). *Masks of Mystery: Explorations in Christian faith and the arts*. Lanham, MD: University Press of America.

Dillenberger, J. (1990). *Image and Spirit in Sacred and Secular Art*. New York: Crossroad.

Dixon, J. W. Jr. (1978). *Art and the Theological Imagination*. New York: Seabury Press.

Farley, E. (2001). *Faith and Beauty: A Theological Aesthetic*. Aldershot, UK: Ashgate Publishing.

Garvin, H. R. (1982). *Literature, Arts, and Religion*. Lewisburg: Buckness University Press.

Harries, R. (1993). *Art and the Beauty of God: A Christian Understanding.* London: Mowbray.

van der Leeuw, G. (1963). *Sacred and Profane Beauty.* Nashville: Abingdon Press.

Spencer, A. B. (1998). "Fiction as a looking glass." *God through the Looking Glass: Glimpses from The Arts.* Grand Rapids: Baker Books.

Viladesau, R. (1999). *Theological Aesthetics: God in Imagination, Beauty, and Art.* New York: Oxford University Press.

Bibliography of Picture Books and Videos

If Nathan Were Here   Ages: 8+
Author: Mary Bahr   Illustrator: Karen A. Jerome
Grand Rapids, MI: Eerdmans Books for Young Readers, 2000
ISBN: 0-8028-5187-8   Other Categories: Death, Friendship

Synopsis: A boy's best friend has died, and he expresses his grief by wondering what Nathan would do if he were still alive. A teacher leads the students to create a memory box to help them deal with their loss.

Review: This book treats a difficult subject in a very sensitive manner without being didactic. The illustrations are soft and gentle.

What Is God?   Ages: 5+
Author: Etan Boritzer   Illustrator: Robbie Marantz
Willowdale, ON: Firefly Books, 1990
ISBN: 0-920668-89-5   Other Categories: Nature of God, Beliefs

Synopsis: This book raises the question of "What is God?" Rather than answering the question, it raises a number of possibilities about what people believe and where they find God.

Review: This is an excellent book to use to start discussions about the nature of God and people's beliefs about where God is found. Even though this book talks about the many places God exists, it does not use inclusive language or show non-traditional metaphors for God.

Pets' Letters to God   **Ages: 5+**
Translated by Mark Bricklin
Rodale Press, 1999
ISBN: 1-57954-208-5   Other Categories: Humor, Prayer

Synopsis: Cats and dogs ask God a variety of questions in the form of prayers.

Review: This is a humorous collection of prayers. Children will enjoy this and may have fun making up their own.

Christopher Is Not Afraid...Anymore   **Ages: 3+**
Author: Craig Burris   Illustrator: Priscilla Burris
Nashville: Thomas Nelson, 1994
ISBN: 0-7852-7978-4   Other Categories: Prayer, Fear, Family

Synopsis: A young boy cries when he is afraid, until his mother shares Psalm 27:1 with him, and he finds courage through prayer.

Review: This book may send the wrong message that it is not okay for boys to cry. This is not to be confused with the excellent Christopher books by Itah Sadu.

Does God Know How to Tie Shoes?   **Ages: 3+**
Author: Nancy White Carlstrom   Illustrator: Lori McElrath-Eslick
Grand Rapids, MI: Wm. B. Eerdmans Publishing Co., 1993
ISBN: 0-8028-5074-X   Other Categories: Nature of God

Synopsis: A young girl walks through the countryside with her parents. As she asks questions about the nature of God, her parents respond using paraphrases of verses from the Psalms.

Review: This is a lovely book about children's honest questions about God. The language is not inclusive, but does include a reference to how God is like "a mother hen protecting her baby chicks." On some pages, the text is difficult to read against the oil paintings.

Every Little Angel's Handbook   **Ages: 5+**
Author and Illustrator: Belinda Downes
London: Methuen Children's Books, 1997
ISBN: 0-7497-3815-4   Other Categories: Angels, Art, Humor

Synopsis: The angels all have different roles and talents. They also have their own style when it comes to clothing and choice of wings. A number of angels are profiled in detail.

Review: This hilarious book takes a tongue-in-cheek look at angels. The illustrations are embroidered and very whimsical.

The Cherry Blossom Tree:
A Grandfather Talks about Life & Death   Ages: 8+
Author: Jan Godfrey   Illustrator: Jane Cope
Augsburg Fortress, 1996
ISBN: 0-8066-2843-X   Other Categories: Death, New Life, Family

Synopsis: Harriet and her grandfather work in the garden on his birthday. When she notices that an old cherry tree has died, she asks if her grandfather will die, too. He teaches her about life and death, and together, they plant a new tree.

Review: This story is not too didactic, but is a conversational way of presenting this difficult topic. The grandfather does not die in the book. The lovely watercolors are soft and comfortable.

Because I Love You   Ages 5+
Author: Max Lucado   Illustrator: Mitchell Heinze
Crossway Books, 2000
ISBN: 0891079920   Other Categories: Parables, Love of God, Family

Synopsis: A man named Shaddai builds a village for children. To protect them from the forest, he builds a wall of stone, but leaves a hole in the wall. A young boy discovers the hole and goes into the forest, but the hole closes behind him. Shaddai searches for him and brings him back home.

Review: This is a lovely, gentle parable of the lost sheep. God is portrayed in both word and illustration as an old, white man with blue eyes and a long white beard.

Just the Way You Are   Ages: 5+
Author: Max Lucado   Illustrator: Sergio Martinez
Crossway Books, 1999
ISBN: 1581341148
Other Categories: Nature of God, Love of God, Family

Synopsis: A king announces he will adopt five orphans, and each child prepares gifts to make them worthy of him. The youngest child has only her heart to give, and finds out that the king accepts her gift but not the others until they are able to make time for him.

Review: This is a lovely story about God's love and acceptance. Some may read the message of the story as a reason not to develop and nurture the gifts and talents God gives us. God is portrayed as a bearded white man.

You Are Special   Ages:5+
Author: Max Lucado   Illustrator: Sergio Martinez
Crossway Books, 1997
ISBN: 0891079319   Other Categories: Self-esteem, Love of God

Synopsis: The judgmental Wemmick people spend their days giving each other stickers – stars for talent or beauty and gray dots for failure and physical imperfection. When Punchinello, covered in gray dots meets a girl without any stickers, she advises him to go see Eli, their maker. Eli tells Punchinello that the stickers will only stick if he gives importance to the Wemmicks' opinions. What really matters is what his creator thinks of him.

Review: This is a touching story about God's love for us in spite of our abilities or looks. The message is the more we turn to God, the less the opinions of others matter. God is portrayed as a white, bearded man.

Making Memories   Ages: 5+
Author: Janette Oke   Illustrator: Cheri Bladholm
Minneapolis: Bethany Backyard, 1999
ISBN: 0-7642-2190-6   Other Categories: Nature, Family

Synopsis: A boy talks to his grandfather about memories and uses all of his senses to appreciate God's world.

Review: This book is set in the country and uses soft acrylics. The story is a bit predictable.

Sanji's Seed   Ages: 8+
Author: B. J. Reinhard   Illustrator: Shelly Hehenberger
Minneapolis: Bethany House Publishers, 2000
ISBN: 0-7642-2210-4
Other Categories: Honesty, Multiculturalism, Morals

Synopsis: A young boy dreams of becoming King, but when he is given a seed to grow, he fails. The others who attempt the task also fail, but replace their seeds with healthy ones. Sanji finds out that in the end, his honesty is rewarded.

Review: This story about honesty depicts multicultural characters. There is a list of discussion starters at the end of the book. The story is about morals, but it makes its point without being too didactic. Children could write or tell their own stories to illustrate the importance of the values of their faiths.

The Prodigal Wolf Ages: 5+
Author: Gary Richmond   Illustrator: Bruce Day
Word Books, 1990
ISBN: 0-8499-0746-2   Other Categories: Parable

Synopsis: A family buys a wolf for a pet. When he runs away, he is taken to the zoo where, by chance, his family finds him five years later.

Review: This is said to be a true story. The wolf is not retuned to his family, as in the story of the prodigal son. The illustrations are poor.

Hey, That's Not What the Bible Says Ages: 8+
Author and Illustrator: Bill Ross
Nashville: Thomas Nelson, 1999
ISBN: 0-8499-5922-5   Other Categories: Satire, Humor

Synopsis: Each story is a twisted retelling of a familiar Bible story, interrupted with "Hey, that's not what the Bible says." This is followed by the "real story" from the Bible.

Review: This funny book has humorous illustrations. The twisted retellings are corrected with the complete original story. It provides a good way for children to compare the sarcastic retellings with the originals.

Hey, That's Not What the Bible Says, Too! Ages: 8+
Author and Illustrator: Bill Ross
Nashville: Thomas Nelson, 2001
ISBN: 0-8499-7592-1   Other Categories: Satire, Humor

Synopsis: The stories of Creation, Abraham and Sarah, Jacob, Joseph, the Exodus, Moses, Gideon, the Birth of Jesus, the Last Supper, and Saul are presented in these sarcastic, humorous retellings.

Review: See review of *Hey, That's Not What the Bible Says*.

Cemetery Quilt Ages: 8+
Authors: Kent and Alice Ross   Illustrator: Rosanne Kaloustian
Boston: Houghton Mifflin, 1995
ISBN: 0-395-70948-2   Other Categories: Death, New Life, Family

Synopsis: A child goes to her grandfather's funeral. At her grandmother's house, she finds the cemetery quilt, which has the name of the dead in coffin-shaped patches.

Review: Children should not read this book alone, as it is a frank examination of one family's way to deal with death.

The Dream Quilt   Ages: 3+
Author: Celeste Ryan   Illustrator: Mary Haverfield
Waterbrook Press, 1999
ISBN: 1-57856-223-6   Other Categories: Prayer, Nature of God

Synopsis: Michael has bad dreams until his mother gives him a dream quilt. When it gets worn, his grandmother takes the quilt away to mend it, and Michael learns that he can rely on God and prayer.

Review: The fabulous illustrations are a mix of watercolors and collage. Some rhymes are mixed in with the story, which allows children to join in the reading. This is a simple, beautiful story.

Cat Heaven   Ages: 3+
Author and Illustrator: Cynthia Ryland
New York: Scholastic (Blue Sky Press), 1997
ISBN: 0-590-10054-8   Other Categories: Poetry, Death, New Life

Synopsis: A cat has a wonderful time in Cat Heaven where it enjoys all its favorite things – catnip, bowls of milk, sleeping on God's bed, etc.

Review: This book may help when a child has lost a pet. God is portrayed as an old man with a white mustache. This may be problematic for those who are uncomfortable with patriarchal images of God. Children could write about or illustrate their understanding of heaven.

God Said Amen   Ages: 5+
Author: Sandy Eisenberg Sasso   Illustrator: Avi Katz
Woodstock, VT: Jewish Lights, 2000
ISBN: 1-58023-080-6
Other Categories: Fables, Cooperation, Problem Solving

Synopsis: Two kingdoms have opposite problems – one has water but no light, the other has light but no water. With the help of royal servants, God answers the prayers of each kingdom.

Review: This complicated fable shows how people can work together and help one another. The servants, not people of privilege, are the ones who are able to solve the problems with God's help.

The Great Dinosaur Mystery and the Bible   Ages: 8+
Author: Paul S. Taylor
Chariot Victor Publishing, 1998
ISBN: 0781430712   Other Categories: Creationism

Synopsis: This book has a very clear creationist perspective. It presents the argument that people and dinosaurs lived at the same time, and posits what life was like for people living with the dinosaurs. It presents the "theory" that dinosaurs became extinct as a result of the Great Flood, but note that it is presented as historical fact, not theory.

Review: This book is interesting, but should be read with caution and guidance. For liberal Christians, it would be fascinating to present the view that some believe that the world is approximately 6,000 years old, and this would make an interesting comparison study between science and creationist beliefs.

My Two Uncles   Ages: 5+
Author and Illustrator: Judith Vigna
Morton Grove, Illinois: Albert Whitman and Company, 1995
ISBN: 0-8075-5507-X   Other Categories: Family, Acceptance

Synopsis: Elly enjoys visiting her Uncle Ned and his partner, and spends some special time with them preparing a gift for Elly's grandparents' 50th anniversary; but when Ned's partner is not invited to the party, Ned decides not to attend. After church the next day, Elly's grandparents stop by to thank Ned for the present.

Review: This is a wonderful story about acceptance. Even though the grandfather is not fully convinced that he wants to have a relationship with Ned and his partner, he concedes a little, thus giving the story a realistic edge. It also shows that Christians can be gay-positive.

The Little Soul and the Sun   Ages: 5+
Author: Neale Donald Walsch   Illustrator: Frank Ricco
Charlottesville, VA: Hampton Roads, 1998
ISBN: 1571740872   Other Categories: Parables, Nature of God
Inclusive Language

Synopsis: The little soul, who is God's creation of light, wants to feel what he is created to be, so he is surrounded by another soul of darkness.

Review: This is a parable, retold from *Conversations with God, Book 1*. Depending on the maturity of the reader this book can be approached from, and appreciated by, people on many levels.

The Broken Promise   Ages: 5+
Author: Ravi Zacharias   Illustrator: Lad Odell
Colorado Springs: Faith Kids, 2000
ISBN: 0-78143-451-3   Other Categories: Morals, Multiculturalism

Synopsis: Asha and Anand decide to start collecting things just like their father. When they decide to trade collections, Anand does not give Asha all his marbles, even though she gives him all her candy. They learn that God always keeps promises.

Review: This story features an East Indian Christian family. The author was born in India, but the illustrator was not. The moral is a bit obvious, but the story is well told.

VeggieTales Books

Pa Grape's Shapes   Ages: 0+
Author: Phil Vischer
Nashville: Tommy Nelson, 1997
ISBN: 0-8499-1507-4   Other Categories: Great Beginnings

Synopsis: Pa Grapes wants to explore the world, but he doesn't have tires for his car. He goes in search of the right shape for his new tires.

Review: Some books in this series have a Christian message, but they are mainly educational. The books are based on characters from the popular VeggieTales series. Rhyming verse is used to teach the lessons.

Archibald's Opposites   Ages: 0+
Author: Phil Vischer
Nashville: Tommy Nelson, 1998
ISBN: 0-8499-1533-3   Other Categories: Great Beginnings

Synopsis: Archibald the Asparagus teaches a lesson about opposites using Larry and Bob as volunteers.

Review: See review for *Pa Grape's Shapes*.

Bob and Larry's ABC's   Ages: 0+
Author: Phil Vischer
Nashville: Tommy Nelson, 1997
ISBN: 0-8499-1508-2   Other Categories: Great Beginnings

Synopsis: This alphabet book is based on scenes from the VeggieTales videos, and some of the names will not make sense unless you are familiar with the video series.

Review: See *Pa Grape's Shapes.*

How Many Veggies?   Ages: 0+
Author: Phil Vischer
Nashville: Tommy Nelson, 1997
ISBN: 0-8499-1488-4   Other Categories: Great Beginnings

Synopsis: Bob sets out to sail his boat, but other vegetables join in until there are too many on board.

Review: See review for *Pa Grape's Shapes.*

Junior's Colors   Ages: 0+
Author: Phil Vischer
Nashville: Tommy Nelson, 1997
ISBN: 0-8499-1487-6   Other Categories: Great Beginnings

Synopsis: Junior likes to color with his crayons, and he shares the colors of all his favorite things.

Review: See review for *Pa Grape's Shapes.*

Time for Tom   Ages: 0+
Author: Phil Vischer
Nashville: Tommy Nelson, 1998
ISBN: 0-8499-1534-1   Other Categories: Great Beginnings

Synopsis: Tom moves through the different times and events in his day. A clock on each page shows the changing time.

Review: See review for *Pa Grape's Shapes.*

VeggieTales Videos

VeggieTales: Rack, Shack & Benny   Ages: **3+**
VIDEO   30 Minutes
Chicago: Big Idea Productions, Everland Entertainment, 1995
Other Categories: Humor, Morals, Retellings

Synopsis: An adaptation of the biblical story of Shadrach, Meshach, and Abednego. In this version, Rack, Shack, and Benny work at a chocolate factory. When they are asked to sing to a 90-foot-tall chocolate bunny, they stand up for what is right, but end up in the furnace.

Review: The VeggieTales series is based on a formula, which most of the videos follow closely. The two main characters, Bob and Larry, answer a question from a child's letter, using stories and songs. About halfway through the video, Larry sings a silly song. At the end of the story, Bob and Larry meet again in the kitchen, of course, and discuss what was learned. This is concluded by a simple Bible verse.

These videos are fun and bouncy, and will hold a child's attention. The messages are simple and straightforward. As in the Bible, most of the characters are male, and almost all the teaching is done by male vegetables. A more inclusive cast of characters would be beneficial, but the videos are still very good. The 3-D computer animation is well done, and the voices are very expressive. There are also funny plays on words that only adults might understand.

Read-along books are also available with bright, colorful illustrations from the videos. These books have the same titles as the videos, but do not have ISBN numbers.

VeggieTales: God Wants Me to Forgive Them?!?   Ages: **3+**
VIDEO   32 Minutes
Chicago: Big Idea Productions, Everland Entertainment, 1994
Other Categories: Humor, Morals, Retellings

Synopsis: There are two stories on this video, both about forgiveness. In "The Grapes of Wrath," Junior Asparagus learns about how hard, but important, it is to forgive the insensitive Grape family.

"Larry's Lagoon" is a spoof on the *Gilligan's Island* television show. Larry is daydreaming when he crashes the boat into a deserted island. The other shipwrecked people learn about why God asks us to forgive others.

Review: See review for *Rack, Shack & Benny*.

VeggieTales: Josh and the Big Wall!   Ages: 3+
VIDEO   30 Minutes
Chicago: Big Idea Productions, Everland Entertainment, 1997
Other Categories: Humor, Morals, Retellings

Synopsis: The promised land awaits, but first, they must go through Jericho. This adaptation of the biblical story of Joshua stresses the importance of listening to God, even if what God wants us to do sounds a bit odd.

Review: See review for *Rack, Shack & Benny*.

VeggieTales: Where's God When I'm S-Scared?   Ages: 3+
VIDEO   30 Minutes
Chicago: Big Idea Productions, 1993
Other Categories: Humor, Morals, Retellings

Synopsis: There are two stories on this video, both handling fear. In "Tales from the Crisper," Junior Asparagus watches a scary movie against his parents' advice. Bob and Larry sing him a song about how God is bigger than any of his fears.

In "Daniel and the Lion's Den," Larry, as Daniel, is thrown into the pit with the lions. This adaptation of the biblical story of Daniel teaches that God is always with us, even when things seem hopeless.

Review: See review for *Rack, Shack & Benny*.

VeggieTales: Are You My Neighbor?   Ages: 3+
VIDEO   30 Minutes
Chicago: Big Idea Productions, 1993
Other Categories: Humor, Morals, Retellings

Synopsis: There are two stories on this video, both about loving our neighbors. "The Story of Flibber-o-loo," retells the biblical story of the Good Samaritan, but in this case, the neighbors identify themselves by what they wear on their heads – either a pot or a shoe.

In "The Gourds Must Be Crazy!" the vegetables are in space about to be hit by a popcorn meteor. They are saved when some strange crew members who are always eating are sent out to dispose of the popcorn, and the others learn that strangers can be our neighbors, too.

Review: See review for *Rack, Shack & Benny*.

VeggieTales: Dave and the Giant Pickle   Ages: 3+
VIDEO   27 Minutes
Chicago: Big Idea Productions, Everland Entertainment, 1996
Other Categories: Humor, Morals, Retellings

Synopsis: In this adaptation of David and Goliath, Dave is a little shepherd boy who cannot measure up to his big brothers. When they go off to battle, the meet the unstoppable 8-foot-tall Giant Pickle. Only Dave, with God's help, is able to bring this Pickle down.

Review: See review for *Rack, Shack & Benny*.

VeggieTales: King George and the Ducky   Ages 3+
VIDEO   30 Minutes   Closed Captioned
Chicago: Big Idea, 2000
Other Categories: Humor, Morals, Retellings

Synopsis: Selfish King George, thinking he is the most important person around, enjoys his bath, and wants all the rubber duckies in the kingdom. Without overt references, this is the story of King David and Bathsheba.

Review: See review for *Rack, Shack, & Benny*.

VeggieTales: Larry-Boy and the Rumor Weed   Ages 3+
VIDEO   30 Minutes   Closed Captioned
Chicago: Big Idea, 1998
Other Categories: Humor, Morals,

Synopsis: Junior and Laura misunderstand an expression and start a rumor about Alfred, Larry-Boy's butler. When they tell the rumor-weed the story, it begins to spread and grow. This spoof of the *Batman* TV series is a story about the power of words.

Review: See review for *Rack, Shack, & Benny*.

VeggieTales: Lyle the Kindly Viking   Ages 3+
VIDEO   37 Minutes   Closed Captioned
Chicago: Big Idea, 2001
Other Categories: Humor, Morals,

Synopsis: In an attempt to bring up the standard of the show, Archibald presents a vegetable rendition of *Hamlet* and a Gilbert and Sullivan styled musical, complete with "Classy Songs by Larry." In the Viking story, Lyle teaches the mean Vikings that sharing is important for everyone.

Review: See review for *Rack, Shack, & Benny.*

VeggieTales: The Toy That Saved Christmas **Ages 3+**
VIDEO   30 Minutes   Closed Captioned
Chicago: Big Idea, 1993
Other Categories: Humor, Morals, Christmas

Synopsis: The citizens of Dinkletown are convinced that Christmas is about getting toys, until one toy sets out to learn about the true meaning of Christmas and the gift of God's love in the baby Jesus.

Review: See review for *Rack, Shack, & Benny.*

VeggieTales: Larry-Boy and the Fib from Outer Space **Ages 3+**
VIDEO   30 Minutes
Chicago: Big Idea, Everland Entertainment, 1997
Other Categories: Humor, Morals,

Synopsis: When Junior Asparagus breaks his father's special collector's plate, he meets a fib from outer space who tells him how to avoid trouble. The real trouble starts when the fib begins to grow out of control. Not even Larry-Boy, the super-hero, can save Junior. Only by admitting to his lie can Junior conquer it.

Review: See review for *Rack, Shack, & Benny.*

VeggieTales: Madame Blueberry **Ages 3+**
VIDEO   30 Minutes   Closed Captioned
Chicago: Big Idea, 1993
Other Categories: Humor, Morals, Retellings

Synopsis: Madame Blueberry longs to buy all the things she does not have, but she cannot be satisfied. She meets a girl who has very little and a boy who is easily satisfied, but the girl and boy are still happy. Madame Blueberry learns that happiness is not found in material goods, and is able to give thanks for all she has.

Review: See review for *Rack, Shack, & Benny.*

VeggieTales: Esther: The Girl Who Became Queen **Ages 3+**
VIDEO   36 Minutes   Closed Captioned
Chicago: Big Idea, 2000
Other Categories: Humor, Morals, Retellings

Synopsis: The King chooses Esther to be his wife and, in spite of her apprehensions, she follows her cousin Mordecai's advice so she can help her people. When Haman threatens to banish their family to the Island of Perpetual Tickling, Esther is the only one who can help. So, she faces her fear to do the right thing with God's help.

Review: See review for *Rack, Shack, & Benny.*

Other Videos

321 Penguins! The Cheating Scales of Bullamanka   Ages 3+
VIDEO   30 Minutes   Closed Captioned
Chicago: Big Idea, 2001
Other Categories: Humor, Morals, Science Fiction

Synopsis: Michelle and her brother, Jason, are playing a game of "Squid, Tac, Toad," when Michelle decides to cheat in order to win. She is then taken into space to Bullamanka with the Penguins to face the cheating Lizard King. There, Michelle learns a lesson about the importance of playing fairly.

Review: This series is not as lively, funny or musical as the VeggieTales series, but it is enjoyable and uses a similar premise – children learn a lesson from the Bible, based on one verse. The main characters are twins, but the outrageous penguins, Zidgel, Midgel, Fidgel, and Kevin steal the show.

321 Penguins! Trouble on Planet Wait-Your-Turn   Ages 3+
VIDEO   30 Minutes   Closed Captioned
Chicago: Big Idea, 2000
Other Categories: Humor, Morals, Science Fiction, Family

Synopsis: Jason and his sister, Michelle, are taken to their grandmom's cottage where there is not much to do, until they discover the attic. While fighting over the telescope, Jason finds a spaceship and is taken to Planet Wait-Your-Turn. There he learns a lesson about turn-taking.

Review: See review for *The Cheating Scales of Bullamanka.*

Books by Children

The 11th Commandment: Wisdom from Our Children　　**Ages: 3+**
Authors: The Children of America
Illustrators: The Children of America
Woodstock, VT: Jewish Lights, 1996
ISBN: 1-879045-46-X　　Other Categories: Humor

Synopsis: "If there were an 11th Commandment, what would it be?" Children from many faiths and cultures answer this question. Their responses are grouped into five categories: Living with Other People, Living with the Earth, Living with Family, Living with Yourself, and Living with God.

Review: Some responses are funny and others are very poignant. This delightful book will be enjoyed by people of all ages.

In God's House　　**Ages: 3+**
Author: Robert Coles　　Illustrators: The Contributors
Grand Rapids, MI: Wm. B. Eerdmans, 1996
ISBN: 0-8028-5126-7　　Other Categories: Nature of God

Synopsis: Children's illustrations and descriptions of God's House.

Review: The contributions to this book are made by children who are "poor, hurt, ailing, abandoned, abused, or victims of bad luck" (quoted from the book jacket). Many of the insights are very touching.

Thank You God: The Prayers of Children　　**Ages: 5+**
Compiled by Fiona Corbridge　　Illustrators: The Contributors
Hillsboro, Oregon: Beyond Words Publishing, 1997
ISBN: 1-885223-53-6　　Other Categories: Prayer, Other Faiths

Synopsis: This is a collection of prayers written and illustrated by Jewish and Christian children.

Review: The prayers in this collection show a wide range of desires, emotions, and requests.

Children's Letters to God: The New Collection　　**Ages: 5+**
Compiled by Stuart Hample and Eric Marshall
Illustrator: Tom Bloom
New York: Workman Publishing, 1991
ISBN: 0-89480-999-7　　Other Categories: Prayer, Praise

Synopsis: This is a collection of questions, wishes, and thanksgivings written by children to God.

Review: This delightful collection of honest letters to God covers a variety of emotions – from funny to serious to poignant.

Just Build the Ark and the Animals Will Come   Ages: 8+
Author: David Heller   Illustrator: Melanie Hope Greenberg
New York: Villard Books, 1994
ISBN: 0-679-42756-2   Other Categories: Humor

Synopsis: Children from a number of Christian denominations and a variety of faiths give their explanations on various topics from the Old Testament such as why Adam was created before Eve, and how Noah's family occupied themselves on the Ark.

Review: As with most books of this type, it may appeal more to adults. Some of the quotations seem to be intentionally silly, especially ones from older children.

Why I Believe in God
and Other Reflections by Children   Ages: 5+
Author: Dandi Daley Mackall   Illustrators: The Contributors
Rocklin, CA: Prima Publishing, 1999
ISBN: 0-7615-1649-2   Other Categories: Nature of God

Synopsis: A collection of short contributions by more than 100 children about the nature of God.

Review: Children between the ages of 5–12 write about their beliefs in God. Adults may find this book more amusing than children.

3

Great Beginnings
Books for Babies
&Toddlers

For it was you who formed my inward parts;
you knit me together in my mother's womb.
I praise you, for I am fearfully and wonderfully made.
Wonderful are your works; that I know very well.
My frame was not hidden from you,
when I was being made in secret,
intricately woven in the depths of the earth.
Your eyes beheld my unformed substance.
In your book were written all the days that were formed for me,
when none of them as yet existed.

PSALM 139:13–16

Reading aloud is one of the most important things a parent, caregiver or teacher can do with a child. It creates a wonderful time for sharing. Reading aloud to a child is one of the most loving acts a person can give. The soothing sound of your voice can calm and reassure children.

When to Read to a Child

It is important to establish reading routines with children from very early on. Reading can and should start at birth or even before. The sounds of the parents' voices are heard in utero. For a parent who has never read to a child, it is good to practice reading aloud even before the baby is born. Not every person is good at reading aloud. For some, it takes practice. Listening to others read aloud is a good way to learn. Visiting the local public library during storytime, volunteering at a local public school, or listening to a visiting author can greatly help people who want to hone their reading skills.

Spending time each night reading together can help form the basis for a lifetime of reading pleasure. Make sure all the chores are done. Turn off the phone. Do not answer the door – you may even want to put a note on the door asking visitors to return later. Remove distractions such as radios, televisions, and computers.

Selecting Books

Books or gift certificates can be given as gifts for infants and toddlers. Gift certificates are great especially for toddlers, because they can choose something of their own. When a child has ownership in a book, they are more likely to take a greater interest in it and are more motivated to read it. With a gift certificate, a parent may want to narrow the options to a few books and let the child choose. By doing this, the parent still has a say in what is going to be read, and the child still feels that they have control of what is chosen.

The quality of books for the very young varies greatly. It is very important to be selective. Some books for young children are scaled-down versions of picture books for older children. While some are well done, others lose their core when they are adapted. Some board books lose the richness of color that was present in the original picture book. Other books are just not suited for adaptation at all. Even though a board book may have the same title and look as the original picture book, the text and illustrations can be quite different.

Cautions

Many books for younger children have cartoon illustrations. As stated in the section on cautions (see Chapter 1 – Introduction), there is a risk in using cartoons to portray characters, as they rarely show nuance or detail. This can lead to stereotypical and extremely shallow portrayals. The images we see, even very early on, can influence the way we see ourselves and others.

Be sure to purchase books that portray people from many cultures, and present these books to children very early. This shows the child the importance of acceptance of all people, and with Christian books, shows that we are all part of God's creation.

Ways to Use the Literature

- Have a selection of literature for young children in the church. At my church, we welcome infants and young children to stay during the worship service if they wish. We keep books and coloring materials in the sanctuary for their use. This also gives a good way to introduce parents to Christian children's literature.

- Talk with your child about the values in the stories you read.

- Collect literature for infants and young children for the nursery and Sunday school. This can calm an anxious child or entertain a bored child. Keep books in the sanctuary to entertain children who do not go out for Sunday school.

- Start a library at your church with good books for parents to borrow. You may be able to solicit donations from people whose children have outgrown their books, or you may ask people to donate books in honor of special events like baptisms or births.

- Begin a ritual of reading aloud with your child from birth. Read every night before prayers and bedtime. Choose a new book to read at least once a week. Let your child select one book, even if it is the same book every night. This may become part of the ritual.

- Encourage older siblings to read to younger ones. This makes the older children feel "grown-up" and responsible, and it creates a special time for siblings to share with one another.

- Let your children read to you. They may memorize familiar stories or may retell from the illustrations. Value their stories and ask questions about what they have told you.

- Tell your child stories. You may want to paraphrase Bible stories or other familiar tales.

- Do not use stories as a reward or punishment.

- Always pack a few books in your diaper bag.

- Read simple books during the Children's Time in church. You may talk with the older children about general themes in the book, and you will have included the youngest by reading something at their level.

- Keep drawing materials on hand for young children to "write" their own books. Using a simple zigzag stitch (at a wide setting or you will just perforate the pages), stitch down the middle of a few pieces of paper on a sewing machine to hold the pages together. This is safer than stapling sheets, as the staples may scratch or come out.

- Visit bookstores and public libraries often. It is a good way to meet other parents and find out what is new. If you know of certain books that should be in their collections, let them know.

- Visit other Sunday school classes to see how they use children's books.

- Plan a child's birthday party around a book theme. Choose a favorite book and dress as characters from the book. You may want to give paperback copies of the book to your guests.

- Read in front of your child. Whether it's the newspaper, the Bible, a paperback novel, or a magazine, it is important for youngsters to see you reading. You may even want to have a special time for each of you to read your own books.

- Talk about what you are reading with your child. Set aside time to tell each other about the books that interest you.

- Find a good children's Bible. Beware of picture Bibles, because many have very poor illustrations. Choose carefully. When reading the Bible with your child, read the same passages in your own Bible.

- Find books about music and learn some special songs. If you do not sing, tapes or CDs make a good alternative.

- Rent or purchase videos for rainy days. Some libraries also have videos available.

- Watch the videos with your child, at least for the first viewing. Do not be afraid to turn off the television if the show is boring, violent, or inappropriate for any reason.

- Tape your child's favorite books. Use a bell to indicate when to turn the pages. This may help you avoid having to read the same book thousands of times, and may free up some time for you to do necessary chores. You can put a number of books on one tape, one following the other.

Bibliography

God Is Like a Mother Hen and Much, Much More   Ages: 0+
Author and Illustrator: Carolyn Stahl Bohler
Louisville: Westminster John Knox Press, 1996
ISBN: 1-57153-200-5   Other Categories: Nature of God
Inclusive Language

Synopsis: Using metaphors from the Bible, each page illustrates the nature of God.

Review: This simple book has spaces for children to fill in their own metaphors about God and gives references to the biblical metaphors. This offers a good way to introduce children to the nature of God and the many ways in which God can be understood.

Count Your Blessings   Ages: 0+
Author: Donna D. Cooner   Illustrator: Kim Simons
Word Books, 1995
ISBN: 0-8499-1199-0   Other Categories: Counting Books, Praise

Synopsis: A counting book about the blessings of everyday life.

Review: The bright, simple illustrations may seem a bit stereotyped. Some of the rhymes don't actually rhyme. Nevertheless, it is a good way to get children to look at the blessings in the world around them.

My First Bible Board Book   Ages: 0+
Editor: Nicola Deschamps
Markham: Scholastic Canada, 2000
ISBN: 0-439-98736-9   Other Categories: Board Books

Synopsis: This board book has labeled illustrations of a variety of things from the Bible.

Review: While there are a number of illustrations of biblical items and animals, one has to wonder about the choice of some of the items and animals portrayed such as watermelon or vultures, parrots, kangaroos, crocodiles, and geckos.

The Presence of God   Ages : 0+

Author: Marie-Agnes Gaudrat   Illustrator: Ulises Wensell

Collegeville, Minnesota: Lutterworth Press/Liturgical Press, 1992

ISBN: 0-7188-2857-7   Other Categories: Board Book, Nature of God

Synopsis: This book compares God to light, rain, a rock, and wind.

Review: This is a companion book to *The Word of God* by the same author. The character in this book is a white girl.

The Word of God   Ages: 0+

Author: Marie-Agnes Gaudrat   Illustrator: Ulises Wensell

Collegeville, Minnesota: Lutterworth Press/Liturgical Press, 1992

ISBN: 0-7188-2858-5   Other Categories: Board Book, Nature of God

Synopsis: This simple book compares God to a present, a promise, favorite stories, and light.

Review: The lovely, doublespread illustrations show a black child and his grandmother who shows him what God is like. A companion book to *The Presence of God*.

The Hidden Treasure (Pop-Up Parables)   Ages: 0+

Author: Jan Godfrey   Illustrator: Chris Saunderson

Nashville: Abingdon Press, 2001

ISBN: 0-687-04950-4   Other Categories: Parables, Retellings, Pop-ups

Synopsis: A very simple retelling of the parable of the Hidden Treasure.

Review: These simple, pop-up books have cartoon-like illustrations. The straightforward language makes the books in this series very accessible.

The Camel and the Needle (Pop-Up Parables)   Ages: 0+

Author: Jan Godfrey   Illustrator: Chris Saunderson

Nashville: Abingdon Press, 2001

ISBN: 0-687-05010-3   Other Categories: Parables, Retellings, Pop-ups

Synopsis: A very simple retelling of the parable of the Camel and the Needle.

Review: See review for *The Hidden Treasure*.

The Lost Sheep (Pop-Up Parables)   Ages: 0+

Author: Jan Godfrey   Illustrator: Chris Saunderson

Nashville: Abingdon Press, 2001

ISBN: 0-687-04930-X   Other Categories: Parables, Retellings, Pop-ups

Synopsis: A very simple retelling of the parable of the Lost Sheep.

Review: See review for *The Hidden Treasure*.

The Two Houses (Pop-Up Parables)   Ages: 0+
Author: Jan Godfrey   Illustrator: Chris Saunderson
Nashville: Abingdon Press, 2001
ISBN: 0-687-05000-6   Other Categories: Parables, Retellings, Pop-ups

Synopsis: A very simple retelling of the parable of the Two Houses.

Review: See review for *The Hidden Treasure*.

Bible Friends: Who's Hiding?   Ages: 0+
Author: Sally Lloyd-Jones   Illustrator: Tracey Moroney
Pleasantville, NY: Reader's Digest Children's Books, 2001
ISBN: 0-570-07147-X   Other Categories: Bible Stories

Synopsis: This lift-the-flap book contains questions and answers about stories from the Old and New Testaments.

Review: The illustrations show only white people. Biblical references for the stories help adults find the story sources.

Bible Friends: Who Says That?   Ages: 0+
Author: Sally Lloyd-Jones   Illustrator: Tracey Moroney
St. Louis: Concordia Publishing House, 2001
ISBN: 0-570-07148-8   Other Categories: Predictable Books

Synopsis: This lift-the-flap book is very simple and predictable.

Review: The book shows how God loves us as a mommy loves her babies. There are references to Bible verses. Jesus is depicted as white.

Lift the Flap Bible   Ages: 0+
Author: Sally Lloyd Jones   Illustrator: Tracey Moroney
Pleasantville, NY: Reader's Digest Children's Books, 2000
ISBN: 1-57584-403-6   Other Categories: Board Book, Retellings

Synopsis: The stories of Creation, Noah, Moses, David, Jonah, Jesus, and some parables are retold with references.

Review: There are 40 flaps for children to explore in this simple book. The pages of this book are glossy, but when you lift the flap, they are dull underneath.

Adam, Adam, What Do You See?   **Ages: 0+**
Author: Bill Martin Jr. and Michael Sampson   Illustrator: Cathie Felstead
Nashville: Tommy Nelson, 2000
ISBN: 0-8499-7614-6   Other Categories: Rhymes, Predictable Books

Synopsis: This rhyming book is based on Bill Martin Jr.'s classic *Brown Bear, Brown Bear, What Do You See?* This new version shows Ruth, Esther, Mary, and men from the Old and New Testaments.

Review: This fun, rhyming book has bold, simple illustrations with mainly white characters. Each page has biblical references.

The Bible Alphabet   **Ages: 3+**
Illustrator: Keith Moseley
Nashville: Broadman and Holman, 1998
ISBN: 0-8054-1288-3   Other Categories: Pop-ups, Art, Alphabet Books

Synopsis: This pop-up alphabet book has separate smaller pages for each letter of the alphabet, which illustrate people and things from Old and New Testaments.

Review: The paper engineering in this book is excellent. Each pop-up is done in white against a brightly colored background. It is odd, however, that J is for Jonah, not Jesus, and there is no letter X (which could also have stood for Jesus).

Counting on Angels: A Pop-Up Counting Book   **Ages: 0+**
Author: Brenda Ward   Illustrator: Sandra Salzillo Shields
Dallas: Word Publishing, 1995
ISBN: 0-8499-1218-0   Other Categories: Angels

Synopsis: A rhyming, counting, pop-up book.

Review: A simple, short rhyme which young children could memorize easily. The pop-ups are well designed.

4

Beautiful Words
Songs, Prayers, & Poems

Praise the Lord!
Praise God in the sanctuary;
praise God in the mighty firmament!
Praise God for mighty deeds;
praise God according to God's exceeding greatness!
Praise with trumpet sound;
praise God with lute and harp!
Praise God with tambourine and dance;
praise God with strings and pipe!
Praise God with clanging cymbals;
praise God with loud clashing cymbals!
Let everything that breathes praise the Lord!
Praise the Lord!

PSALM 150 (INCLUSIVE LANGUAGE PSALMS)

Children's literature based on songs, poems, and prayers is rich and varied. Books with songs, poems, and prayers connect easily with the Bible. They provide a way to understand and connect with the importance of music, poetry, and prayer in worship and daily life throughout the ages. To God, music is not a frill or an extra, but an integral part of our lives. Music often expresses what words alone cannot speak. Poetry condenses thought and exemplifies beauty in verse. Prayers are how we speak and listen to God. All three are vitally important to our being and our relationships with God.

Songs

One category of books about songs explains the origin or effect that song has had through the ages. *Silent Night: The Song from Heaven*, by Linda Granfield and illustrated by Nelly and Ernst Hofer fits into this category. This book not only gives the history of the song, but also tells the Christmas story as two children experience the crèche at their church in Oberndorf, Austria in 1818, the origin of the carol.

Some books, such as *From a Distance*, by Julie Gold and illustrated by Jane Ray, take a single song and illustrate it in a way that takes the text and reflects it by illustrating the lyrics, or extends it by telling a story in the pictures themselves. A number of musical interpretations of this song have been recorded, and this would be a wonderful way to compare the different recordings.

Music can also help us to connect with different cultures. The words of many African American spirituals, for example, often have codes used by people who were attempting to escape slavery by the Underground Railroad.

Prayers

For the parent who is not entirely comfortable with extemporaneous prayer, a book with a collection of prayers may be a wonderful way for both parent and child to pray without worrying about the words. This may offer a way to begin new family rituals of prayers around meal and bedtimes, sharing blessings, and giving thanks.

Many different books explore prayers that may or may not be a part of the traditional worship services at church. Some of the most beautiful books take prayers, such as the Lord's Prayer and illustrate them, so that the illustrations tell a story of their own.

Other collections may be more eclectic such as *The Children's Book of Poems, Prayers and Meditations*, compiled by Liz Attenborough, with various illustrators. One of the benefits of eclectic collections is that they usually draw on traditional prayers for much of their collection. This is a wonderful way to introduce children to the prayers which may be used still in worship or other rituals. When children are more familiar with the various readings and recitations in worship, they are more able to be a part of it. Worship is much less of a mystery when a child is more knowledgeable about the various components of the liturgy.

Poems

Some books take a biblical poem, song, or prayer and illustrate it. Author and illustrator Bijou Le Tord has created many fine examples, such as *The River and the Rain*, a retelling of the Lord's Prayer with an environmental theme; and The Little Shepherd, a retelling of Psalm 23, told through the eyes of a young shepherd boy.

Other books are compilations of poems. Poems are gathered from a variety of sources into an anthology. These may be brought together on a particular theme such as *A Child's Book of Blessings*, compiled by Sabrina Dearborn and illustrated by Olwyn Whelan, which gathers blessings from around the world into one volume. These books provide a great resource for those working in church settings, as it is easy to find a poem or prayer that will work with the theme or readings for a service.

A poetry book need not be collections of poems, but can also be a poem on its own. A beautiful example is *Where Does God Live?* by Holly Bea and exquisitely illustrated by Kim Howard using paste-paper techniques. This book uses poetry to show a child's search for God.

For the musical or linguistic child, books such as these may link their musical abilities and gifts with print. Through music, the child may be better able to express or understand their faith, because that is the way that particular child learns best. These books may help validate the importance of that gift, and may give witness to the importance of music to God and God's people. For a child with linguistic intelligence, the use of beautiful words to explore and express God's love may touch their heart in a way nothing else can.

Ways to Use the Literature

- Read one of the books such as *The River and the Rain* instead of the traditional prayers during an intergenerational worship service.

- Learn one of the songs that has inspired a book such as *First He Made the Sun*, by Harriet Ziefert and illustrated by Todd McKie.

- Work through a book of prayers, praying one or two prayers before bedtime. You can take turns reading the prayers, read them together, or read them silently.

- Write a prayer for a special occasion. You might want to give it to someone as a gift or read it during a service.

- Collect your favorite prayers and make them into a book of your own. You might want to add ones you have written. Illustrate your book.

- Perform a choral reading of a poem. Older children might like to perform a rap using percussion instruments, which may be improvised using found objects such as keys and 5-gallon drums.

- Memorize and recite a poem.

- Use the structure of a poem to create a poem of your own.

- Learn about different types of poems such as cinquains, haiku, free verse, limericks.

- Choreograph a dance to go along with a song from one of the books, or learn a folk dance from another culture.

- Collect books about songs along a certain theme, such as Christmas carols or folk songs from a variety of cultures.

- Use books about African American spirituals to learn about the history of slavery in America and Canada.

- Use books about folk songs to learn about the cultures represented in the songs. Find out about the origins of the folk songs and their meaning.

- Find different songs in the Bible. Compare the number of songs in the Old and New Testaments. Why is there such a difference?

- Learn about the importance of song in the Jewish temples. Compare that with the way songs and music are used in worship in your own church today.

- Find out about which instruments were used in biblical times. Some of those instruments are still widely used, while others are more rare. Try to borrow some of those instruments, or invite someone who plays one to perform during worship.

- Take your favorite song, poem, or prayer and illustrate it.

- Make a list of different musicians in the Bible.

- The Bible contains some famous songs. Find a famous song and read it aloud, or put it to music.

- Write a poem of your own and make it into a book. If you are not a great illustrator, get a friend to do the illustrations. Many authors do not illustrate their own books. We each have different gifts!

Bibliography

All Things Bright and Beautiful   Ages: 3+
Author: Cecil Frances Alexander   Illustrator: Bruce Whatley
HarperCollins, 2001
ISBN: 0-06-026617-1   Other Categories: Nature, Animals

Synopsis: A young girl explores a farm, the animals and
the countryside, and later shares her experience with her family.

Review: The words of the famous hymn are illustrated delightfully. The
girl shows respect and appreciation for everything in her world.

The Children's Book of Poems, Prayers and Meditations   Ages: 5+
Compiled by Liz Attenborough
Illustrators: Bee Willey, Thomas Taylor, Stephen Lambert, Allan
Drummond, Jill Newton, Colin Williams, Valeria Petrone, Maryclare Foa,
Peter Bailey, and Rosemary Woods
Boston: Element Children's Books, 1998
ISBN: 1-90188-185-7   Other Categories: Meditation, Poetry, Prayer

Synopsis: This is an anthology of hundreds of poems, prayers, and
meditations, mainly from traditional sources. The anthology has ten different
subjects, each with a different illustrator.

Review: Each chapter of the anthology ends with a lovely guided meditation
which could be led by a teacher, minister, parent, etc. The meditation is
meant to allow the child to reflect on the poems and prayers in the collection.
The illustrations are disappointing, and can detract from the text.

My Spiritual Alphabet Book   Ages: 3+
Author: Holly Bea   Illustrator: Kim Howard
Tiburon, CA: H. J. Kramer, Inc. – Starseed Press, 2000
ISBN: 0-915811-83-9   Other Categories: The Environment
Inclusive Language

Synopsis: This lovely poem explores an appreciation for the creation of
heaven and earth and the importance of spiritual values.

Review: Kids will love to read this bouncy poem. The illustrations are bright
and fun. Mother Earth is one topic that is focused on.

Where Does God Live?   Ages: 5+
Author: Holly Bea   Illustrator: Kim Howard
Tiburon, CA: H. J. Kramer, Inc., 1997
ISBN: 0-915811-73-1   Other Categories: Nature of God

Synopsis: Hope asks many questions, but most of all, she wants to know where God lives. The friends and animals she meets each have different answers.

Review: This beautiful poem shows that God is in all creation. The illustrations show paste-paper techniques and depict multicultural characters.

A Child's Book of Prayer in Art   Ages: 8+
Author: Sister Wendy Beckett   Illustrator: Various Classical Painters
New York: DK Publishing, 1995
ISBN: 1-56458-875-0   Other Categories: Prayer, Art, Informational

Synopsis: Twelve aspects of prayer – respect, love, family, understanding, learning, forgiveness, choosing heaven, true happiness, thinking, determination, selflessness, and listening are examined using lessons from classical paintings.

Review: Using both the entire painting and two studies, Sister Wendy Beckett discusses the various aspects of prayer as they relate to the paintings. Some of the paintings are religious, while others are not.

Shalom, Salaam, Peace   Ages: 3+
Author: Howard I. Bogot   Illustrator: Norman Gorbaty
Central Conference of American Rabbis 2000
ISBN: 0881230820   Other Categories: Other Religions, Peace

Synopsis: This poem about peace is written in English, Arabic, and Hebrew. The book opens and reads from right to left.

Review: This fabulous book will be a great teaching tool for anyone who is working for issues of peace. The text is in three languages, side by side, and includes quotations from children about peace. A portion of the sales is donated to agencies working towards peace in the Middle East. Superb!

Grandpa, Is There a Heaven?   Ages: 8+
Author: Katherine Bohlmann   Illustrator: David Erickson
St. Louis: Concordia Publishing House, 2001
ISBN: 0-570-07136-4   Other Categories: Grandparents, Death, New Life

Synopsis: A child and his grandfather discuss death and heaven.

Review: This poem is interspersed with Bible verses. This takes a soft, gentle look at what heaven is like.

What About Heaven?   Ages: 0+
Author: Kathleen Long Bostrom   Illustrator: Elena Kucharik
Wheaton, Illinois: Tyndale House Publishers, 2000
ISBN: 0-8423-73353-5   Other Categories: Great Beginnings

Synopsis: This rhyming poem about heaven is based on biblical references.

Review: The poem answers a number of questions that young children may have about heaven. The illustrations are multicultural and rather stereotypical, especially the depiction of the Asian girl.

Thanks Be to God: Prayers from Around the World   Ages: 5+
Author and Illustrator: Pauline Boynes
New York: MacMillan, 1990
ISBN: 0-02-708541-4   Other Categories: Prayer

Synopsis: A collection of traditional prayers, some contemporary, some old.

Review: None of the prayers has inclusive language, but this does reflect the reality of traditional prayers. The illustrations are gentle.

Can I Pray with My Eyes Open?   Ages: 3+
Author: Susan Taylor Brown   Illustrator: Garin Baker
Hyperion Press, 1999
ISBN: 0786803282   Other Categories: Multiculturalism

Synopsis: This simple poem shows a girl wondering about how and when to pray, only to find out that prayer has no bounds.

Review: You can feel the emotions in Baker's oil paintings, which show a young black girl in her search for God. This book will take the pressure off people who are hoping to find the "right" way to pray.

Sleepytime Prayers:
Thoughts and Readings for Bedtime   Ages: 0+
Author: Yolanda Browne   Illustrator: Kathy Couri
Pleasantville, NY: Reader's Digest Children's Books, 2000
ISBN: 1-57584-665-9
Other Categories: Prayers, Board Books, Informational, Great Beginnings

Synopsis: The left-hand page of this board book has information about God, angels, nighttime, etc. with a matching prayer on the right-hand page.

Review: These are nice, simple prayers of thanksgiving for bedtime.

Daytime Prayers: Thoughts and Readings for Everyday Ages: 0+
Author: Yolanda Browne   Illustrator: Kathy Couri
Pleasantville, NY: Reader's Digest Children's Books, 2000
ISBN: 1-57584-664-0
Other Categories: Prayers, Board Books, Informational, Great Beginnings

Synopsis: The companion to *Sleepytime Prayers*.

Review: See *Sleepytime Prayers*.

Glory   **Ages: 3+**
Author: Nancy White Carlstrom   Illustrator: Debra Reid Jenkins
Grand Rapids, MI: Wm. B. Eerdmans Publishing Co. 2001
ISBN: 0-8028-5143-6
Other Categories: Nature, Praise, Prayer, Poetry

Synopsis: This poem is an offering of praise to God for the joy of nature.

Review: The illustrations show a girl trying on different costumes and masks of each animal, species, fish, or bird as they are mentioned in the poem. The oil paintings ribbon through each page of the book.

What Does the Sky Say?   **Ages: 5+**
Author: Nancy White Carlstrom   Illustrator: Tim Ladwig
Grand Rapids, MI: Wm. B. Eerdmans Publishing Co., 2001
ISBN: 0-8028-5208-4
Other Categories: Life, Nature, Multiculturalism

Synopsis: A little girl watches the ever-changing sky through the seasons and notices her changing feelings and growth.

Review: This lovely, non-rhyming poem shows a girl of color exploring her world and her own emotions. The language and artwork are beautifully matched to create a truly delightful book.

Absolutely Angels: Poems for Children & Other Believers Ages 5+
Selected by: Mary Lou Carney   Illustrator: Viqui Maggio
Honesdale, PA: Boyds Mills Press, 1998
ISBN: 1-56397-708-7   Other Categories: Angels, Poetry, Prayer

Synopsis: A collection of poems and prayers about angels.

Review: This collection is illustrated with cut-outs of Victorian angels, decorations, paintings, and found items. While the angels in the cut-outs are mainly white, others are portrayed in the illustrations. Angels have been popularized lately, but they have also had popularity during other times in our history, especially in Victorian times.

We Are Not Alone, We Live in God's World   Ages: 3+
Author: A New Creed of the United Church of Canada
Illustrator: Gary Crawford
Toronto: United Church Publishing House, 1996
ISBN: 1-55134-064-X   Other Categories: Beliefs, Creeds, Creation

Synopsis: An illustrated version of the New Creed of the United Church of Canada.

Review: This book shows people at various ages and stages of their life in the nature of God's creation. The illustrations include people of all races, social standing, and abilities.

My First Prayers and Psalms   Ages: 0+
Illustrator: Anna Curti
New York: Random House, 1999
ISBN: 0-375-80235-5
Other Categories: Board Books, Prayer, Multiculturalism

Synopsis: This is a collection of biblical prayers and psalms as well as traditional and poetic prayers.

Review: The prayers are very simple and straightforward with multicultural illustrations.

A Child's Book of Blessings   Ages: 3+
Author: Compiled by Sabrina Dearborn   Illustrator: Olwyn Whelan
New York: Barefoot Books, 1999
ISBN: 1-84148-010-X   Other Categories: Informational

Synopsis: This collection of blessings from around the world represents a variety of religions and traditions.

Review: Exquisite watercolor and ink illustrations accompany a number of short blessings that can be used at different times of the year. There is a list of sources and resources about the blessings. As an extension, children could follow the examples in this book and write their own blessings or collect blessings from people they know.

One Wide River to Cross   Ages: 3+
Author: Barbara Emberley   Illustrator: Ed Emberley
Little, Brown and Company, 1966/1992
ISBN: 0-316-23445-1   Other Categories: Multiculturalism

Awards: Caldecott Honor, 1967

Synopsis: Based on the African American spiritual, this rhyming counting book tells the story of the animals coming to the Ark.

Review: This wonderful book has different colored pages, illustrated with woodblocks. The music to the song of the same title is included.

Morning Has Broken   Ages: 5+
Author: Eleanor Farjeon   Illustrator: Tim Ladwig
Grand Rapids, MI: Wm. B. Eerdmans Publishing Co., 1996
ISBN: 0-8028-5127-4   Other Categories: Art

Synopsis: The text is taken from the 1931 hymn by Farjeon.

Review: Tim Ladwig enhances the beauty of this hymn as he captures each moment in time with photographic detail. He depicts different scenes for each line of the hymn.

A Book about God   Ages: 5+
Author: Florence Mary Fitch   Illustrator: Henry Sorensen
New York: Lothrop, Lee, and Shepard, 1998
ISBN: 0-688-16128-6   Other Categories: Nature of God, Poetry

Synopsis: This poetic narrative compares different things in nature to the nature of God.

Review: The text was written in 1953, and while it does not use inclusive language, it is lovely. The heavy oil illustrations do not really capture the beauty of Fitch's narrative.

Barnyard Prayers   Ages: 3+
Author: Laura Godwin   Illustrator: Brian Selznick
New York: Hyperion Books for Children, 2000
ISBN: 0-7868-0355-X   Other Categories: Prayers, Nature, Humor

Synopsis: A young city boy dreams that he visits different animals on his toy farm. Each animal has a different prayer to offer.

Review: Some of the prayers are funny, and some are adapted from traditional prayers, which may not sit well with some people because of their irreverent nature.

From a Distance   Ages: 5+
Author: Julie Gold   Illustrator: Jane Ray
New York: Dutton Children's Books, 1998
ISBN: 0-525-45872-7   Other Categories: Songs, Poetry, War, Justice

Synopsis: Based on the lyrics of the Grammy Award winning song by Julie Gold.

Review: Jane Ray's beautiful pastel and watercolor illustrations bring out the true beauty of this song about war, injustice, peace, and friendship on earth. Woven into the illustrations are familiar images of war, as one child's neighborhood is torn apart. This is, however, a book about hope and beauty, in spite of people's injustice to each other.

Amazing Grace: The Story of the Hymn   Ages: 8+
Author: Linda Granfield   Illustrator: Janet Wilson
Toronto: Tundra Books, 1997
ISBN: 0-88776-390-1   Other Categories: History

Synopsis: This is the story of the hymn, "Amazing Grace," and its composer, a slave trader who was caught in a storm and prayed to be delivered. After he was saved, he worked to abolish slavery.

Review: This fascinating story of a changed life may be a bit complicated and some of the history may need to be explained to children. The illustrations are very dark, but fit the text.

The Next Place   Ages: 5+
Author and Illustrator: Warren Hanson
Minneapolis: Walman House, 1997
ISBN: 0-931674-32-8   Other Categories: Death, New Life

Synopsis: A poem about what life is like after earthly life is done.

Review: This beautiful book uses a variety of artistic media including mosaic tile borders to illustrate the hope of new life. This is a truly comforting way to explain death to children.

Prayers & Graces:
A Lovely Collection for Boys & Girls   Ages: 3+
Author: Gail Harvey
New York: Derrydale Books, 1993
ISBN: 0-517-09276-X   Other Categories: Prayer

Synopsis: A collection of Prayers of Love, Graces, and Prayers for Bedtime.

Review: Some prayers are from the Bible, and others are from classical authors. The illustrations, like the prayers, are old and traditional.

The Gentle Dark:
Nighttime Poems & Prayers for Children   Ages: 3+
Author: Alyson Huntly   Illustrator: Chao Yu
Spruce Grove, Alberta: ParseNip Press
ISBN: 0-9683421-1-6 and
Etobicoke, Ontario: United Church Publishing House, 1999
ISBN: 1-55134-105-0   Other Categories: Nighttime

Synopsis: A collection of 18 poems and prayers about the dark.

Review: In her note, Huntly explains that she is attempting to reclaim the dark as a positive image, rather than the negative and racist one she grew up with. The watercolor illustrations show people from a wide variety of backgrounds, and the poems name children with names from many parts of the world.

The Goodbye Boat   Ages: 5+
Author: Mary Joslin   Illustrator: Claire S. Little
Grand Rapids, MI: Wm. B. Eerdmans Publishing Co., 1999
ISBN: 0-8028-5186-X   Other Categories: Death, New Life, Changes

Synopsis: This is a simple poem about saying goodbye.

Review: The lovely illustrations in this book leave lots of space to discuss losing a loved one who has moved or died.

Glory of Creation   Ages: 8+
Illustrator: Thomas Kinkade
Eugene, OR: Harvest House Publishers, 1998
ISBN: 1-56507-764-4   Other Categories: Art

Synopsis: A collection of poetry from Western poets and biblical quotations.

Review: Beautiful calligraphy and Kinkade's richly detailed oil paintings enhance this collection. The biblical quotations are not precisely referenced.

I Wanted to Know All about God   Ages: 3+
Author: Virginia L. Kroll   Illustrator: Debra Reid Jenkins
Grand Rapids, MI: Wm. B. Eerdmans Publishing Co., 1994
ISBN: 0-8028-5078-2
Other Categories: Community, Nature, Friends, Multiculturalism

Synopsis: Children wonder about God and find God in nature and people.

Review: This excellent poem has simple, yet deep language. The oil color
illustrations show a variety of races.

> *"I wanted to know what colors God likes*
> *Then I met several children of other races."*

Because Nothing Looks Like God   Ages: 3+
Author: Lawrence Kushner and Karen Kushner
Illustrator: Dawn Majewski
Woodstock: Jewish Lights, 2000
ISBN: 1-58023-092-X   Other Categories: Nature of God

Synopsis: This poem about the Nature of God takes the form of questions
and answers: Where is God? What does God look like? and How does God
make things happen?

Review: This beautiful, open book about who God is and what God does
shows God in everyday situations of our lives. There is also a board book
called *Where Is God?* which is based on this book.

The Lord's Prayer   Ages: 5+
Illustrator: Tim Ladwig
Grand Rapids, MI: Wm. B. Eerdmans Publishing Co., 2000
ISBN: 0-8028-5180-0   Other Categories: Prayer, Multiculturalism

Synopsis: A young girl and her father help an elderly neighbor. The girl
finds a beautiful pendant of the Lord's Prayer and returns it to the woman,
who then gives it to the girl.

Review: The story is told in the illustrations which match the text of the
Lord's Prayer. The family in this story is black. The beautiful watercolors
show the emotions and love of this family.

Goodnight Blessings   Ages: 3+
Author and Illustrator: Karen Mezek Leimert
Nashville: Thomas Nelson, 1994
ISBN: 0-8499-1134-6   Other Categories: God's Love

Synopsis: A young girl gets ready for bed and takes time to look back on her day. She gives thanks for all the blessings she has received.

Review: In this circular poem, each page leads to the next one. This lovely, gentle story reminds children (and adults) about God's love. Children could write their own blessings.

In Every Tiny Grain of Sand:
A Child's Book of Prayers and Praise   Ages: 3+
Compiled by Reeve Lindbergh
Illustrators: Christine Davenier and Bob Graham
Candlewick Press
ISBN: 0-7636-0176-4   Other Categories: Other Faiths, Prayer, Praise
Inclusive Language

Synopsis: Contains 77 prayers for the day, night, home, and earth from many cultures and faith traditions.

Review: The cultural origin of each prayer is given in this inclusive collection. The beautiful illustrations portray children from many cultures. Some of these prayers are well known, and others are more obscure. This gives a good introduction to the spirituality of different peoples, and a good way to foster respect and understanding for a variety of traditions.

The Circle of Days   Ages: 3+
Author: Reeve Lindbergh   Illustrator: Cathie Felstead
Cambridge, Mass: Candlewick Press, 1998
ISBN: 0-7636-0357-0   Other Categories: Praise, Environment, Poetry

Synopsis: Based on the "Canticle of the Sun" by St. Francis of Assisi, this adaptation is a song of praise for nature around us.

Review: This is a beautiful book of thanksgiving in both text and paper collage artwork. This adaptation is written by the daughter of Charles Lindbergh, the famous aviator.

A Child's Garden of Prayer　　　　　　　　　**Ages: 5+**
Author: Steve and Becky Miller　　Illustrator: Kathryn A. Fincher
Harvest House Publishers
ISBN: 0-7369-0117-5　　Other Categories: Prayer

Synopsis: A collection of 50+ prayers (some old and some new) and Bible verses.

Review: The paintings which accompany the prayers and verses have a soft, old-fashioned quality. Unfortunately, there is only one depiction of a non-white child.

The ABC Bible Storybook　　　　　　　　　**Ages: 3+**
Author: Karen Ann Moore　　Illustrator: Becky Farley
Colorado Springs: Faith Kids, 2000
ISBN: 0-78143-390-8
Other Categories: Alphabet Books, Retellings, Poetry

Synopsis: This is an alphabet book of poetry about stories in the Bible.

Review: Each poem has references to the biblical stories which inspired it. The illustrations are mainly white characters. Children could take other Bible stories and write their own poems about them, which could be staged for pageants, etc.

Good Night, God Bless　　　　　　　　　**Ages: 3+**
Author: Susan Heyboer O'Keefe　　Illustrator: Hideko Takahashi
New York: Henry Holt, 1999
ISBN: 0-8050-6008-1　　Other Categories: Community

Synopsis: In this good night poem, various members of the community settle in for the night.

Review: This may be a comforting bedtime ritual for children. One of the illustrations shows a mother bottle feeding her child; a depiction of breast-feeding may have been preferable.

Gates of Wonder:
A Prayerbook for Very Young Children　　　**Ages: 3+**
Authors: Robert Orkand, Joyce Orkand, and Howard I. Bogot
Illustrator: Neil Waldman
New York: Central Conference of American Rabbis, 1989
ISBN: 0-88123-009-X　　Other Categories: Judaism

Synopsis: This simple prayer book explains the basics of Jewish worship.

Review: Beautiful watercolors enhance the prayers. The Hebrew expressions have a pronunciation guide and English translation.

The Gift of an Angel:
For Parents Welcoming a New Child   Ages: 3+
Author and Illustrator: Marianne Richmond
Waldman House Press, 2000
ISBN: 0-931674-43-3   Other Categories: Poetry

Synopsis: God chooses a guardian angel for a child who is about to be born.

Review: This would be a lovely gift for expectant parents about God's care for each child. The beautiful illustrations are very soft and whimsical. There is some opposition to the concept of guardian angels, so caution is warranted.

Words of Gold:
A Treasury of the Bible's Poetry and Wisdom   Ages: 5+
Selected and Introduced by: Lois Rock
Illustrator: Sarah Young
Grand Rapids, MI: Wm. B. Eerdmans Publishing Co., 2000
ISBN: 0-8028-5199-1   Other Categories: Retellings

Synopsis: Short retellings of Old and New Testament stories with biblical references and introductions.

Review: A short paragraph introduces each reading, which uses the NRSV and Good News Bible. Gold borders and decorations enhance the readings.

Safe This Night:
Night-Time Prayers for Little Children   Ages: 3+
Author: Lois Rock   Illustrator: Louise Rawlings
Colorado Springs: Lion Publishing, 1997
ISBN: 0-7459-3616-4

Synopsis: This is a collection of prayers and poems for nighttime.

Review: The prayers are repetitive, and children could easily join in for the refrains. They could be read separately or as a whole. This offers a good way to introduce prayers if a parent is not comfortable making them up. The illustrations are framed with handmade paper, and portray some multicultural characters.

Bless This House   Ages: 3+
Author and Illustrator: Leslie Staub
San Diego: Harcourt, 2000
ISBN: 0-15-201984-7   Other Categories: Prayer

Synopsis: A child blesses his home, family, and the world as he prays before bed.

Review: This simple book could be used to help establish a prayer routine for children at bedtime. The sweet, bold illustrations are bright, and painted in oils.

One Earth, One Spirit:
A Child's Book of Prayers from Many Faiths & Cultures Ages: 3+
Author: Tessa Strickland
San Francisco: Sierra Club Books for Children, 1997
ISBN: 0-87156-978-7
Other Categories: Other Faiths, Prayer, Inclusion
Inclusive Language

Synopsis: Contains 17 prayers from around the world with photographs. Notes are provided for adults to help children understand the prayers.

Review: This is a beautiful collection of prayers and photographs. The photos are of excellent quality. Prayers have both male and female imagery.

A Child's Book of Prayers:
New & Traditional Prayers for Children   Ages: 0+
Author: Glenda Trist   Illustrator: Carol Hill
Toronto: DK Publishing, 1999
ISBN: 1-55144-214-0   Other Categories: Prayer, Children's Writing

Synopsis: This is a collection of short, simple prayers for different times and feelings (night, day, friends, family, animals, etc.).

Review: While the photos are very staged, some of these short prayers are written by children. This could be used to inspire children to write or collect their own prayers. See also: *A Child's Book of Values* by Lesley Wright.

God of the Sparrow   Ages: 3+
Author: Jaroslav J. Vajda   Illustrator: Preston McDaniels
Morehouse Publishing, 1999
ISBN: 0-8192-1745-X   Other Categories: Songs, Poetry, Nature

Synopsis: The modern Lutheran hymn "God of the Sparrow" (also written by Vajda) is presented in poetry.

Review: This is a beautiful, gentle poem about the nature of God. This book presents a sense of awe and reverence about the beauty of God's world.

God Answers My Prayers   Ages: 3+
Author: Denise Vezey   Illustrator: Victoria Ponikvar Frazier
Colorado Springs: Chariot Victor Publishing, 1999
ISBN: 0-78143-086-0   Other Categories: Prayer

Synopsis: Features three stories about a child's prayers to God.

Review: This simple book addresses why answers to prayer are not always what they seem or what we expect. The book is a bit didactic.

The Prayer of Jabez for Little Ones   Ages: 3+
Author: Bruce Wilkinson   Adapted by: Melody Carlson
Illustrator: Alexi Natchev
Nashville: Tommy Nelson, 2001
ISBN: 0-8499-7943-9   Other Categories: Prayer, Poetry

Synopsis: Adapted from the bestselling adult book *The Prayer of Jabez* by Bruce Wilkinson, this board book takes the prayer found in 1 Chronicles 4:10 and breaks it down into a poem for children.

Review: This is a lovely rendition of the phenomenally successful adult book. The prayer adaptation is simple, and the illustrations match the poem nicely.

The Prayer of Jabez for Kids   Ages: 10+
Author: Bruce Wilkinson   Adapted by: Melody Carlson
Illustrator: Dan Brawner
Nashville: Tommy Nelson, 2001
ISBN: 0-8499-7944-7   Other Categories: Young Teen Books, Prayer

Synopsis: An adaptation of the bestselling adult book *The Prayer of Jabez* by Bruce Wilkinson for older children.

Review: This chapter book is not as nice as the board book. It sets out a plan for children to follow, based on saying the prayer, reading and rereading the book, and involving others.

Emma and Mommy Talk to God   **Ages: 3+**
Authors: Marianne Williamson and Emma Williamson
Illustrator: Julia Noonan
HarperCollins Juvenile Books, 1996
ISBN: 0-06-026464-0   Other Categories: Family, Love of God

Synopsis: A child asks her mom about God, and learns about God's love for her.

Review: This is Marianne Williamson's first children's book. This lovely, gentle book about God's love would be wonderful as a bedtime story.

Making the World   **Ages: 5+**
Author: Douglas Wood   Illustrators: Yoshi and Hibiki Miyazaki
New York: Simon and Schuster Books for Young Readers, 1998
ISBN: 0-689-81358-9   Other Categories: Nature, Community

Synopsis: Different things happen in nature, and each impacts on the world around, helping to "make the world."

Review: The illustrations show people and animals all around the world, and emphasize the interdependence of people and animals and elements of nature. The simple poem has a repeated last line, allowing pre-readers to join in.

A Child's Book of Values   **Ages: 3+**
Author: Lesley Wright
New York: Dorling Kindersley, 2001
ISBN: 0-7894-6518-3   Other Categories: Children's Writing

Synopsis: This eclectic collection looks at 12 values. Each value has a definition, Bible stories, quotations from children, discussion points, a Bible verse, and a prayer written by a child.

Review: While the photos look staged, they do portray children from a variety of cultures. This book is a bit didactic, but it could be used as a tool to encourage children to think of other values and describe them. See also: *A Child's Book of Prayers* by Glenda Trist.

5

God & the Earth
Children's Environmental Literature

God saw everything that God had made, and indeed, it was very good.
And there was evening and there was morning, the sixth day.

GENESIS 1:31

Let the heavens praise your wonders, O Lord,
your faithfulness in the assembly of the holy ones.
For who in the skies can be compared to the Lord?
Who among the heavenly beings is like the Lord?

The heavens are yours, the Earth also is yours;
the world and all that is in it – you have founded them.

PSALM 89:5–6, 11

Children will be the caretakers of the legacy we leave behind. So far, we have not given them a great gift, nor have we set good examples for our children to follow. Children are often more in touch with the importance of the environment than adults. Children spend more time outdoors than most adults. Children relate to animals on a level that adults do not. Ultimately, our world is theirs, and it is what we do now that will determine their ability to carry on and care for that world.

The Bible and the Earth

The Bible is full of stories about the earth, the environment, and our connection to it. We are a part of nature, and are not separate from it. As a part of nature, we are impacted by the way we treat nature, ourselves and each other. Our role is described as having "dominion" over the earth. That does not mean controlling or ruling the world, but having deep and shared responsibility for the earth and all the things in it. God is found in the earth, not apart from it.

Connection to the land was integral to the lives of the people in biblical times. People relied on the land to provide food, water, and shelter. Animals were kept (and sacrificed), fish were caught, storms were feared, harvest was celebrated. In modern Western society, we have lost much of that connection. Most of us have shelter, and food is usually purchased at supermarkets, brought in from afar. Animals are companions, not meals unless they are processed elsewhere. But such was not the case in the Bible.

Many of the stories of Jesus take place in different environments, and often, the environment influences the story. Jesus prayed in the wilderness, walked on water, calmed the storms, preached on a mountaintop. But his main concern was the people of the earth and their relationship to each other and the world around them. As a human, Jesus was a part of his environment. As God, the Christ inspires us to bring glory to God on the earth.

There are not many Christian books about the environment. You can, however, bring other books and merge them with this topic. Books about creation, and about our role in creation are also well-suited to the theme of the environment. Do not forget that people form part of nature and the environment, and our role as creations of a loving God also makes up a part of the environment.

Native Spirituality

A study of the environment and creation could tie in nicely with Native Studies and learning about Native spirituality. The reverence for Mother Earth and Creator can be paralleled with biblical nature stories. There are many beautiful books by First Nations writers which talk about the environment and how they are called to care for it. We can learn a lot from these teachings.

Other Related Topics

Destruction
Stewardship
Creation

Responsibility
God's Gifts
Trees and Plants

Animals
Humans

Ways to Use the Literature

- *The River and the Rain* is a retelling of the Lord's Prayer using the environment to tell a story in the illustrations. Choose another prayer or story from the Bible and retell it, showing how it impacts our world.

- The Bible contains many stories about the environment. Noah's Ark is one, so is the story of Joseph and the time of famine. Collect as many biblical environment stories as you can find.

- List as many different environments as you can, both indoors and outdoors. Start with your room and work your way out. Name your favorite things in each environment. Name your least favorite.

- List ways to improve these environments. Be specific for each one. Set aside time every day to make one of these improvements.

- Weather plays an important role in many biblical stories. Snow is even mentioned in the Bible. Collect as many biblical stories as you can which have weather as an important factor for the outcome of the story.

- There are many animal stories in the Bible, such as the story of Jonah. Collect all the biblical animal stories you can find.

- Make a list of all the animals in the Bible.

- Make a list of all the trees and plants in the Bible.

- Make a list of all the people in the Bible!

- Ask if you can have some space in your church/schoolyard for a garden. Plant vegetables which can be used in church suppers or for a local shelter. Try to plant some plants or herbs that are mentioned in the Bible. Plant trees in memory of church members who have died or lost family members.

- Read *Grandad's Prayers of the Earth*. Write your own prayers for the earth and read them during a service.

- Plan activities for Earth Day. Make posters from recycled paper. Brainstorm activities that you can do to make the earth better, starting in your own community.

- The Book of Revelation promises a new heaven and a new earth. What do you think they will look like? What will be our role in them?

- Have a worship service outdoors. Go to a park, the beach, a field, the woods, a mountaintop, a valley, the rocky shoreline, a desert, a garden, a schoolyard, a conservation area, or another place of your choosing.

- Read *God in Between* by Sandy Eisenberg Sasso. List the places you find God in the world. List the ways you find God in others. List the ways you are a blessing to others.

- Learn about the way First Nations peoples care for and revere Mother Earth. Visit a Native Center, or attend a pow-wow. Invite a Native person to share their spirituality with you.

- Read *A Prayer for the Earth: The Story of Naamah, Noah's Wife* by Sandy Eisenberg Sasso. Write a story about an unnamed woman or man in the Bible. Name that person and write about an important thing they might have done.

- Read *Sing a New Song: A Book of Psalms* by Bijou Le Tord. Find other nature stories in the Bible.

 Bibliography

This Is the Earth That God Made   **Ages 3+**
Author: Lynn Downey   Illustrator: Benrei Huang
Minneapolis: Augsburg Fortress, 2000
ISBN: 0806639601   Other Categories: Activities, Poetry

Synopsis: This predictable book is based on "The House that Jack Built."

Review: This book can be used for drama activities, chants, and choral readings. At the end of the book, there is a section called "Family Fun in the Earth That God Made" which contains instructions and ideas for environmental things to do and make.

Seeds of Heaven   Ages: 5+
Author: Kim M. Henry   Illustrator: Mary Anne Lard
Harrisburg, PA: Morehouse Publishing , 1999
ISBN: 0819217913   Other Categories: Family, Heaven
Inclusive Language

Synopsis: A boy walks with his father and experiences the wonder of God's creations on Earth. Each scene is paired with a verse from the New Testament.

Review: This book states that heaven is here among us; and emphasizes the importance of seeing and experiencing the beauty of God's creation. This book could be used to explore the places in scripture where heaven is described, where nature is found, and where people's role as keepers of the earth is defined. The illustrations are soft and gentle. Lovely.

When God Made the Tree   Ages: 5+
Author: Virginia Kroll   Illustrator: Roberta Collier-Morales
Nevada City: Dawn Publications, 1999
ISBN: 1883220971   Other Categories: Information, Multiculturalism

Synopsis: We are introduced to different trees in God's creation around the world. Each tree is used by the people in its particular part of the world.

Review: This book also contains an information sections about the trees named in the book. This book can be used to introduce the multicultural aspects of our world as well as the importance of using resources in responsible ways. Unfortunately, this book does not use inclusive language.

The River and the Rain: The Lord's Prayer   Ages 3+
Author and Illustrator: Bijou Le Tord
New York: Bantam Doubleday Dell Books for Young Readers, 1996
ISBN: 0-385-32034-5   Other Categories: Prayer, Art, Retellings

Synopsis: A retelling of the Lord's Prayer with illustrations which show the need to care for Earth.

Review: This is a beautiful retelling, using alternative language for the Lord's Prayer. The soft watercolors show the destruction of Earth and the need for us to care for it.

Sing a New Song: A Book of Psalms   **Ages 3+**
Author and Illustrator: Bijou LeTord
Grand Rapids, MI: Wm. B. Eerdmans Publishing Co., 1997
ISBN: 0802851398   Other Categories: Retellings, Prayer

Synopsis: This book explores the theme of nature in the Psalms.

Review: This by no means presents an exhaustive study of this theme, and the book could be used as a starting point to search out more places in the Psalms (and other books) where nature is praised. LeTord's interpretation is a wonderful celebration and prayer for harmony in nature.

The Blessing Seed:
A Creation Myth for the New Millennium   **Ages 5+**
Author: Caitlin Matthews   Illustrator: Alison Dexter
Bristol, UK: Barefoot Books,1998
ISBN: 1-901223-280   Other Categories: Retellings, Blessings
Inclusive Language

Synopsis: God sings creation into being and entrusts Earth to the care of Man and Woman. The blessing seed is their gift from God, and they are instructed to spread God's blessings throughout Earth.

Review: This book takes an inclusive look at the creation story. It can be used to encourage children to see the blessings they have been given, as well as to encourage the sharing of their gifts with others.

God in Between   **Ages 5+**
Author: Sandy Eisenberg Sasso   Illustrator: Sally Sweetland
Woodstock, VT: Jewish Lights Publishing, 1998
ISBN: 1879045869   Other Categories: Legends, God's Immanence

Synopsis: Poor villagers look for God, only to find that God is within them and in the relationships they have with others.

Review: This is a beautiful exploration of the importance of people as part of God, and the place God has in our lives. The story stresses the need to see God in others.

A Prayer for the Earth:
The Story of Naamah, Noah's Wife   Ages 5+
Author: Sandy Eisenberg Sasso   Illustrator: Bethanne Anderson
Woodstock, VT: Jewish Lights Publishing, 1996
ISBN: 1879045605   Other Categories: Animals, Family

Synopsis: Naamah collects seeds to save the plants of Earth from the flood.

Review: This is not a retelling, but the story of Noah's unnamed wife caring for the earth's plants is delightful. Not only does it name her, but it gives her an important and overlooked role in saving the plants while her husband cares for the animals.

God's Quiet Things   Ages: 3+
Author: Nancy Sweetland   Illustrator: Rick Stevens
Grand Rapids, MI: Wm. B. Eerdman's Publishing, 1994
ISBN: 0-8028-5082-0   Other Categories: Prayer, Poetry

Synopsis: A young boy explores God's creation in nature.

Review: The rhyming text is very soft and open. The pastel illustrations have an interesting variety of perspectives.

Grandad's Prayers of the Earth   Ages 5+
Author: Douglas Wood   Illustrator: P. J. Lynch
Cambridge, MA: Candlewick Press, 1999
ISBN: 0-7636-0660-X   Other Categories: Prayer, Family

Synopsis: As a child and his granddad walk and talk, Grandad answers the boy's questions about prayer. Grandad shows the boy the different ways trees, stones, water, grasses, birds, and animals, and people all pray.

Review: This exploration of the nature of prayer is very freeing and open-minded. This book could be used to teach children about prayer and to explore the different ways that they pray. This book could also be used effectively in many adult discussion and learning groups. The intricately detailed watercolor illustrations capture instants in time and show a variety of perspectives.

6

Rejoice & Be Glad
Christian Holidays & Celebrations

I will greatly rejoice in the Lord,
my whole being shall exult in my God.

Isaiah 61:10

Rejoice in the Lord always; again I will say, Rejoice.

Philippians 4:4

The holidays offer a wonderful time to introduce children to Christian literature and give us a time to pass along traditions and stories to younger generations. They are an opportunity to share and remember God's love for us. Holidays are also a time when you can give Christian books to friends and relatives without apology. There is a plethora of books about these seasons available, many of them more secular than Christian.

Because of the time-specific nature of books about holidays, they may not be a wise investment for some. These books may only be brought out for a few weeks a year, and it may be better to purchase less expensive paperback editions of books if they are available. Unfortunately, when it comes to Christian books, it is often difficult to find inexpensive editions. Other options include libraries, borrow-a-book programs from schools, secondhand stores, garage sales, used book sales, friends and neighbors, and older children. Do not forget to donate your old books once your children have outgrown them, but be sure to get their permission, so you do not throw out any treasures.

The books I have reviewed for this chapter deal specifically with the story of Christ's birth, death, or resurrection; or deal with Christian values of giving, forgiving, and sharing as they are experienced around those holidays. There are many other wonderful mainstream Christmas books such as *The Polar Express* by Chris van Allsberg, which I am not including with this collection. I am not overlooking them for any reason other than to be specific about the focus in this collection.

Other Traditions

Many schools, especially in the public school system, recognize Christmas as part of the larger winter season. Often, it is celebrated along with other festivals at this time of year as a Festival of Lights. It is possible for children to not hear the Christmas story, so even if we assume it is familiar and known, that may not be the case. This is a time to ensure that we read the Christmas story to children and familiarize them with it.

As a teacher, I know that it is often difficult to deal with holidays such as Christmas and Easter from a religious context. I always read the stories to my students and present them as stories of what some people believe. By presenting them in an informational context, I am not proselytizing, even though my students know I am a practicing Christian. I also read stories about other holidays, such as Eid, Divali, and Passover, so my students have a well-rounded understanding of many traditions.

I often ask my students to share information about their celebrations with the class. They are often eager to do so, but I never force a reluctant child to speak and share. At times, students have brought in parents to cook special holiday dishes, decorate hands with henna, light a menorah and sing the blessing. All these experiences open us up to learning about each other and foster respect for the different cultures represented in our inner-city school community.

Easter

The Easter story is a difficult one. It tells a story of torture and murder. It is also the story of the most generous love imagined, and the most wonderful hope possible. How we tell this story is important, and it is vital to know the audience with whom we are sharing. The details may disturb the very young child. The focus on the death of Jesus without the promise of new life may be frightening in the least and utterly pointless at best.

Stories of bunnies and chicks abound at this time of year. They are not necessarily bad and do not have to detract from the Easter story. Each talks about new life and the promise it holds. If we read these cute stories about modern secular Easter traditions, we can relate them to the Easter story if we connect them with the circle of life, the promise of new beginnings, and renewal that is our hope in Christ.

Christmas

There are countless books about Christmas, and the quality of the books is constantly improving. It is important, also, to recognize the other times of the Christian year which surround Christmas. Advent – when we prepare for the Christ child to arrive – begins the Christian calendar. There are a few books about this time of anticipation, which should not be overlooked.

Epiphany, the time when the Wise Ones arrived to bring gifts to the Child, follows Christmas and coincides with the time when Orthodox Christians celebrate the birth of Christ. As with Advent, there are some beautiful books about Epiphany which can help bring closure to the Christmas season, with the acknowledgement of Christ as a gift for all people.

Other Holidays

The other significant times in the Christian year are not so popular in children's literature. There is little mention of the baptism of Jesus (except in books that deal with the entire life of Jesus). Pentecost is rarely mentioned as the beginning of the Christian church. The reign of Christ could be recognized with a variety of books about Jesus' life. A few books like *Come Worship with Me: A Journey through the Church Year* deal specifically with the Christian year, and could be used in worship to explain the different festivals and their symbolism.

Ways to Use the Literature

- Use a children's book as the basis for the Christmas pageant. You could even do a reader's theatre, where one person reads the book and the children act out the parts. This is particularly good for younger children who may be shy or may forget lines.

- Videotape the Christmas pageant for shut-ins or people in your congregation who cannot make it to the service. Have a special showing so that the performers can see the pageant.

- Read *The Best Christmas Pageant Ever* and discuss God's gift of Christ for all people.

- Compare the stories in different retellings of the Christmas story with the biblical versions of Christ's birth.

- Compare the biblical versions of Christ's birth in the gospels. Read about the promise of Christ's birth in Isaiah.

- Make a list of all the different names for Jesus. There are some in the Old Testament and in the New Testament. We may also have our own names for Jesus, such as Teacher or Example.

- Learn about Christmas celebrations around the world. Find out how people from other countries have brought their celebrations to their new homes in North America.

- Try different holiday foods from other cultures.

- Some people follow the Julian calendar and celebrate Christmas in January. Learn about the differences between the Gregorian and Julian calendars.

- Some people fast before Christmas, abstaining from certain foods and alcohol. Learn more about fasting and why people fast. Some religions require fasting. Invite a Muslim to talk about why and how they fast for Ramadan.

- Advent is the time before Christmas when we anticipate the birth of Jesus. It begins the Christian year. Learn more about the Christian year and why some churches follow it. Find out why some churches do not follow the Christian year.

- On a large piece of paper, draw a circle. Starting with Advent, place the different festivals of the Christian year on this circle.

- Make Christmas crafts. Take them to a local nursing home or hospital to brighten the season for people who cannot get out. Christmas can be a time of sadness for people who are lonely.

- Start a "mitten tree" at your church. Encourage people who can knit to donate mittens. Collect the mittens during the offering and put them on the tree. Take the mittens to a local women's shelter. Read *The Mitten* by Jan Brett.

- Learn to knit.

- Learn about the celebrations of other cultures. Divali and Hanukkah occur near Christmas time. Try to take part in one of these celebrations with a friend or with a youth group from a local temple or synagogue. If you live in a large city, see if there are special celebrations in East Indian or Jewish neighborhoods.

- Read *Silent Night: The Song from Heaven* and *Joy to the World*. Learn these carols and sing them during Children's Time in church, or go out caroling one evening with your church group. You could visit shut-ins or go to a local nursing home.

- Epiphany is an important part of Christmas, and it is a time that is often overlooked following the frenzy of Christmas. Epiphany recognizes the time when the Wise Ones visited Jesus and brought gifts. Read the story of Epiphany and learn about the importance of Jesus as a gift for all peoples of the world.

- Think about the gifts brought by the Wise Ones to the Christ Child. What gifts do you bring? How do you share your gifts with others? How do others share their gifts with you? How do you give thanks to God for all these gifts?

- Pentecost celebrates the beginning of the Christian Church. Learn about the history of your church. Ask older members for their memories of the early years of your church. You may want to write the history of your church.

- Make a list of different holidays from Christianity and other faiths. How many can you list? Learn about the ones that are unfamiliar to you.

Bibliography

Advent

A Christmas Carousel   **Ages: 3+**
Author and Illustrator: Francesca Crespi
San Francisco: Chronicle Books, 1999
ISBN: 0-8118-2614-7   Other Categories: Movable Books

Synopsis: A pop-up carousel book with ribbon ties and Advent calendar doors to open.

Review: This beautiful book may not stand up to much repeated use, but makes a lovely alternative to a traditional Advent calendar.

Waiting for Noel: An Advent Story **Ages: 5+**
Author: Ann Dixon   Illustrator: Mark Graham
Grand Rapids: Eerdmans Books for Young Readers, 1996/2000
ISBN: 0-8-28-5192-4   Other Categories: Family

Synopsis: As they light the Advent candles, Noel, a young girl, listens to the story of her birth and how the family waited anxiously for her to be born, just as we await the birth of the Christ child during Advent.

Review: This is a beautiful story of the delight in the birth of a newborn baby. This book would be a nice present for a new parent or for a child who needs to be affirmed as a wanted and loved part of the family.

'Twas the Month Before Christmas: **Ages: 3+**
A Coloring & Family Activity Book   **(with adult supervision)**
Author: Martha H. King
Harrisburg, PA: Morehouse Publishing, 1999
ISBN: 0-8192-1785-9   Other Categories: Activities

Synopsis: A coloring and craft book for Advent.

Review: This book has a number of simple activities, and the contents can be photocopied legally.

The Manger Where Jesus Lay **Ages: 0+**
Author: Martha Larchar   Illustrator: Karen Clark
Cincinnati, Ohio: Standard Publishing Company, 1996
ISBN: 0-7847-0357-4   Other Categories: Predictable Books

Synopsis: This predictable book is based on "The House that Jack Built."

Review: This is a fun book for young children. The main words use rebus symbols, allowing children to join in when they recognize a symbol.

Jacob's Gift **Ages: 5+**
Author: Max Lucado   Illustrator: Robert Hunt
Nashville: Tommy Nelson, 1998
ISBN: 0-8499-5830-X   Other Categories: Giving

Synopsis: Jacob is an apprentice carpenter who is chosen by the Rabbi to work on a special project, which turns out to be the manger for the Christ child.

Review: The soft pastels are lovely, but they depict white people. The story is nice, but is a bit predictable.

Before & After Christmas:
Activities & Ideas for Advent and Epiphany   **Ages: 5+**
Author: Debbie Trafton O'Neal   Illustrator: David La Rochelle
Minneapolis: Augsburg Fortress, 1991
ISBN: 0-8066-2534-1   Other Categories: Activities

Synopsis: A collection of activities to focus on the Christmas story throughout the season, and especially when the commercialization of Christmas arises.

Review: Each day of the season has an activity. The instructions are simple, with good, clear illustrations. Some of the activities will require adult assistance.

Christmas

An Amish Christmas   **Ages: 5+**
Author: Richard Ammon   Illustrator: Pamela Patrick
New York: Atheneum, 1996
ISBN: 06898037X   Other Categories: Family

Synopsis: Amish schoolchildren prepare for Christmas. The book explains that for these Amish children, Christmas is a two-day celebration, after which, they return to school.

Review: The simple text and photo-like pastel illustrations depict everyday scenes in the life of the Amish. There are translations of the Pennsylvania Dutch expressions. This gives a good introduction to Amish traditions and beliefs. See also: *An Amish Year*.

Joy to the World: A Family Christmas Treasury   **Ages: 5+**
Editor: Ann Keay Beneduce   Illustrator: Gennady Spirin
New York: Atheneum Books for Young Readers, 2000
ISBN: 0-689-82113-1   Other Categories: Songs, Poetry

Synopsis: This comprehensive collection of poems, stories, and music is divided into five sections based on traditional Christmas symbols of the Star, the Manger, Gift Givers, the Tree, and Christmas Everywhere.

Review: Some of the short stories are written by famous authors. There is sheet music for the carols. The book is illustrated with watercolors and colored pencils and has lovely decorations on the pages.

Christmas Crafts and Activities   Ages: 3+
Author: Children's Ministry Resources
Ventura, CA: Gospel Light, 1998
ISBN: 0-8307-2359-5   Other Categories: Activities

Synopsis: A collection of ideas and instructions for snacks, activities, stories, games, and crafts for children from early childhood through upper elementary school ages.

Review: These good and simple ideas can be completed with readily available materials. There are clear instructions with black and white illustrations. This makes a great resource for teachers, ministers, Sunday school leaders, etc.

The Baby Who Changed the World   Ages: 5+
Author: Sheryl Ann Crawford   Illustrator: Sonya Wilson
Colorado Springs: Faith Kids, 2000
ISBN: 0-78143-431-9   Other Categories: Animals, Gifts

Synopsis: The animals of Bethlehem anticipate the birth of Jesus. Each animal thinks the child will have traits like its own.

Review: This story is charming, but has little to do with the biblical story. The watercolors are rather muddy and the characters are white.

The Little Crooked Christmas Tree   Ages: 5+
Author: Michael Cutting   Illustrator: Ron Broda
Willowdale, ON: Firefly Books, 1990
ISBN: 1-895565-76-6   Other Categories: Giving, Sacrifice

Synopsis: A young spruce tree wants to know what a Christmas tree is. When a dove lands in the tree and builds a nest, the tree bends its branches to protect the baby doves. The chicks grow and it comes time for the dove family to return to their home, but before they leave, the mother dove explains Christmas to the tree who has given her so much. Later, the surrounding trees are cut down, and only the little crooked tree is left, but when a park springs up magically around it, children come to decorate the spruce tree and sing carols around it.

Review: This touching and beautiful story of giving and sacrifice is made spectacular by Ron Broda's paper sculpture. The illustrations are outstanding, as is all of Broda's work.

Silent Night: Carols for Christmas   **Ages: 5+**
Embroideries by Belinda Downes
London: Mammoth, 1995
ISBN: 0-7497-2965-1   Other Categories: Songs

Synopsis: Contains12 carols with sheet music, illustrated with embroideries.

Review: Each carol is illustrated with a lovely embroidery using a naive style. The embroideries show people of different cultures and races.

The Christmas Book:
Stories, Songs, Traditions, Things to Do & Make   **Ages: 5+**
Author: Moira Eastman
Melbourne, Australia: Collins Dove, 1978/1986
ISBN: 0-85924-101-7   Other Categories: Songs, Activities

Synopsis: A short collection of activities, gift-making ideas, discussion starters, stories, and activities from Advent to Epiphany.

Review: The ideas are fairly simple and well explained.

While Shepherds Watched   **Ages: 5+**
Author: Jenni Fleetwood   Illustrator: Peter Melnyczuk
Nashville: Broadman and Holman, 1999
ISBN: 080542036-3   Other Categories: Faith of Children

Synopsis: Matthias, a young shepherd boy, spends his first night in the fields on his eighth birthday. He cares for a newborn sheep when an angel appears to tell of the birth of Jesus. Matthias visits the child and gives him a whistle as a birthday present.

Review: This charming story could be enacted for a Christmas pageant. Some of the characters are white.

Joy to the World   **Ages: 3+**
Carols selected by Maureen Forrester   Illustrator: Frances Tyrrell
Toronto: Lester Publishing, Ltd., 1992
ISBN: 1-895555-19-1   Other Categories: Songs

Synopsis: Twelve Christmas carols from around the world are presented in song and art.

Review: In addition to the music for the carols, a section explains the history of each carol. Tyrrell's intricate artwork and borders show a good variety of cultural representations.

Bethlehem Ages: 5+
Author and Illustrator: Fiona French
HarperCollins, 2001
ISBN: 0-06-029623-2 Other Categories: Art, Retellings

Synopsis: The Christmas story up to the flight to Egypt is taken from the King James Version of the Book of Luke.

Review: The beautiful illustrations by award-winning illustrator Fiona French are made to look like stained glass windows.

The Candymaker's Gift:
The Inspirational Legend of the Candy Cane Ages: 8+
Author: Helen Haidle Illustrator: David Haidle
Tulsa, OK: Honor Books, 1996
ISBN: 1-56292-150-9 Other Categories: Giving, Legends

Synopsis: A candymaker creates a candy cane for his granddaughter as a reminder of the gift of Jesus at Christmas.

Review: This beautiful, sweet story introduces the meanings behind the candy cane. The book includes ideas for recipes and decorations, with references to biblical verses behind the candy cane.

The Living Nativity:
The Story of St. Francis & the Christmas Manger Ages: 8+
Author: Helen Haidle Illustrator: David Haidle
Tulsa, OK: Honor Books, 1998
ISBN: 1-56292-537-7 Other Categories: People

Synopsis: A young handicapped boy meets a monk who takes the child in. Together, they help prepare the first Living Nativity in Greccio, near Assisi, Italy.

Review: While this book uses the term "lame" to describe the boy, it is a sweet story about how a child can help share the gospel story with others. This book has ideas for parents and teachers as well as additional Bible readings.

Bright Star Shining: Poems for Christmas   Ages: 3+
Selected by Michael Harrison and Christopher Stuart-Clark
Illustrators: Stephen Lambert, Louise Rawlings, Susan Scott
Grand Rapids, MI: Wm. B. Eerdmans Publishing Co., 1993
ISBN: 0-8028-5177-0   Other Categories: Poetry

Synopsis: A collection of Christmas poems by famous authors such as e. e. cummings, Kenneth Grahame, and Michael Rosen.

Review: This lovely collection is very well designed with illustrations to accompany each poem. This is a good book to introduce children to traditional poetry.

Away in a Manger   Ages: 5+
Author: Sarah Hayes   Illustrator: Inga Moore
Toronto: Overlea House, 1987
ISBN: 0-7172-2168-7   Other Categories: Songs

Synopsis: The Christmas story is told using both prose and matching carols for each portion of the story.

Review: This would make a very good resource to use when planning a Christmas pageant or carol service to tell the Christmas story. The characters are mainly white.

An Angel Just Like Me   Ages: 5+
Author: Mary Hoffman
Illustrators: Cornelius van Wright and Ying-Hwa Hu
London: Frances Lincoln, 1997
ISBN: 0-7112-1179-5   Other Categories: Multiculturalism

Synopsis: Tyler, a young black child complains that he never sees dark-skinned angels. When he tells his wish to his friend Carl, an art student, Carl makes Tyler a beautiful dark angel out of wood, and all his friends of different races want an angel that looks like them, too.

Review: This is a beautiful story with very realistic illustrations. This is a good book to use to question assumptions about how the Divine is portrayed.

Easy Ways to Christmas Plays Ages: 3+ (with adult supervision)
Author: Vicki Howie   Illustrator: Sarah Laver
Oxford, UK: The Bible Reading Fellowship, 1998
ISBN: 1-84101-017-0   Other Categories: Activities

Synopsis: This book has three complete plays for Christmas with scripts, activity sheets, posters, and stage plans.

Review: This provides an excellent resource to liven up the usual pageant. It has good ideas to extend the experience as well as interesting introductions.

A Northern Nativity: Christmas Dreams of a Prairie Boy   Ages: 5+
Author and Illustrator: William Kurelek
Montreal: Tundra Books, 1976
ISBN: 0-912766-41-7   Other Categories: Art, Social Justice

Synopsis: William, a young boy, dreams about different Nativity scenes based on his history and geography lessons. If the Christ child could be born to a poor family in Bethlehem, why not here, too?

Review: This outstanding book reminds us to welcome everyone as if they were the Christ. The different Canadian scenes with their humble settings remind us of the humility and humanity of the birth of Christ. Kurelek uses the words "Eskimo" and "Indian" (the book was written in 1976), and it would be a good way to introduce the way words have changed through the years.

The City That Forgot about Christmas   Ages: 5+
Lutheran Television, Screen Images, Inc., Gateway Films, 1987
VIDEO   22 Minutes   Other Categories: Giving

Synopsis: Benji has a bad day and wishes that Christmas would just go away. He visits his grandfather, who tells him about a city that forgot about Christmas. Then, Matthew, a stranger, comes and brings back the joy of Christmas to the people, reminding them that Christmas was when God came to live on earth.

Review: This video uses poor animation, but the story is lovely. Based on the book of the same name by Mary Warren, published by Concordia Publications.

The ABC's of Christmas   Ages: 5+
Author: Francine M. O'Connor   Illustrator: Bartholomew
Liguori, MO: Liguori Publications, 1994
ISBN: 0-89243-581-X   Other Categories: Poetry

Synopsis: This is not, as the title would seem to imply, an alphabet book, but is a poem about the birth of Jesus. It starts with the prophecy of Isaiah and ends with a child praying before the Nativity scene.

Review: The illustrations throughout most of the book are sepia colored, until you reach the point in the story when the baby is born. The poem details many aspects of the Christmas story.

Holiday Facts and Fun: A Multicultural Christmas   Ages: 5+
VIDEO   23 Minutes
Rainbow Educational Video, Colman Communications Corporation, 1993
Other Categories: Multiculturalism

Synopsis: Five real American families are profiled celebrating Christmas. Each family comes from a different cultural background, and brings different traditions to the holiday.

Review: This video shows Norwegian, Korean, Native American, Mexican, and Ethiopian families and their traditions. The narration explains the traditions and food which is shared. The Ethiopian family have come from a refugee camp and they are celebrating their first Christmas in America.

The Nativity   Ages: 3+
Author and Illustrator: Jane Ray
Toronto: Doubleday Canada, 1991/1999
ISBN: 0-385-25983-2   Other Categories: Art, Retellings

Synopsis: The words of the Christmas story are adapted from the gospels. At the back of the book is a 3-dimensional Nativity scene with characters to place around the crèche.

Review: Ray's illustrations are incomparable. She brings the story to life. The paper doll characters can be moved around the Nativity scene to tell the Christmas story.

S Is for Star: A Christmas Alphabet   Ages: 5+
Author: Cynthia Furlong Reynolds   Illustrator: Pam Carroll
Chelsea, MI: Sleeping Bear Press, 2001
ISBN: 1-58536-064-3   Other Categories: Alphabet Books, Poetry

Synopsis: Each letter has a mix of religious and secular symbols for Christmas, with some detail about the symbols.

Review: There is a mixture of poems and text about the symbols, and information about Christmas traditions around the world. The illustrations are old-fashioned.

The Best Christmas Pageant Ever   **Ages: 8+**
Author: Barbara Robinson   Illustrator: Judith Gwyn Brown
HarperTrophy, 1972/Reprint 1998
ISBN: 0064402754   Other Categories: Chapter Books, Humor

Synopsis: It is time for the Sunday school to put on the annual Christmas pageant. The real problems start when the six terrible Herdman children, the neighborhood bullies, show up and become the stars of the show. In the process, they learn about the Christmas story, while adding a few details of their own.

Review: This book is riotously hilarious with delightful and memorable descriptions. A classic!

Elijah's Angel   **Ages: 5+**
Author: Michael J. Rosen   Illustrator: Aminah Brenda Lynn Robinson
San Diego: Harcourt Brace and Company, 1992
ISBN: 0-15-225394-7   Other Categories: Multiculturalism

Synopsis: A young Jewish boy befriends Elijah, an old black man. One year, Christmas and Hanukkah coincide and the two exchange gifts made with love.

Review: This is a beautiful, authentic story of intergenerational, interracial and interfaith relationships, based on the life of Elijah Pierce (1892–1984).

The Nativity: From the Gospels of Matthew & Luke   **Ages: 3+**
Illustrator: Ruth Sanderson
Toronto: Little, Brown and Company, 1993
ISBN: 0-316-77113-9   Other Categories: Retellings, Art

Synopsis: A retelling of the birth of Jesus from the visit of the angel to Mary, up to the return of the holy family to Nazareth following the flight to Egypt.

Review: Sanderson's illustrations are wonderful. There is a feeling of iconography in her work, which reflects her Orthodox faith.

How the Grinch Stole Christmas   **Ages: 3+**
Author and Illustrator: Dr. Seuss
New York: Random House, 1957/1985
ISBN: 0-394-80079-6   Other Categories: Poetry

Synopsis: The mean Grinch decides to steal Christmas from the Who's, but after he takes all their material possessions, the Grinch sees the Who's celebrating Christmas anyway, and repents by changing his ways.

Review: This classic story can lead into wonderful discussions about repentance, renewal and the real meaning of Christmas. A video is also widely available.

Lift the Flap Nativity　　　　　　　　　　　　　　**Ages: 3+**
Retold by: Allia Zobel-Nolan　　Illustrator: Tracey Moroney
Pleasantville, NY: Reader's Digest Children's Books, 2001
ISBN: 1-57584-831-7　　Other Categories: Board Books

Synopsis: The story of the birth of Jesus from the visit of the angels to the visit of the Wise Ones is retold with flaps for children to open.

Review: There are 40 flaps for children to explore in this simple book. The pages of this book are glossy, but when you lift the flap, they are dull underneath.

Epiphany

The Little Drummer Boy　　　　　　　　　　　　**Ages: 5+**
Music by Katherine Davis, Henry Onorati, and Harry Simeone
Illustrator: Kristina Rodanas
New York: Clarion Books, 2001
ISBN: 0-395-97015-6　　Other Categories: Songs

Synopsis: An illustrated version of the traditional Christmas song in which a poor young child visits the Christ child but has no gift except the music he can play.

Review: The charming illustrations are done in colored pencil and watercolors. The book has the sheet music for the song.

What Can I Give Him?　　　　　　　　　　　　**Ages: 3+**
Author and Illustrator: Debi Gliori　*(Based on a poem by Christina Rosetti)*
New York: Holiday House, 1998
ISBN: 0-8234-1392-6　　Other Categories: Giving

Synopsis: A young girl in modern times prepares for Christmas and searches for a gift for the Christ child. In parallel illustrations, a young girl in the time of Jesus helps prepare the stable and leads the Wise Ones to the child.

Review: This simple book is a treasure. The two stories told in the illustrations happen side by side and parallel each other.

A Night the Stars Danced for Joy   Ages: 5+
Author: Bob Hartman   Illustrator: Tim Jonke
Colorado Springs: Lion Children's Books, 1999
ISBN: 0-7459-4086-2   Other Categories: Retellings, Dance

Synopsis: Angels visit the shepherds and announce the birth of Jesus. They dance in the sky before disappearing as the shepherds set off to find the child.

Review: This nice story includes a shepherd's wife, even though she remains nameless. It could be used to introduce liturgical dance to people.

The Gift of the Magi   Ages: 8+
Author: O. Henry   Illustrator: Lisbeth Zwerger
New York: Aladdin Paperbacks, 1982
ISBN: 0-689-81701-0   Other Categories: Family, Giving

Synopsis: Della longs for combs to put in her beautiful hair, but knows she and her husband cannot afford them. With little money to buy a present for her husband, Jim, Della sells her hair to buy him a watch fob; but Jim has sold his precious gold watch to buy Della hair combs.

Review: This classic story by O. Henry is brought to life with Zwerger's illustrations. The lesson of irony is that the giver who sacrifices is the wisest.

The Gift of the Magi   Ages: 8+
(Based on the short story by O. Henry)
Encyclopedia Britannica Educational Corporation, 1980
VIDEO   15 Minutes   Other Categories: Family, Giving

Synopsis: Della longs for combs to put in her beautiful hair, but knows she and her husband cannot afford them. With little money to buy a present for her husband, Jim, Della sells her hair to buy him a watch fob; but Jim has sold his precious gold watch to buy Della hair combs.

Review: The video remains faithful to O. Henry's story of irony and true giving. The acting is a bit understated, but the point comes across.

Three Wise Women   **Ages 5+**
Author: Mary Hoffman,
London, UK: Frances Lincoln, 1999
ISBN: 0-7112-1423-9   Other Categories: Multiculturalism

Synopsis: Three women from different parts of the world meet on a path
and follow a star to bring a special gift to the Christ child. The young White
woman bakes him bread, the Indian grandmother tells him a story of hope,
and the Black woman holds out her child to kiss the newborn.

Review: This beautiful book for Advent expresses the gifts that women
bring to the world and to the Christ. The illustrations are lovely and soft.

The Greatest Gift of All   **Ages: 0+**
Author: Kimberley Rinehart   Illustrator: Georgia Rettmer
New York: Inspirational Press, 1987
ISBN: 0-88486-185-6   Other Categories: Retellings

Synopsis: The characters in this retelling of Luke 2:1–20 each offer something
to the Christ child, but it is the child who offers the greatest gift of all.

Review: This simple pattern book could be used for the perennial Christmas
pageant. The illustrations are simple, torn paper designs that could be easily
re-created by children.

The Fourth Wise Man   **Ages: 8+**
(Based on the story by Henry Van Dyke)
Author: Susan Summers   Illustrator: Jackie Morris
New York: Dial Books for Young Readers, 1998
ISBN: 0-8037-2312-1   Other Categories: Legends

Synopsis: Artaban, a Zoroastrian, follows the star to find the King of Kings.
When he stops to help a man, the other three Wise Ones go on without
him. Artaban spends his life looking for the Promised One, whom he finds
on the day of the crucifixion.

Review: This book is based on the traditional legends of the fourth Wise
One. The book is very well designed with beautiful watercolors. Summers
had used this story in her teaching before writing it, and her storytelling
style comes through wonderfully.

The Last Straw   **Ages: 5+**
Author: Fredrick H. Thury   Illustrator: Vlasta van Kampen
Toronto: Key Porter Books, Ltd., 1998
ISBN: 1-55263-022-6   Other Categories: Music

Synopsis: Hoshmakaka, a whining camel, is asked to carry gifts to the newborn King. He agrees, in spite of his many ailments; but on his journey, he meets others who ask him to take their gifts, too. He agrees, until a young boy gives him a piece of straw to take for the baby's bed. This breaks the camel's back, and Hoshmakaka finally falls to his knees before the manger.

Review: This beautiful story is based on the author's libretto (performed by the Toronto Children's Chorus). The illustrations are bold and wonderful. This is an excellent book for Epiphany.

Easter and Pentecost

Usborne Bible Tales: The Easter Story   **Ages: 3+**
Author: Heather Amery   Illustrator: Norman Young
London: Usborne, 1998
ISBN: 0-7460-3358-3   Other Categories: Retellings

Synopsis: This very simple retelling of the Easter story begins with Jesus' entry into Jerusalem and ends with his reappearance to the disciples.

Review: The language is very simple and is good for younger readers. The characters are white.

Easter around the World   **Ages: 8+**
CLASSROOM VIDEO   20 Minutes
Burnaby, BC: Undated
Other Categories: Informational

Synopsis: This video looks at the origins of Easter and Easter symbols around the world. It also shows a family celebrating the Passover Seder.

Review: An Australian production, this video also shows the differences between the hemispheres, as Easter falls in the autumn in Australia. There is a study guide for different grade levels. While the video is a little dry, the information explains the rituals and symbols well.

He Is Alive   Ages: 5+
Author: Helen Haidle   Illustrator: Joel Spector
Grand Rapids, MI: Zonderkidz, 2001
ISBN: 0-310-70033-7   Other Categories: Retellings

Synopsis: A retelling of the death and resurrection of Jesus.

Review: This book has dramatic ¾ page illustrations, some of which are scary. The story focuses on the importance of the Resurrection.

Jesus Is Risen   Ages: 3+
Author: Rolf Krenzer   Illustrator: Constanza Droop
Translated by: Linda M. Maloney
Collegeville, MN: Liturgical Press, 1999
ISBN: 0-8146-2764-1   Other Categories: Retellings

Synopsis: A retelling of the ministry, death, and resurrection of Jesus.

Review: This straightforward retelling has bright illustrations, with detailed cartoonlike characters. The illustrations are not scary or gory.

Easter   Ages: 8+
Illustrator: Jan Pienkowski
London: Puffin Books, 1989
ISBN: 0-14-054486-0   Other Categories: Retellings

Synopsis: The story of Easter, taken from the KJV's four gospels.

Review: The book is pieced together from the four gospels to create one story. The language of the King James Version is difficult for young children. Dark silhouettes contrast with the delicate designs highlighted with gold.

The Easter Story   Ages: 5+
Author and Illustrator: Brian Wildsmith
Oxford, UK: Oxford University Press, 1993
ISBN: 0- 19-279952-5   Other Categories: Retellings

Synopsis: A retelling of the Easter story. The story covers the time from the entry into Jerusalem to the ascension, as seen through the eyes of the donkey who carried Jesus.

Review: The amazing color and perspective make this story elegant and radiant. This book is rich in gold decoration, typical of Wildsmith's style. This is almost too beautiful to tell the story of the death of Jesus, but captures wonderfully the spirit of resurrection.

Thanksgiving

Gracias, The Thanksgiving Turkey   Ages: 5+

Author: Joy Cowley   Illustrator: Joe Cepeda

New York: Scholastic, 1996

ISBN: 0-590-46977-0   Other Categories: Multiculturalism

Synopsis: Miguel's dad sends him a turkey to fatten up for Thanksgiving, but it quickly becomes a friend and part of the family. Gracias follows Miguel to mass where the priest blesses Gracias. On Thanksgiving Day, the family has turkey for dinner – Gracias eats at the table while the family dines on chicken.

Review: This is a lovely story with multicultural, inner-city characters. The rich oil paintings set the moods and match the text well. The book includes a glossary of Spanish terms used in the story.

7

Tell Me the Stories
Bible Stories Retold

But blessed are your eyes for they see and your ears for they hear.
MATTHEW 13:16

Just before Easter one year, I told my Grade 3 students the Easter story of the death and resurrection of Jesus. Afterwards, Luke, a bright, interested student came to me with wide eyes full of wonder and asked if anyone had ever thought to write that story down. "It would make a really good book," he insisted. I assured him that it had been written, almost 2000 years ago and many times since then. He looked a bit disappointed, because he was sure he was really on to something. Luke will be a publisher one day, I am sure.

This chapter looks at two ways to retell a story. Obviously, we will look at books that retell stories or passages from the Bible. We will also look at the act of retelling a story as a way to engage with a text and make it come alive.

The Bible contains many wonderful stories. And, while many of the modern translations such as the NRSV make the Bible much more accessible to people, it still can be a very intimidating book. Many churches do not fare well at teaching the Bible, and it remains a mystery to many, even those who consider themselves a part of the church. Bible study can be frightening for those who do not have much knowledge of the Bible. Even knowing where to find the different books of the Bible can make the novice uncomfortable.

Bridging the Gap

For children (and adults!), retellings of Bible stories in the form of picture books are a wonderful way to bridge the gap. When a retelling of a Bible story is well done, it can bring the story to life and enable the reader to make personal connections in a way that makes the story real and effective. Children are very visual, and seeing a story in picture can help the child imagine what life was like when the story took place, what the people may have looked like, and understand the land in which the story is set. Or, when more modern illustrations accompany a retelling, the child can connect that story to his or her own world.

Retellings have the advantage of putting together a story that may be broken up in the Bible. The life of David, for example, is found in a number of different books in the Bible. In a retelling of the life of David, the author or storyteller can take the events found in the different biblical books and bring them together to form a story that follows chronologically and cohesively.

The life of Jesus is found throughout the four gospels and is written about differently in each. Some have events that others do not mention. Some stories differ in gospel presentations. Rarely do retellings look at these differences. For the most part, a retelling such as *Easter* by Jan Pienkowski, which takes information from all four gospels to tell the story of the death of Jesus, takes the parts of the story from the most familiar or detailed source.

Purpose of Retelling Bible Stories

Why would an author take a perfectly good biblical story and need to retell it? Should you just stick with the Bible, the original source for these stories? Why mess with perfection? Of course the Bible is our source and inspiration for these stories, but truth is found in many ways and places.

A retelling may act as a conduit. Once a person has read or heard a story in the form of a retelling, they may be encouraged to go back to the source material, i.e., the Bible, for the story. Or maybe the retelling will stick with a person in a way that the words alone will not. We all have different learning strengths. I am a visual learner. Once I have seen something I usually remember it, but often forget or do not process what I hear. This means that I have "heard" many sermons and not learned a thing! For others, it may mean that the story must be heard aloud, or acted out, or sung. The source is important, but I believe that God honors any way in which we seek and find God's Spirit and truth.

Retellings and Teaching

Teachers often use retelling to both teach and assess learning. When a student is invited to retell a story, either aloud or in writing, the act of retelling helps the student consolidate learning and understanding. By retelling a story, the child needs to recall information, events, and characters; sequence events so they make sense; and tell the story in a way to engage and convince the audience.

Listening to a child retell a story the child has heard or read allows the teacher to see the depth of interaction the student has experienced with the story. A child who has really connected with a story would be better able to retell it in a convincing manner. The teacher can use a retelling to evaluate where the student has made connections, memorized or understood words and phrases, followed the plot, or where the child has failed to engage with the text in a meaningful way.

Retelling stories can provide an easy way to move into drama. For those who are not comfortable with teaching or leading drama, retelling a story can act as a way to support a production or even a small, unrehearsed learning experience. You can read the story aloud as the children act out the parts, or the reading can be developed into a full-fledged extravaganza with costumes, sets, and lighting.

When children retell a story, they take ownership of the story. When the story is in their control, children can place the emphasis on certain characters or events that are particularly significant to them. In a retelling, the child may interpret certain expressions in a way that another person would not. This does not mean that if a child becomes stuck or frustrated that the teacher or leader should not step in and support the child with a key phrase that may restart the flow of the story. Above all, the teacher is there to help the child, not only to evaluate.

Of course, when a child is retelling a story, the most important thing to remember is to celebrate the child's accomplishment. It takes courage to stand up and speak before an audience, even an audience of one.

Types of Retellings

There are five different types of retellings which can be found in Christian children's literature: the exact quotation, the factual retelling, the loose retelling, the satirical retelling, and the illustrative retelling. Each type has advantages and disadvantages, and each may be used for vastly different purposes.

The first type is the *exact quotation*. In this genre of retellings, the story is quoted directly from the Bible and is illustrated. An example of this type is

To Every Thing There Is a Season: Verses from Ecclesiastes, illustrated by the fabulous husband and wife team of Leo and Diane Dillon. Strangely, the version most often used in an exact quotation retelling is the King James Version, which, while it has beautiful and poetic language, is not very accessible to children. The words seem stilted and foreign.

In the second type, *factual retelling*, the writer takes the story as it is written and rewrites it in modern language. This type of retelling is more practical for teaching the events and characters of a story. An example of this type is *Parables: Stories Jesus Told*, written by Mary Hoffman and illustrated by Jackie Morris.

The third type is the *loose retelling*. In this genre, the author takes a story and adds imagined details. This may create a wonderful, interesting story, but it can confuse children, especially when they later read the biblical story. An example of this type is *Lydia*, by Marty Rhodes Figley and illustrated by Anita Riggio. Loose retellings may have changes in setting, character, plot, or all three. This type is good for reading as a story, but not for teaching facts or events.

The fourth type of retelling is the *satirical retelling*. In this genre, the author takes a biblical story and plays on the words and themes to create a sarcastic twist on the story. Some may dislike this genre and may regard this as mockery or contemptuous, but this genre can be wonderful for adults or the very knowledgeable child who is able to understand the plays on language. All of Mike Thaler's books, such as *David, God's Rock Star* fall into this category. As with the loose retellings, stories in this genre may lead to much confusion for the child who does not have a good understanding of the biblical version of the story being satirized. It is not good to use satirical retellings as a way to introduce children to stories.

A fifth type of retelling, the *illustrative retelling*, may be an exact quotation or factual retelling, but the illustrations in this retelling tell a story of their own. In *The Lord's Prayer*, illustrated by Tim Ladwig, for example, the story in the illustrations shows a girl and her father helping an elderly neighbor. The girl finds a beautiful pendant of the Lord's Prayer and returns it to the neighbor, who then gives it to the girl. The story is told through the beautiful and realistic paintings and is connected by the discovery of the pendant. Children could retell a completely different story from the illustrations alone.

Ways to Use the Literature

There are many ways to use retellings. They are a gold mine of information and inspiration. Here are a few examples of ways to use retellings:

- Find a story in the Bible and create your own retelling. This is a great way to find out more about words or phrases that children do not understand.

- Take a passage and create an illustrative retelling. The illustrations should tell their own story that goes along with the biblical passage.

- Take an illustrative retelling and show the pictures without the text. Encourage the listeners to guess which passage is being illustrated.

- Take a retelling and act it out.

- Use the picture from a retelling as inspiration for a set design for a play or pageant.

- Create a library collection of retellings in your church or school. The Bible itself is a library – a collection of books – and you could make your own Bible from collected books.

- Take a passage from the Bible and illustrate it yourself. It does not have to be a story. You may even wish to take one very meaningful verse and create a series of illustrations to express what that verse means to you.

- Compare one passage from different versions of the Bible. Choose one or mix and match the versions to create an interesting retelling.

- Take a retelling and find the verses in the Bible that match with the lines in the story. This is a good exercise for teaching people how to use a concordance.

- Discuss satire and why it is offensive to some people but hilariously funny to others. Read a satirical retelling and compare it to the original story. Invite children to offer their own opinions on it.

- Learn about plays on words from satire. Discuss how Jesus used this to teach.

- Invite children to read or act out a retelling during an intergenerational service instead of the usual scripture reading.

- Take a factual retelling and extend it into a loose retelling. You may want to write about what happens next in the story, or write the story in a different place and time. You might throw in a different character, or even yourself, to complicate the plot.

- Take a loose retelling and bring it back to a factual retelling by taking out the pieces of the story that do not belong with the original, biblical text.

- Use drama to act out a story. Pretend you are traveling back in time and space to become part of the Bible story being retold.

- Invite a storyteller to lead worship.

- Set a story to music. Sing your retelling, or find songs about the story you are reading and make it a part of your own retelling.

- Rap a psalm.

- Record the story onto a tape so younger children can "read" the story while looking at the pictures.

- Take a factual retelling and cut it up into pieces. Try to re-create the story, getting the events into their correct order.

- Collect a number of retellings of the same story. Compare the books and discuss why some are better than others.

- Write to the author and/or illustrator of a favorite retelling. Do the same for a retelling that you did not like. Include a stamped, self-addressed envelope.

- Ask an older member of the congregation to tell you one of their favorite stories.

- Ask younger members of the congregation to tell you their favorite stories.

- Collect these stories and make an anthology of stories from your congregation. Sell the books as a fundraiser.

- Do an author study. Choose an author and collect as many books by that person as possible. Look at the author's personal style. Find patterns in the books. Compare earlier and more recent books.

- Do an illustrator study. Look at the media and techniques used by that illustrator. Try to copy that style.

Biblical Characters

Noah

Noah's Ark   **Ages: 3+**
Author: Georgie Adams   Illustrator: Anna C. Leplar
London: Orion Publishing House, 2000
ISBN: 0805420371   Other Categories: Great Beginnings

Synopsis: This is a simple retelling of the story of Noah's Ark.

Review: The illustrations depict a white Noah. The language is very simple.

Two by Two by Two   **Ages: 3+**
Author and Illustrator: Jonathan Allen
New York: Dial Books for Young Readers, 1994
ISBN: 0-8037-1838-1   Other Categories: Humor

Synopsis: The animals board the ark, but trouble ensues. Noah tries to distract them with games and entertainment.

Review: This is not a strict retelling, but a fun story nonetheless. The pages are filled with animals, which are each labeled.

The Ark   **Ages: 3+**
Author and Illustrator: Arthur Geisert
Boston: Houghton Mifflin Co., 1988
ISBN: 0-395-43078X   Other Categories: Art

Synopsis: This loose retelling of the story of Noah's Ark looks at what life was like on the ark for its passengers.

Review: The detailed ink drawings provide excellent perspective and points of view. The book portrays animals from all parts of the world.

Noah's Ark   **Ages: 5+**
Author: Heinz Janisch   Illustrator: Lisbeth Zwerger
Translator: Rosemary Lanning
New York: Scholastic, 1997
ISBN: 0-7358-1419-8   Other Categories: Art

Synopsis: A retelling of the story of Noah.

Review: This retelling has very unusual illustrations of people from Edwardian times, while fish swim in and out of large buildings. There are some biology textbook illustrations and lovely watercolors. While the illustrations are wonderfully eccentric, the text maintains the spirit of the original.

Aardvarks, Disembark   **Ages: 5+**
Author and Illustrator: Ann Jonas
New York: Greenwillow Books, 1990
ISBN: 0-688-07206-2   Other Categories: Environment, Informational

Synopsis: The flood is over and it is time for the animals to disembark, but Noah does not know all their names. When he calls for all the animals to disembark, they pass before him. What follows is a collection of unusual animals that are not normally found in children's books.

Review: Jonas has carefully researched the animals for this book. There is a long list of the animals, a pronunciation guide, the countries of origin, as well as markers indicating if they are extinct or endangered. Very well done.

Noah's Trees   **Ages: 3+**
Author and Illustrator: Bijou Le Tord
HarperCollins, 1999
ISBN: 0-06-028235-5   Other Categories: Environment

Synopsis: A tree lover, Noah plants trees in hopes of giving them to his three sons. God had other plans for the trees and tells Noah to build an ark. The animals come, and Noah also brings saplings of his beloved trees.

Review: This is not actually a retelling, but it is a lovely story. The heavy watercolors are different from most of Le Tord's work.

Noah's Ark   **Ages: 0+**
Author and Illustrator: Peter Lippman
New York: Workman Publishing, 1994
ISBN: 1-56305-662-3
Other Categories: Great Beginnings, Board Books, Counting, Poetry

Synopsis: The story of Noah's Ark is retold in the form of a rhyming counting book.

Review: This is a structural, 3-dimensional board book.

The Story of Noah and the Ark   Ages: 5+
Retold by: Michael McCarthy   Illustrator: Giuliano Ferri
New York: Barefoot Books, 2001
ISBN: 1-84148-361-3   Other Categories: Poetry

Synopsis: A poetic retelling of Noah and the Ark, adapted from the RSV, New Jerusalem Version, and other translations.

Review: Children could perform this fun retelling as a choral reading or a rap. The watercolor and colored pencil illustrations are fabulous.

How Noah Knew What to Do   Ages: 3+
Author: Karen Ann Moore   Illustrator: Kersten Brothers Studios
Colorado Springs: Faith Kids, 2000
ISBN: 0-78143-440-8   Other Categories: Poetry, Humor

Synopsis: Noah has to build an ark to prepare for the flood, but he knows he is not fully qualified for the job.

Review: This is a fun, lively poem for young children. A parent guide at the back of the book lists ways to extend learning. The illustrations use a primitive style with little detail and depict a white Noah.

Noah's Ark   Ages: 3+
Author and Illustrator: Jane Ray
Toronto: Doubleday Canada Limited, 1990
ISBN: 0-385-25274-9   Other Categories: Art

Synopsis: A retelling of the story of Noah's Ark using words from the King James Version.

Review: The words hold the beauty of the KJV's poetry, but may be difficult for a young child to appreciate and understand. Ray's artwork, however, is outstanding. She captures the story in panels, and includes rich detail and borders, with characters of color.

Two by Two   Ages: 3+
Author and Illustrator: Barbara Reid
Richmond Hill: North Winds Press, 1992
ISBN: 0-590-73656-6   Other Categories: Art, Poetry

Synopsis: A poetic retelling of the story of Noah's Ark.

Review: Barbara Reid's artwork makes this retelling really come alive. Reid uses Plasticine to create intricately detailed illustrations with depth and beauty. Includes a version of the song "Who Built the Ark," with additional verses written by Reid.

A Stowaway on Noah's Ark   **Ages: 3+**
Author and Illustrator: Charles Santore
New York: Random House, 2000
ISBN: 0-679-88820-9   Other Categories: Humor

Synopsis: Noah chooses pairs of animals to go on the ark, but little Achbar the mouse is not chosen. He feels this is unfair and sneaks onto the ark, hiding among the animals.

Review: Wow! This is not a real retelling, but it is a very fun story with amazing illustrations. The detail is outstanding and the perspective is very realistic.

Noah and His Ark   **Ages: 0+**
Author: Jane Scarsbrook   Illustrator: Jan Lewis
London: Prospero Books, 2001
ISBN: 1-55267-127-5   Other Categories: Great Beginnings, Poetry

Synopsis: A simple retelling of the story of Noah and the Ark.

Review: See review of *Daniel in the Lion's Den*.

Noah's Ark   **Ages: 0+**
Author and Illustrator: Peter Spier
Picture Yearling, 1992 (paperback reissue)
ISBN: 0-385-09473-6   Other Categories: Great Beginnings, Art

Synopsis: A wordless picture book retelling of the story of Noah.

Review: The richly detailed and humorous watercolors are wonderful and deserving of its Caldecott Medal. Children will revisit this book and find new details in the illustrations with each reading. See also, *Noah's Ark*, the video.

Noah's Ark *(Based on the book by Peter Spier)*   **Ages: 5+**
Oakville, ON: Oak Street Video, Magic Lantern Communications
VIDEO   27 minutes   Other Categories: Art, Music

Synopsis: This animated video is based on the Caldecott Medal winning book by Peter Spier.

Review: Although narrated wonderfully by James Earl Jones, this video does not approach the quality and depth of Spier's illustrations. The music by Stewart Copeland is beautiful.

Noah and the Big Boat　　　　　　　　　　　**Ages: 0+**
Author: Brenda C. Ward
Nashville: Broadman and Holman, 1998
ISBN: 080541779-6　　　Other Categories: Great Beginnings

Synopsis: A retelling of the story of Noah and the Ark.

Review: This cute series contains very simple retellings accompanied by photos of babies dressed in costumes to illustrate the stories.

Joseph

Joseph Had a Little Overcoat　　　　　　　**Ages: 3+**
Author and Illustrator: Simms Taback
New York: Viking, 1999
ISBN: 0-670-87855-3　　　Other Categories: Song, Poetry, Judaism
Awards: Caldecott Medal

Synopsis: Based on a Yiddish folk song (included in the book), this is the story of Joseph, who started with a coat that continued to be recycled until all he ended up with was a story.

Review: This is a lovely book with wonderful illustrations and endpages. The die-cut holes reveal what the coat will turn into next. The folk song could be sung and acted out.

Joseph　　　　　　　　　　　　　　　　**Ages: 5+**
Author and Illustrator: Brian Wildsmith
Grand Rapids, MI: Wm. B. Eerdmans Publishing Co., 1997
ISBN: 0-8028-5161-4　　　Other Categories: Art

Synopsis: A retelling of the story of Joseph.

Review: The huge doublespread illustrations are well researched. Wildsmith's work has amazing detail and perspective. Outstanding!

Moses

Moses in Egypt   Ages: 0+
Author: Jane Scarsbrook   Illustrator: Jan Lewis
London: Prospero Books, 2001
ISBN: 1-55267-126-7   Other Categories: Great Beginnings, Poetry

Synopsis: A simple retelling of the life of Moses

Review: See review of *Daniel in the Lion's Den.*

Exodus   Ages: 5+
Author and Illustrator: Brian Wildsmith
Grand Rapids, MI: Wm. B. Eerdmans Publishing Co., 1999
ISBN: 0802851754   Other Categories: Art

Synopsis: The story of the life of Moses is retold from his birth until, following Moses' death, Joshua leads the people into the Promised Land.

Review: While Wildsmith's paintings are beautiful, the faces in this book are predominately white. You do, however, get a feel for the large numbers of people involved in the Exodus from the drama of Wildsmith's detailed paintings.

David

David & Goliath   Ages: 8+
Hanna Barbera (The Greatest Adventure: Stories from the Bible)
Turner Home Entertainment, 1993
VIDEO   Closed Captioned.   Other Categories: Science Fiction

Synopsis: Three young people travel through time to find themselves in ancient Israel. There they meet David, the only Israelite brave enough to stand up to the Philistine giant Goliath.

Review: This 30-minute video contains quite a lot of violence, which, with the exception of the modern time-travelers, stays true to most of the biblical story. The animation is quite simple.

David & the Trash-Talkin' Giant   Ages: 5+
Author: Joel Anderson   Illustrators: Abe Goolsby and Joel Anderson
Nashville: Tommy Nelson, 1999
ISBN: 0-8499-5918-7   Other Categories: Activities, Environment

Synopsis: A rhyming retelling of 1 Samuel 16–17 illustrated with found items.

Review: See review for *Jonah's Trash...God's Treasure*.

David and Goliath **Ages: 0+**
Author: Jane Scarsbrook Illustrator: Jan Lewis
London: Prospero Books, 2001
ISBN: 1-55267-128-3 Other Categories: Great Beginnings, Poetry

Synopsis: A simple retelling of the story of David and Goliath.

Review: See review of *Daniel in the Lion's Den*.

David, God's Rock Star **Ages: 8+**
Author: Mike Thaler Illustrator: Dennis Adler
Colorado Springs: Faith Kids, 2000
ISBN: 0-78143-49-7 Other Categories: Satire

Synopsis: Loose retellings of the stories of the Tower of Babel, Joseph, David, Solomon, and Job.

Review: See review of *Daniel, Nice Kitty*.

David & Bubblebath-Sheba **Ages: 8+**
Author: Mike Thaler Illustrator: Dennis Adler
Colorado Springs: Faith Kids, 2000
ISBN: 0-78143-511-0 Other Categories: Satire

Synopsis: Five stories of men from the Old Testament (Jacob, David, Solomon, Uzziah, Balaam).

Review: See review of *Daniel, Nice Kitty*.

Solomon

King Solomon & the Bee **Ages: 5+**
Author: Dalia Hardot Renberg Illustrator: Ruth Heller
HarperCollins, 1994
ISBN: 0-06-022899-7 Other Categories: Legends, Repentance

Synopsis: King Solomon could talk to the animals. One day, a bee stings him and Solomon calls all the stinging animals to appear before him. When the Queen of Sheba visits Solomon with pretend flowers and asks him to tell which is real. Solomon, in his wisdom opens the window and asks his friend the bee for help. The bee is able to repay Solomon for his sin of stinging him.

Review: Taken from a traditional tale, this story uses biblical characters but is not a true retelling. The story is well told with bold illustrations.

The Wisdom Bird: A Tale of Solomon & Sheba   **Ages: 8+**
Author: Sheldon Oberman   Illustrator: Neil Waldman
Honesdale, PA: Boyds Mills Press, 2000
ISBN: 1-56397-816-4   Other Categories: Legends, Multiculturalism

Synopsis: Sheba presents Solomon with a challenge – to build a palace out of bird beaks. The hoopoe bird teaches Solomon the importance of the beaks and why they must not be changed. Solomon learns that promises must be broken sometimes in order to do what is right.

Review: This story blends tales from African, Yemeni, European, and Jewish traditions. The illustrations are multicultural, and it is important to note that it is Sheba who teaches Solomon a lesson.

Elijah

Elijah, Prophet Sharing   **Ages: 8+**
Author: Mike Thaler   Illustrator: Dennis Adler
Colorado Springs: Faith Kids, 2000
ISBN: 0-78143-512-9   Other Categories: Satire

Synopsis: Stories of Elijah, Daniel, Elisha; Shadrach, Meshach, and Abednego; Abraham and Isaac.

Review: See review of *Daniel, Nice Kitty*.

Daniel

Daniel and the Lion   **Ages: 3+**
Author and Illustrator: Sekiya Miyoshi
Cleveland, OH: Pilgrim Press, 2001
ISBN: 0-8298-1452-3   Other Categories: Great Beginnings

Synopsis: A retelling of the story of Daniel.

Review: Japanese artist Miyoshi depicts Daniel with pastels as a sweet white boy with green hair. The illustrations are cute and would appeal to very young children.

Daniel in the Lion's Den   **Ages: 0+**
Author: Jane Scarsbrook   Illustrator: Jan Lewis
London: Prospero Books, 2001
ISBN: 1-55267-129-1   Other Categories: Great Beginnings, Poetry

Synopsis: Daniel 5:30 – 6:24 retold in rhyme.

Review: This fun rhyming retelling could be sung as a rap. The simple illustrations show dark-skinned characters, but without any distinguishing features.

Daniel, Nice Kitty   **Ages: 8+**
Author: Mike Thaler   Illustrator: Dennis Adler
Colorado Springs: Faith Kids, 2000
ISBN: 0-7814-3432-7   Other Categories: Satire

Synopsis: Humorous retellings of the stories of Daniel, Hezekiah, Naaman, Absalom, and Moses.

Review: Adults will appreciate the plays on words, but the humor may be over the heads of children. The retellings may confuse those who are not familiar with the biblical stories. Only the stories of men from the Old Testament are retold. Each retelling has references to the "real story."

Jonah

Jonah's Trash...God's Treasure   **Ages: 5+**
Authors: Joel Anderson and Abe Goolsby
Photographer: David Bailey
Nashville: Tommy Nelson, 1998
ISBN: 0-8499-5825-3   Other Categories: Activities, Environment

Synopsis: A retelling of the story of Jonah.

Review: Children will revisit this book often to look for the objects hidden in the illustrations which are made from found objects. There is a list of items to find in the pictures (similar to *I Spy* books).

Jonah and the Two Great Fish   **Ages: 3+**
Author and Illustrator: Mordicai Gerstein
New York: Simon and Schuster Books for Young Children, 1997
ISBN: 0-689-81373-2   Other Categories: Legend, Judaism

Synopsis: Jonah tries to escape from God's call and ends up in a fish which is very spacious and well furnished. Inside the fish, Jonah spends three comfortable days until God sends another fish which is dark and crowded and unpleasant. Jonah will promise anything to get out of this fish. When God releases him, Jonah goes to Ninevah to prophesy to the people.

Review: This retelling makes use of legends from the Jewish tradition to add to the familiar biblical tale. The humorous and detailed artwork is created with oil on vellum. Children should know the biblical story before reading this retelling to minimize confusion.

Jonah and the Whale   Ages: 3+
Author and Illustrator: Geoffrey Patterson
London: Frances Lincoln, 1998
ISBN: 0-7112-0663-5   Other Categories: Art

Synopsis: A retelling of the story of Jonah until his decision to warn the Ninevites of their fate.

Review: This book does not follow through and tell the whole story of Jonah, thus missing the climax of the story. The illustrations are dramatic double-page spreads.

Jonah and the Big Fish   Ages: 0+
Author: Brenda C. Ward
Nashville: Broadman and Holman, 1998
ISBN: 080541780-X   Other Categories: Great Beginnings

Synopsis: A retelling of the story of Jonah.

Review: This cute series contains very simple retellings accompanied by photos of babies dressed in costumes to illustrate the stories.

Biblical Women

Queen Esther, The Morning Star   Ages: 5+
Author and Illustrator: Mordicai Gerstein
New York: Simon and Schuster, 2000
ISBN: 0-689-81372-4   Other Categories: Women, Purim

Synopsis: A retelling of the Book of Esther.

Review: The illustrations in this retelling are fun and lively. This book does not introduce Purim, but it is a good retelling of the story of Esther, who saves her people from the evil king of Persia.

Daughters of Fire: Heroines of the Bible   **Ages: 5+**
Author: Fran Manushkin   Illustrator: Uri Shulevitz
San Diego: Silver Whistle-Harcourt, Inc., 2001
ISBN: 0-15-201869-7   Other Categories: Women

Synopsis: Ten retellings of the stories of women in the Hebrew Bible.

Review: These retellings are based on a variety of sources – the Hebrew Bible, the Midrash, and the Talmud. The clearly told stories give a well-rounded view of these women with strengths and weaknesses. The illustrator has won Caldecott medals for other books he has written and illustrated.

Eve and Her Sisters: Women of the Old Testament   **Ages: 3+**
Author: Yona Zeldis McDonough   Illustrator: Malcah Zeldis
New York: Greenwillow Book, 1994
ISBN: 0-688-12512-3   Other Categories: Women, Judaism

Synopsis: Retellings of the stories of 14 women from the Old Testament.

Review: The very simple retellings would provide a good starting point for further reading. The bright and simple folk art illustrations match the text.

Daughters of Eve: Strong Women of the Bible   **Ages: 8+**
Author: Lillian Hammer Ross   Illustrator: Kyra Teis
New York: Barefoot Books, 2000
ISBN: 1-902283-82-1   Other Categories: Women, Judaism

Synopsis: Detailed retellings of nine women from the Old Testament and the Apocrypha. Some of the information is from the Midrash not found in scripture.

Review: Each story has an introduction, and there is a glossary of terms. The characters are multicultural. The language is not inclusive, which does not match with the theme of this book.

Tapestries: Stories of Women in the Bible   **Ages: 5+**
Author and Illustrator: Ruth Sanderson
Little Brown, 1998
ISBN: 0316770930   Other Categories: Women, Art

Synopsis: The lives of 24 women from the Old and New Testaments are retold in short, simple stories.

Review: The retellings are extremely simple, which parallels the scant presentation of women in the Bible. This contrasts with the exquisite, detailed illustrations with beautiful borders.

Stories

To Everything   Ages: 3+
Illustrator: Bob Barner
San Francisco: Chronicle Books, 1998
ISBN: 0-8118-2086-6   Other Categories: Art

Synopsis: A retelling of some passages from Ecclesiastes 3.

Review: This outstanding book has bold paper-collage illustrations. At the end of the book, there is a guide for ways to use the book, with discussion questions and activities.

The Creation: God's Busy Week   Ages: 3+
Author: Cathy Capozzoli   Illustrator: Mary Hamilton
Nashville: Broadman and Holman, 1996
ISBN: 6-5135-6285-6   Other Categories: Creation

Synopsis: This is a retelling of Genesis 1:1 – 2: 3.

Review: The illustrations are simple at first, then become more and more crowded as animals, birds, fish, and people are created.

To Every Thing There Is a Season:
Verses from Ecclesiastes   Ages: 3+
Illustrators: Leo and Diane Dillon
New York: Scholastic, 1998
ISBN: 0590478877   Other Categories: Poetry, Art

Synopsis: Verses are adapted from the King James Version of Ecclesiastes "To every thing there is a season..." and illustrated in diverse ways, showing the timelessness of the verses and of God's love.

Review: Each panel has an illustration from a different time, era, and culture. While such appropriation may be problematic in some cases, it is clear that the Dillons research the subjects carefully. At the end of the book, there are explanations about the illustrations, with information about the contents and techniques used. Outstanding!

Creation   Ages: 5+
Author: Helen Haidle   Illustrator: David Haidle
Zondervan, 2000
ISBN: 0-310-70018-3   Other Categories: Animals

Synopsis: The myth of creation is retold and each segment is paired with a matching passage from the Psalms.

Review: This is really two separate books that could stand alone. One part is about creation, and the other looks at the different animals of creation. The illustrations are rich and varied.

The Creation   Ages: 5+
Author: James Weldon Johnson   Illustrator: Carla Golembe
Boston: Little, Brown and Company, 1993
ISBN: 0-316-46744-8   Other Categories: Poetry, Multiculturalism

Synopsis: Taken from the non-rhyming poem "God's Trombones: Seven Negro Sermons in Verse" written in 1919 and first published in 1927. This is a retelling of the creation story, based on a sermon by a black country preacher.

Review: Even though God is referred to as "He," Johnson does compare God to "a mammy bending over her baby," as God creates people who then celebrate their creation. The rich illustrations are monotypes, a combination of painting and printing.

The Little Shepherd   Ages: 0+
Author and Illustrator: Bijou Le Tord
New York: Bantam Doubleday Dell Books for Young Readers, 1991
ISBN: 0-440-40961-6   Other Categories: Art, Great Beginnings

Synopsis: A little shepherd boy retells Psalm 23 in simple language.

Review: This is a touching adaptation of a favorite Psalm. Le Tord's soft watercolor illustrations are delightful.

When the World Was New   Ages: 3+
Author and Illustrator: Alicia Garcia de Lynam
Broadman and Holman, 1998
ISBN: 0-8054-1880-6   Other Categories: Art, Nature of God

Synopsis: A book about creation and what would have happened if God had not made certain things in our world.

Review: The beautiful watercolor illustrations portray God as an old white man with white hair, a long white beard, and wearing a white robe. This could be used to discuss our ideas of the images and portrayals of God.

The Creation Story   Ages: 3+
Illustrator: Norman Messenger
New York: DK Publishing, 2001
ISBN: 0-7894-7910-9   Other Categories: Nature, Creation

Synopsis: A retelling of the creation story from Genesis 1 from the New Living Translation.

Review: The richly detailed illustrations show animals, plants, and birds from around the world, but the book does not give details about what is depicted. Adam and Eve are white.

The Angel and the Donkey   Ages: 5+
Author: Katherine Paterson   Illustrator: Alexander Koshkin
New York: Clarion Books, 1996
ISBN: 0-395-68969-4   Other Categories: Animals, Angels

Synopsis: A retelling of the story of Balaam's donkey from Numbers 22 – 24. Greedy Balaam, a soothsayer, is prevented from delivering a curse upon the Israelites by his talking donkey, who is able to see the angel of the Lord.

Review: This is a beautiful story about one of only two talking animals in the Old Testament. The illustrations are well researched and look very authentic. There is information about different biblical sources in the afterword.

The Story of the Creation   Ages: 3+
Author and Illustrator: Jane Ray
London: Orchard Books, 1992
ISBN: 0-385-25394-X   Other Categories: Art

Synopsis: A retelling of the seven days of creation.

Review: Jane Ray's work, as always, is outstanding. She uses different shapes for the illustrations, giving the book a sense of design unequalled in most children's books. Her words follow the biblical text, but are retold in an understandable and approachable way. This book celebrates creation.

Finding the Fruits of Peace: Cain and Abel — Ages: 5+
Author: Sandy Eisenberg Sasso   Illustrator: Joani Keller Rothenberg
Woodstock, VT: Jewish Lights, 2001
ISBN: 1-58023-123-3   Other Categories: Legends

Synopsis: When God created the world, each tree bore fruit of many kinds. But when Cain killed Abel, the trees went into mourning, and only bore one type of fruit from then on.

Review: This story is from the Jewish Midrash. The book also has notes about how to discuss the topic of anger with children.

The Ten Commands: From God's Own Hands — Ages: 5+
Author: Phil A. Smouse
Wheaton, IL: Chariot Victor Publishing, 1999
ISBN: 0-7814-3259-6   Other Categories: Poetry

Synopsis: Features ten Bible stories retold in rhyme to illustrate the ten commandments.

Review: The emphasis in these fun rhymes is clearly on the love of God rather than what people should not do. The cartoon illustrations portray white characters. Commandment #7 (You shall not commit adultery) is changed to "Guard your heart."

In the Beginning — Ages: 0+
Author: Steve Turner   Illustrator: Jill Newton
Colorado Springs: Lion Publishing, 1996
ISBN: 0-7459-3605-9   Other Categories: Poetry

Synopsis: God speaks and the world comes into being in this simple retelling of the creation story.

Review: This fun rhythmic poem could be performed by children as a rap. Jill Newton's watercolors are bright and bold. One caution: while Adam is referred to as a "man," Eve is referred to as a "girl."

The Creation Story — Ages: 0+
Author: Brenda C. Ward
Nashville: Broadman and Holman, 1998
ISBN: 080541778-8   Other Categories: Creation, Great Beginnings

Synopsis: A retelling of the first creation story from Genesis 1.

Review: This cute series contains very simple retellings accompanied by photos of babies dressed in costumes to illustrate the stories.

The Creation   Ages: 3+
Author and Illustrator: Brian Wildsmith
Brookfield, CT: Millbrook Press, 1996
ISBN: 0-7613-0144-5   Other Categories: Art

Synopsis: A retelling of the creation story with pop-ups.

Review: The story of creation is hidden beneath the flaps of this outstanding pop-up book. The paper engineering is fabulous, and typical of Wildsmith's brilliant work. A treasure!

Genesis   Ages: 8+
(Text adapted from the King James Version)
Illustrator: Ed Young
HarperCollins, 1997
ISBN: 0-06-025356-8   Other Categories: Creation, Art, Environment

Synopsis: This is an adaptation of the King James Version Genesis 1:1 – 2:3.

Review: The difficult language of the KJV and the dark pastel illustrations in this book make it more suitable for older children. This book can also be used to discuss environmental issues which Young presents in the names of endangered and extinct animals which make up the endpages.

First He Made the Sun   Ages: 0+
Author: Harriet Ziefert   Illustrator: Todd McKie
New York: G. P. Putnam's Sons, 2000
ISBN: 0-399-23199-4   Other Categories: Songs, Multiculturalism

Synopsis: Based on lines from a traditional African American folk song "First He Made a Sun," this book expands on the song to retell the creation myth.

Review: Bright folk art paintings illustrate this beautiful song which could be rapped or sung. Children could make a project out of finding a folk song and retelling it in the same manner.

Collections of Bible Stories – Old and New Testament

The Bible Storybook   **Ages: 5+**
Author: Georgie Adams   Illustrator: Peter Utton
London: Dolphin, 1997
ISBN: 1-85881-2143   Other Categories: Humor

Synopsis: This is a collection of retellings of ten Bible stories from the Old and New Testaments.

Review: The retellings are very simple. The illustrations are humorous, but depict white characters.

The Usborne Children's Bible: The Old Testament   **Ages: 5+**
Author: Heather Amery   Illustrator: Linda Edwards
E D C Publications, 1998
ISBN: 0746030436   Other Categories: Story Collections

Synopsis: Simple retellings of 21 Old Testament Stories.

Review: The stories are simple and short. The drawings are fun and lively, but have mainly white characters.

The Children's Book of Faith   **Ages: 8+**
Author: William J. Bennett   Illustrator: Michael Hague
New York: Doubleday Books for Young Readers, 2000
ISBN: 0-385-32771-4   Other Categories: Traditional Stories

Synopsis: A collection of 34 stories from the Bible, American history, the lives of the saints, and others.

Review: The illustrations are dark and old-fashioned, and it is doubtful that they will appeal to children. Some of the stories are classics, but they are not in a collection that makes cohesive sense.

Interactive Bible Stories for Children: Old Testament Ages: 3+
Editor: Lois Cougher
Group Publishing, 1994
ISBN: 1-55945-190-4   Other Categories: Family

Synopsis: Fifteen stories from the Old Testament are retold, with questions built into the stories. This book includes the stories of Esther and Ruth.

Review: These books serve as a good introduction for people with little experience reading aloud to children; the questions can guide the discussion surrounding the stories. The black and white illustrations are uninspiring.

Interactive Bible Stories for Children: New Testament   Ages: 3+
Editor: Lois Cougher
Group Publishing, 1994
ISBN: 1-55945-291-9   Other Categories: Family

Synopsis: Retellings of stories from the New Testament.

Review: See review of *Interactive Bible Stories for Children: Old Testament.*

The Bible: The Really Interesting Bits   Ages: 5 +
(Great Events from the Bible)
Illustrator: Brian Deif
Tyndale House, 1999
ISBN: 1-894451-00-7   Other Categories: Information

Synopsis: Retellings of 12 stories from the Bible.

Review: This large format book contains good illustrations. The stories are chopped up into small bits. One wonders from the title if they are implying that the rest of the Bible is boring.

Out of the Ark: Stories from the World's Religions   Ages: 8+
Author: Anita Ganeri   Illustrator: Jackie Morris
San Diego: Harcourt Brace and Company, 1996
ISBN: 0-15-200943-4
Other Categories: Other Faiths, Multiculturalism, Legends
Inclusive Language

Synopsis: This is a collection of stories from Christianity, Sikhism, Judaism, Islam, Hinduism, Aborigine spirituality, Native spirituality, Incan beliefs, Shinto, and Buddhism. The stories are broken into the following categories: Creation Stories, Flood Stories, Animal Stories, Birth, Courtship and Marriage Stories, War, Pestilence and Persecution Stories, and the Lives of Religious Leaders.

Review: The stories are short and well written. This is an excellent book for comparing how different faiths have used stories to express their beliefs and make sense of the world. Morris' exquisite watercolors capture the spirit of each culture in a very sensitive manner.

God's Mailbox: More Stories about Stories in the Bible Ages: 8+
Author: Marc Gellman   Illustrator: Debbie Tilley
New York: Beech Tree, 1998
ISBN: 0-688-16363-7   Other Categories: Humor
Inclusive Language

Synopsis: This is a collection of 18 stories, both humorous and serious about Old Testament stories.

Review: These are not retellings of Bible stories, but are stories which have been inspired by Bible stories. Each story has references to the biblical verses which served as the inspiration for the story.

Picture That! Bible Storybook   Ages: 3+
Author: Tracey Harrast   Illustrator: Garry Colby
Zondervan Publishing House, 1998
ISBN: 0310926009   Other Categories: Great Beginnings

Synopsis: A collection of 65 stories from the Old and New Testament.

Review: This is a very simple collection of stories. Each story contains rebus symbols (icons which stand for words), which allows the pre-reader to take part in the reading. The stories are accompanied by questions about the text.

Bible Stories from the Old Testament   Ages: 3+
Author: Joy La Brack   Illustrator: Kathy Mitchell
New York: Random House, 2001
ISBN: 0-375-81016-1   Other Categories: Men

Synopsis: Retellings of 12 stories from the Old Testament.

Review: With the exception of Eve, only stories about men in the Bible are retold in this mediocre collection. The characters are portrayed as white. See also: *Bible Stories from the New Testament.*

The Family Story Bible   Ages: 5+
Author: Ralph Milton   Illustrator: Margaret Kyle
Kelowna, BC: Northstone Publishing, 1996
ISBN: 1-55145-092-5   Other Categories: Information
Inclusive Language

Synopsis: Retellings of more than 100 stories from Hebrew and Christian scriptures, with biblical references.

Review: The author has used the scriptures as the basis for these retellings, but has also added his own details of things that might have happened, or the way things may have been at the time. The watercolor illustrations capture the essence of the text and are wonderfully honest, such as the boy holding his nose because of the smell on the Ark, and Hannah breastfeeding her baby.

Tomie dePaola's Book of Bible Stories   Ages: 3+
Illustrator: Tomie dePaola
New York: G. P. Putnam's Sons/Zondervan, 1990
ISBN: 0-310-91235-0   Other Categories: Art

Synopsis: Retellings of Old and New Testament stories from the New International Version of the Bible.

Review: Award-winning illustrator Tomie dePaola creates his illustrations with a naive style that has a medieval appearance. His characters are approachable and central to each illustration. This is a good collection of illustrated Bible stories.

Discovering the Bible:
Noah's Ark and other First Bible Stories   Ages: 8+
Retold by: Victoria Parker
Lorenz Books, 1999
ISBN: 0754802051   Other Categories: Information

Synopsis: This is a collection of Old Testament retellings combined with explanations of related words, theories, information about archaeology, history, etc.

Review: This collection presents a variety of beliefs. It contains a glossary of terms, as well as maps and photos of important sites.

The Bible Made Easy:
A Pop-Up, Pull-Out, Interactive Bible Adventure   Ages: 3+
Author: Linda Parry   Illustrator: Alan Parry
Nashville: Thomas Nelson, 1999
ISBN: 0-8499-5902-0   Other Categories: Art, Information

Synopsis: A pop-up book of Bible stories from Creation, the Exodus, Joseph, Jonah, Jesus, and Revelation.

Review: This is a fun book with snippets of information about each story. The book may not stand up to much repeated use. The characters are mainly white.

Let There Be Light   **Ages: 5+**
Illustrator: Jane Ray
New York: Dutton Children's Books, 1997
ISBN: 0-525-45925-1   Other Categories: Art

Synopsis: The stories of Creation, Noah's Ark, and Christmas using the King James Version.

Review: This book is exquisitely beautiful. Each richly decorated page leaves many openings for discussion and wonder. The design of this book weaves the text with the illustrations, with whimsical and fascinating borders.

A Family Bible Treasury: Everlasting Stories   **Ages: 5+**
Author: Lois Rock   Illustrator: Christina Balit
Oxford, UK: Lion Publishing, 2001
ISBN: 0-8118-3258-9   Other Categories: Art

Synopsis: Retellings of stories from the Old and New Testaments.

Review: The retellings are simple and some have biblical quotations. The bright, detailed illustrations are done in watercolor, gouache, and gold ink.

Crafts from Your Favorite Bible Stories   **Ages: 3+**
Author: Kathy Ross   Illustrator: Sharon Lane Holm
Brookfield, CT.: Millbrook Press, 2000
ISBN: 0-7613-1295-1   Other Categories: Activities

Synopsis: Contains 27 crafts to match stories from the Old and New Testaments.

Review: This book has good illustrations, clear instructions, and materials lists for each project. There are biblical references for each activity. The activities are easy to follow and make.

The Loving Arms of God   **Ages: 5+**
Author: Anne Elizabeth Stickney   Illustrator: Helen Cann
Grand Rapids, MI: Wm. B. Eerdmans Publishing Co., 2001
ISBN: 0-8028-5171-1   Other Categories: Prayer

Synopsis: A collection of retellings of stories from the Old and New Testaments. Each story has an introduction to relate the story to modern life or explain it.

Review: Along with the retellings is a section for each story called Meeting God; with a Bible verse, questions to think about, and a guide for prayer. There are lovely illustrations for each story.

The Bible Story   Ages: 3+
Author: Philip Turner   Illustrator: Brian Wildsmith
Oxford University Press, 1989
ISBN: 0192731602   Other Categories: Art

Synopsis: This book contains retellings of 48 stories from the Old and New Testaments.

Review: The short, simple retellings are enhanced by the intense watercolor illustrations that are so typical of Wildsmith's art.

Bible Stories   Ages: 8+
Author: Carol Watson   Illustrator: Kim Woolley
Columbus: McGraw-Hill
ISBN: 1-57768-761-2   Other Categories: Technology

Synopsis: This collection of facts about life in Bible lands features very short retellings of biblical stories. The book and CD highlight the stories of men from the Bible – Abraham, Isaac and Jacob, Joseph, Joshua, David, and Jesus.

Review: The characters are white. Some illustrations may be disturbing, such as a picture of a dead child in the Passover, and the Egyptians drowning in the Red Sea.

God Speaks to Us in Water Stories   Ages: 8+
Author: Mary Ann Getty-Sullivan
Illustrator: Marygrace Dulski Antkowski
Collegeville, MN: Liturgical Press, 1996
ISBN: 0-8146-2364-6   Other Categories: Environment

Synopsis: Retellings of stories from the Bible that involve water including Noah, the crossing of the Red Sea, Water comes out of the rock, Naaman, the baptism of Jesus, Jesus walking on the water, and Jesus and the Samaritan Woman.

Review: The dark pastel illustrations give a heavy feel to this collection of stories. The retellings are fair.

God Speaks to Us in Feeding Stories   **Ages: 8+**
Author: Mary Ann Getty-Sullivan
Illustrator: Marygrace Dulski Antkowski
Collegeville, MN: Liturgical Press, 1998
ISBN: 081463654   Other Categories: Food

Synopsis: Retellings of eight Bible stories about feeding.

Review: See review of *God Speaks to Us in Water Stories.*

The Life of Jesus

Tell Me the Story of Jesus   **Ages: 5+**
Author: V. Gilbert Beers   Illustrator: Cheri Bladholm
Wheaton, IL: Tyndale Kids, 2001
ISBN: 0-8423-3868-3   Other Categories: Information

Synopsis: Retellings of certain events in the life of Jesus.

Review: This is an extensive collection of retellings in short 1- or 2-page stories. The illustrator used live models, which are sometimes not believable.

Celebration Song   **Ages 3+**
Author: James Berry   Illustrator: Louise Brierley
London, UK: Hamish Hamilton, 1994
ISBN: 0-241-00209-5   Other Categories: Song, Multiculturalism

Synopsis: On Jesus' first birthday, Mary tells him the story of his birth in song.

Review: The illustrations are set in the Caribbean and picture the Holy family as black. The words are written on ribbons, which wind through the story. This is a wonderful book to use with all children to show how people portray Jesus in ways that they can relate to him.

Mary's Story   **Ages: 5+**
Author: Sarah Jane Boss   Illustrator: Helen Cann
New York: Barefoot Books, 1999
ISBN: 1-901223-44-2   Other Categories: Biography, Legend

Synopsis: The story of the Virgin Mary (part biblical, part legendary) from the Annunciation to the Assumption.

Review: The watercolor, graphite, and collage illustrations in this presentation are inspired by Italian Renaissance paintings and may not appeal to younger children. Some may find it difficult to separate the legend from biblical information about Mary. There are references in the author's note.

The Parable of the Leaven   Ages: 3+
Author and Illustrator: Helen Caswell
Nashville: Abingdon Press, 1992
ISBN: 0-687-30024-X   Other Categories: Parables

Synopsis: A retelling of the parable of the leaven from Matthew 13:33. A young girl buys flour and yeast to make bread.

Review: The old-fashioned, sweet illustrations are a bit stereotypical. Her breadmaking is compared to the kingdom of heaven, but the parable is not fully explained.

Lydia   Ages: 5+
Author: Marty Rhodes Figley   Illustrator: Anita Riggio
Grand Rapids, MI: Wm. B. Eerdmans, 1999
ISBN: 0-8028-5141-X   Other Categories: Prayer, Community

Synopsis: Lydia loves all things purple and becomes a seller of purple cloth. When she converts to Christianity and opens her house for meetings, her precious things are ruined, but when Paul and Silas are imprisoned, she realizes that people are more precious than things.

Review: This is not a precise retelling, but is based loosely on the story of Lydia in Acts 16. Lydia learns about the importance of prayer and devotion to God and her friends. The illustrations show many items which do not fit with the time and setting of the story.

The Story of Zacchaeus   Ages: 5+
Author: Marty Rhodes Figley   Illustrator: Cat Bowman Smith
Grand Rapids, MI: Wm. B. Eerdmans Publishing Co., 1995
ISBN: 0-8028-5092-8   Other Categories: Humor

Synopsis: A retelling of the story of Zacchaeus, the tax collector.

Review: Figley adds many details that are not in the biblical story, but creates a humorous retelling. This is a story about the possibility of transformation.

Stories and Songs of Jesus   **Ages: 5+**
Authors: Paule Freeburg, D.C. and Christopher Walker
Illustrator: Jean Germano
Portland, OR: OCP Publications, 1994
ISBN: 0-915531-27-5   Other Categories: Songs

Synopsis: Each biblical retelling (from Gabriel's announcement to the Resurrection) has a song to go with it.

Review: The songs were written for the book, and can be used to introduce song as prayer. The songs have different musical styles and easy lyrics. The characters are white.

More Stories and Songs of Jesus   **Ages: 5+**
Authors: Paule Freeburg, D.C. and Christopher Walker
Illustrator: Jean Germano
Portland, OR: OCP Publications, 1999
ISBN: 0-915531-78-X   Other Categories: Songs

Synopsis: See synopsis of *Stories and Songs of Jesus*.

Review: See review of *Stories and Songs of Jesus*.

My Own Story of Jesus   **Ages: 3+**
Illustrator: Heinz Giebeler
Toronto: Canadian Bible Society, 1997
ISBN: 0-88834-296-9   Other Categories: Retellings

Synopsis: Retellings of the life of Jesus (birth, Jesus and his friends, the parables, and his death and resurrection) taken from the Contemporary English Version of the Bible.

Review: The retellings are very short with watercolor illustrations, and are good for very young children. This gives a good introduction to the Bible, with biblical references.

What Did Jesus Promise?   **Ages: 3+**
Author: Helen Haidle   Illustrator: Cheri Bladholm
Grand Rapids, MI: Zonderkidz, 1999
ISBN: 1-57673-649-0   Other Categories: Information

Synopsis: Bible verses about the promises of Jesus are presented in sidebars, with a short discussion of each verse.

Review: The language is nice and straightforward, explaining the Bible verse in simple terms. The illustrations portray children from many races and a child in a wheelchair.

Parables: Stories Jesus Told   Ages: 5+
Author: Mary Hoffman   Illustrator: Jackie Morris
London: Frances Lincoln, 2000
ISBN: 0-7112-148-9   Other Categories: Parables

Synopsis: Retellings of eight parables told by Jesus.

Review: Each parable has an introduction that relates it to modern life, and is followed by questions for ways to relate personally to the parable. The watercolors are beautiful, and the page design gives a variety of views.

Love Is...   Ages: 3+
(Adapted from 1 Corinthians 13)
Illustrator: Wendy Anderson Halperin
New York: Simon and Schuster Books for Young Readers, 2001
ISBN: 0-689-82980-9   Other Categories: Art

Synopsis: This presentation of 1 Corinthians 13 bases its picture-story on portions of the King James, the New International, and the Revised Standard versions of the Bible.

Review: This is a treasure! The exquisite, detailed illustrations cannot be described adequately. Halperin has created a work of art with great attention to detail. This book can be read again and again and the reader will see new things each time. Children could draw their own illustrations to show what love means to them.

The Sunflower Parable   Ages: 5+
Author: Liz Curtis Higgs   Illustrator: Nancy Munger
Nashville: Thomas Nelson, 1997
ISBN: 0-7852-7171-6   Other Categories: Parables, Death, New Life

Synopsis: Logan wants to grow large sunflowers and is disappointed when fall comes and they stop growing. Through this, Logan learns about the cycle of life.

Review: Each page has Bible verses that relate to the text. The parable is simple and straightforward. The farmer is a man.

The Parable of the Lily   Ages 5+
Author: Liz Curtis Higgs   Illustrator: Nancy Munger
Nashville: Thomas Nelson, 1997
ISBN: 0785272313   Other Categories: Parables, New Life

Synopsis: A girl receives a box of earth as a present from her father. She throws it out, only to find an Easter lily has grown from the bulb in the earth.

Review: See review for *The Sunflower Parable*.

The Tale of Three Trees   Ages: 8+
Author: Angela Elwell Hunt   Illustrator: Tim Jonke
Oxford: Lion Publishing, 2001
ISBN: 0-7459-4593-7
Other Categories: Folk Tales, Legends, Board Book

Synopsis: Three trees each dream of a different goal – to hold treasure, to become a boat, and to point to God. One day, the trees are cut down. The first becomes the manger, the second a fishing boat for Jesus and the disciples, and the third becomes the cross on which Jesus was killed.

Review: Although this is a board book, it is not for very young children, as the images are a bit jarring. The illustrations are quite dark, but the story presents a lovely retelling of a traditional tale.

Bible Stories from the New Testament   Ages: 3+
Author: Meredyth Inman   Illustrator: Kathy Mitchell
New York: Random House, 2001
ISBN: 0-375-81017-X   Other Categories: Parables

Synopsis: A retelling of stories from the life of Jesus and the parables he told.

Review: This collection's short passages come only from the four gospels, not from the entire New Testament as the title implies. Characters are portrayed as white. See also: *Bible Stories from the Old Testament*.

Miracle Maker: A Life of Jesus, Retold & Remembered   Ages: 5+
Retold and compiled by: Mary Joslin   Illustrator: Francesca Pelizzoli
Colorado Springs: Lion Children's Books, 1998
ISBN: 0-7459-4081-1   Other Categories: Songs, Poetry

Synopsis: A collection of Bible passages, poems, and stories about the miracles of Jesus.

Review: The passages are short, combined with small illustrations, bordered pages, and decorations. The book stresses that internal change is also a miracle.

The Glorious Impossible   Ages: 5+
Author: Madeleine L'Engle   Illustrator: Giotto
New York: Simon and Schuster Books for Young Readers, 1990
ISBN: 0-671-68690-9   Other Categories: Art

Synopsis: The story of Jesus from the Annunciation to Pentecost is retold using illustrations taken from the Giotto frescoes of the Scrovegni Chapel in Padua, Italy.

Review: The 700-year-old frescoes, originally commissioned in an attempt to purchase indulgences, have been carefully preserved in the Scrovegni Chapel. These images form the illustrations of this beautiful book. The scenes are passionate and remarkably clear. A wonderful introduction to classical Christian art.

Young Jesus of Nazareth   Ages: 12+
Author: Marianna Mayer
New York: Morrow Junior Books, 1999
ISBN: 0-688-16727-6   Other Categories: Art

Synopsis: This book uses mainly apocryphal writings to retell the story of Jesus' youth.

Review: A collection of classical paintings (many by James Tissot) illustrate this book. It is interesting to compare the various portrayals of the young Jesus. There are notes on story sources as well as a bibliography. This may be an interesting book for adult study.

The Twelve Apostles: Their Lives and Acts   Ages: 8+
Author: Marianna Mayer   Editor: Phyllis Fogelman
Phyllis Fogelman Books, 2000
ISBN: 0803725337   Other Categories: History, Legends, Biography

Synopsis: Scripture, Apocrypha, and legend give insight into the character of the apostles, and the history of their acts.

Review: There is a list of sources and references for the information presented in the book. The illustrations are paintings by many classical European artists.

The Life of Jesus in Masterpieces of Art   **Ages: 8+**
Author: Mary Pope Osborne
New York: Penguin Group, 1998
ISBN: 0-670-87313-6   Other Categories: Art

Synopsis: Retelling of certain events in the life of Jesus taken from the four gospels, using the King James Version and the Revised Standard Version of the Bible.

Review: This book is illustrated with paintings from the 15th and 16th centuries, and includes works by Botticelli and Fra Angelico. The text is straightforward and easy to understand, merging the four gospels into a chronological order. A synopsis of the pictures used is reproduced at the end of the book.

I Want to Know about Jesus   **Ages: 8+**
Who Jesus Is, What He Did, and Why He Died for Me
Authors: Rick Osborne and K. Christie Bowler
Grand Rapids, MI: Zondervan, 1998
ISBN: 0-310-22087-4   Other Categories: Informational

Synopsis: This is an informational book about the life of Jesus, the history of his time, his miracles and teachings, and his promises.

Review: This makes a good resource to introduce children to the life and times of Jesus. It contains a section about how women were important to Jesus, but the book does not use inclusive language. It does portray people from a variety of races.

The Miracles of Jesus   **Ages: 5+**
Author and Illustrator: Tomie dePaola
New York: Holiday House, 1996
ISBN: 0823412113   Other Categories: Art

Synopsis: This book retells the stories of 12 miracles of Jesus, from calming the seas to raising the dead, with references to the scriptural texts.

Review: The very simple retellings match the simple watercolors painted in the distinct style of dePaola. Note that the faces are white.

Little Jesus, Little Me   **Ages: 0+**
Author: Dorris Rikkers   Illustrator: Dorothy Stott
Grand Rapids, MI: Zondervan Publishing House, 2000
ISBN: 0-310-23205-8   Other Categories: Great Beginnings

Synopsis: The significant events in the childhood of Jesus are compared to those of the typical child today.

Review: This simple pattern book emphasizes the humanity of Jesus, and how Jesus can relate to people of today. Jesus is depicted as white.

Paul, God's Message Sent Apostle Post   **Ages: 8+**
Author: Mike Thaler   Illustrator: Dennis Adler
Colorado Springs: Faith Kids, 2000
ISBN: 0-78143-433-5   Other Categories: Satire, Retellings

Synopsis: Loose retellings of the stories of Pentecost, Ananias and Sapphira, Simon, Peter and Cornelius, and Paul.

Review: The main characters in these sarcastic retellings are all men. This book may appeal more to adults, and may be confusing for children.

The Story of Jesus:
Photographed As If You Were There   **Ages: 3+**
Author: Henry Wansbrough   Photographer: Tony May
Barrons Juveniles, 1997
ISBN: 0764150480   Other Categories: Informational

Synopsis: Stories of the New Testament are retold with photos which help re-create the scenes.

Review: This offers an interesting concept which could bring alive the stories and settings of the life of Jesus. Unfortunately, Jesus and most of the models in this book are white.

Jesus   Ages: 5+
Author and Illustrator: Brian Wildsmith
Oxford, UK: Oxford University Press, 2000
ISBN: 0- 19-27905905   Other Categories: Art

Synopsis: A retelling of the life of Jesus from Gabriel's announcement to Pentecost.

Review: Exquisite illustrations are in the shape of windows. The gold borders have various Christian symbols and shapes in their design.

My Bible Village: Martha and Mary's House   Ages: 0+
Author: Allia Zobel-Nolan   Illustrator: Linda Clearwater
Grand Rapids, MI: Zonderkidz, 2000
ISBN: 0-310-98254-5
Other Categories: Board Books, Great Beginnings

Synopsis: Retells the story of Jesus' visit to the home of Mary and Martha.

Review: Very young children will like the peek-a-boo illustrations. Unfortunately, the velcro closure is too strong, and the front cover is easily damaged in opening.

My Bible Village: Zaccheus' House   Ages: 0+
Author: Allia Zobel-Nolan   Illustrator: Linda Clearwater
Grand Rapids, MI: Zonderkidz, 2000
ISBN: 0-310-98253-7
Other Categories: Board Books, Great Beginnings

Synopsis: Retells the story of Jesus' visit to the home of Zaccheus.

Review: Very young children will like the peek-a-boo illustrations. Unfortunately, the velcro closure is too strong, and the front cover is easily damaged in opening.

8

A New Creation
Inclusive Creation Stories & Myths

So God created humankind in God's own image,
in the image of God, God he created them;
male and female God created them.

GENESIS 1:27

There is in Wisdom a spirit that is intelligent, holy, unique, manifold, subtle,
mobile, clear, unpolluted, distinct, invulnerable, loving the good, keen,
irresistible, beneficent, humane, steadfast, sure, free from anxiety, all-
powerful, overseeing all, and penetrating through all spirits that are
intelligent, pure and altogether subtle.

WISDOM 7:22–23

As a child, my image of a male, authoritarian, judgmental God was never challenged. I was not encouraged to think otherwise. As an adult and a feminist, my view of God changed to a Spirit that is beyond our earthly images of male and female. This new view was liberating, but until I found a faith community that shared this view, I thought I had a dirty little secret about my God.

Children will encounter traditional, stereotypical images of God and people throughout their lives. They will see people trying to fulfill the expectations of what they think their roles ought to be. They will encounter language that omits and excludes them. They will see images of domination and disregard for those who lack what our society considers power. Children's literature cannot right these wrongs, but it can give children alternative language to use, different views to hold and an openness to possibility that includes all people, regardless of their place in society or some people's attitudes towards them.

The same is possible when it comes to presenting an image of God. Too often, those traditional images have excluded people – Father, white, old, almighty, Lord – these images do not reflect the majority of the world's population. People have not been able to see themselves in God's image, even though they were created in that image. It is possible to re-create the image of God – inasmuch as an image is necessary – so people can reclaim their place with a God that can free them to see themselves.

Gender and Books

Within the realm of mainstream children's literature, there are many wonderful books that are empowering for girls and young women. Books, such as those profiled in *Gender Positive! A Teachers' and Librarians' Guide to Nonstereotyped Children's Literature, K-8.* (Roberts, P., Cecil, N. and Alexander, S., 1993. Jefferson, NC: McFarland & Company) and *Great Books for Girls* (Odean, K., 1997. NY: Ballantine Books) show women in non-traditional roles, with positive assertive traits and in a variety of occupations. There are also many biographies of women who serve as positive role models and examples.

Inclusive Language and Children's Books

In children's literature for faith development, however, there are not as many works that use inclusive language and show strong women and girls of faith. God is often still referred to using masculine pronouns. The stories of biblical men are highlighted, perhaps because so many of them have names! Women are often shown as mothers and homemakers lacking other roles or characteristics.

Thus began my search for children's literature for faith development that would use inclusive language and would contain positive, varied images of women and men. While my main goal was to find books that would empower girls and young women, it is important to note that these books are also empowering for boys and young men. Inclusive literature allows boys to see themselves in a variety of roles and encourages a wider interpretation and understanding of a God of all peoples. These books are not just for girls. They are for all the children of God.

Creation and Women

The biblical Creation Story and "The Fall" as it has been erroneously described is a particularly difficult one for women. The creation story in Genesis 1:26–31 describes man and woman created equally, male and female in God's image, yet this is often overlooked in favor of the "rib story" (Genesis 2:18–24) where Eve is created from man as a helper. Blame, shame, and guilt are also heaped upon women for "the fall from grace."

How are girls and young women to remove themselves from these negative images in these most basic of Bible myths? What damage do these images inflict on people of faith, male and female, who are struggling to find their role within society and the church? What role can children's literature play in helping to reverse these perceptions?

It seems so fitting that creation stories be associated with the female image – woman, who brings life into the world and sustains it. The strength of the creative spirit in women makes it a natural connection. As an artist, my right-brained creative side connects me with my God. My prayer is expressed through my creativity. It is how I relate to my Creator God, because we have something in common!

The Creation Myths

The following reviews look at children's books that portray alternate views of creation myths. These books and stories all use inclusive language, and are suitable for use by people of any faith tradition to empower and encourage their children in opening up to a more holistic interpretation of scripture. While many are picture books, they can be used to open discussion at any age level.

I hope these books will help women and girls of all ages reclaim their positive role in Creation, and that they will encourage men and boys to be open to non-traditional views of God and language which uses positive references to God, regardless of gender specificity.

Ways to Use the Literature

- Learn more about inclusive language. What is your church's stance on it? How is it carried out in your church? Do some leaders use more inclusive language than others? Can you encourage people to use inclusive language?

- We do not need to put down men and boys in order to empower girls and women. Brainstorm ways you can include the male members of your school, church, community in your attempts to be more inclusive to all.

- Find a creation story that is not written with inclusive language and rewrite it. Create inclusive illustrations, too.

- Write to authors and publishers and encourage them to use inclusive language in their books.

- Collect creation stories from different faith traditions. Read the stories and compare them. Some traditions are very open to inclusive language, while others are not.

- Write a creation story of your own. You may base it on a story you have heard or it may be completely your own idea.

- Compare scientific facts about creation with creation stories. Find out why some faith traditions reject science in favor of more literal biblical interpretation.

- Visit a planetarium or observatory. Learn more about the universe and our place in it.

- Read a creation story for Earth Day.

- Make a list of all the different names you could use for God. Share this list with your minister and encourage him or her to use these names in the prayers and sermons. Do not throw out the traditional names, but include them and balance them with non-traditional names.

- Have a creation celebration. Read creation stories. Bring items to create with. You might create music, art, poetry, writing, good works, or ideas. Remember not to criticize creations, but celebrate them.

- There are many ways to be inclusive. How about ability? Or sexuality? Or socio-economic class? Or level of education? Or marital status? Or age? Or race? Or religion? How many others can you think of?

- Take your list of ways to be inclusive and think about ways to make your church/school more inclusive. Could you invite speakers to discuss these topics? Could you try to make your church/school more accessible for the handicapped? What else could you do to include others?

- What are some of the reasons we exclude people? This may be difficult to discuss, but it is very important to examine our own behaviors and attitudes.

- There are probably many people in your own school/congregation/ youth group who are very creative. Find out how and why they express themselves through their creativity.

- Make a list of all the different ways you can think of to be creative. What is your favorite creative expression? Why do you enjoy it? How can you express it to be a blessing to others?

- There are two creation stories in the Bible, and they are quite different. Read them both and compare them.

 Bibliography

Mama God, Papa God: A Caribbean Tale　　Ages: 5+
Author: Richardo Keens-Douglas　　Illustrator: Stefan Czernecki
Vancouver: Tradewind Books, 1999　　ISBN: 1-896580-24-6
Inclusive Language　　Other Categories: Multiculturalism

Synopsis: This is a Caribbean retelling of the creation story. In creating people, they ask each other what they look like. "Love, pure love." So that is what they created!

Review: The illustrations are bright and bold, and the story presents a simple, fun expression of God's love. Keens-Douglas is a storyteller, and this comes through in his writing. This is a wonderful book for reading aloud.

In the Beginning　　Ages: 5+
Told by: Virginia Hamilton　　Illustrator: Barry Moser
Orlando, Florida: Harcourt Brace and Company, 1988
ISBN 0-15-238742-0　　Other Categories: Environment, Multiculturalism
Inclusive Language

Synopsis: Four inclusive creation stories are found in this collection:

1. *Moon and Sun: Mawu-Lisa the Creators* (a myth from the Fon people of Benin). The Great Mother, Nana Buluke, creates the world, has twins, and then does nothing else. The twins then become the Mother and Father of all.

2. *The Woman Who Fell from the Sky: Divine Woman the Creator* (a Huron myth). A Divine Woman falls to the world when only water covered it. The water animals try to find earth so she can live on it. Twin boys are born, one being good and the other evil.

3. *Separation of Earth and Sky: Sedi and Melo the Creators* (a myth of the Minyong people, a tribal group in northeast India). Woman Earth and Man Sky marry, but the fearful men decided to beat Melo and he retreated to the heavens. Sedi's daughters and granddaughters bring light to the world.

4. *The Coming of All Things: The Greek Creators* (traditional Greek mythology). The female Earth was created so the gods and goddesses would have a place to stand. It is Earth that brings forth the Heavens; and the Sea and the Titans, her children.

Review: This collection of 25 creation stories from around the world also contains an extensive bibliography of useful sources on the subject of this genre. A synopsis and explanation about its origin follows each story. Two of the 25 myths are about female creators, and in two others, Mother Earth plays an important role.

Song of the Earth   Ages: 5+
Author: Mary Hoffman   Illustrator: Jane Ray
London, England: Orion Children's Books, 1995
ISBN 1-85881-341-7   Other Categories: Environment
Inclusive Language

Synopsis: Mother Goddess, who gave birth to all living things; Yin and Yang; the Zodiac signs; and Mother Earth are just some of the pieces of the elements that have held importance to ancient and modern peoples.

Review: The roles of the four elements of life – earth, water, fire, and air – are examined by Hoffman, with exquisite illustrations by Jane Ray, using rich, earthy colors and metallics. The place the elements have in spirituality, both modern and historical, is documented in stories, non-fiction articles, and poems. This book deals equally with male and female images.

The Tale of the Heaven Tree   Ages: 5+
Author: Mary Joslin   Illustrator: Meilo So
Grand Rapids, MI: Wm. B. Eerdmans Publishing Co., 1999
ISBN: 0-8028-5190-8   Other Categories: Environment
Inclusive Language

Synopsis: The Great Maker creates a wonderful paradise on earth, but it is destroyed by people's greed. One day, the Great Maker talks to a girl and tells her to plant a seed, which eventually grows into a home for birds and animals and the garden below.

Review: This wonderful, inclusive story has superb watercolor illustrations. The tree in this story is based on the *ailanthus altissima*, a Chinese tree called the "Tree of Heaven." Outstanding!

When the Beginning Began:
Stories about God, The Creatures & Us   Ages: 12+
Author: Julius Lester   Illustrator: Emily Lisker
San Diego: Harcourt Brace (Silver Whistle), 1999
ISBN: 0-15-201238-9   Other Categories: Environment, Judaism
Inclusive Language

Synopsis: Each chapter takes a short passage of scripture and tells a story around it, adding to the Jewish Midrash tradition.

Review: The stories are well told, but certain terms and expressions, while humorous or challenging, may be uncomfortable for some people. The stories are not retellings, but expand on the passages. Lester uses many images of God – male and female as well as images from nature.

The Blessing Seed:
A Creation Myth for the New Millennium   Ages: 5+
Author: Caitlin Matthews   Illustrator: Alison Dexter
Bristol, UK: Barefoot Books, 1998
ISBN 1-901223-28-0   *Inclusive Language*
Other Categories: Environment, Art, Nature of God

Synopsis: In this version of "The Fall," Adam and Eve are not portrayed as sinners, but as having a special gift to be the most like God, and a duty to learn and to care. God explains that people were made for their longing to know, and sends Adam and Eve to discover four paths to help them learn and care – the path of wonder, the path of emptiness, the path of making, and the path of coming home.

Review: The watercolors created by Alison Dexter show beautiful richness of color, particularly the apple-bedecked endpages. In the story, Adam and Eve are dark skinned, but without distinct features of any particular people. God is described in the text as "Mother and Father of All," who sings creation into being. The text allows for an interpretation of the seeking of knowledge as an exploration of different paths towards growth, explaining that it is respect for creation that will end our separation from God.

Heart Talks with Mother God   Ages: 5+
Authors: Bridget Mary Meehan and Regina Madonna Oliver
Illustrators: Betsy Gowen, Barbara Knutson, and Susan Sawyer
Collegeville, Minnesota: The Liturgical Press, 1995
ISBN 0-8146-2069-8   *Inclusive Language*
Other Categories: Environment, Image of Woman

Synopsis: Creation is described as "God Birthing the World" (pages 12–13) in a meditation of Mother God, who, as a pregnant mother, gives birth to new life. Knutson's illustration shows a mother welcoming her child, while both are embraced by the outstretched hands of God.

Review: This book takes ten female images of God and uses them to develop meditations that can be used with children. The simple language speaks clearly to a child, using examples of situations from a child's world. At the back of the book, there is a section to help parents, teachers, and caregivers prepare for using the book within a meditation time and guides for presenting each story.

A Creation Story   Ages: 3+
Author: Carolyn Pogue   Illustrator: Chao Yu
Spruce Grove, Alberta: ParseNip Press
ISBN 0-9683421-0-8 and
Toronto, Ontario: United Church Publishing House, 1998
ISBN 1-55134-094-1   *Inclusive Language*
Other Categories: Environment, God's Relationship to People

Synopsis: A lonely God searches for people to talk to. First, Girl is created from a black ball of mud "with lots of parts, something like the reflection in the water." Boy is created next from reddish-brown mud. God continues to create many peoples from different colors of mud.

Review: This simple book shows a God with emotions and a deep desire for communication with creation. A female or transcendent God is implied by the creation of the girl from a reflected image of God. Yu's watercolors show God as a blue being, neither male nor female.

But God Remembered:
Stories of Women from Creation to the Promised Land Ages: 5+
Author: Sandy E. Sasso   Illustrator: Bethanne Andersen
Woodstock, Vermont: Jewish Lights Publishing, 1995
ISBN: 1879045435   *Inclusive Language*
Other Categories: Environment, Women, Legends

Synopsis: Adam and Lilith lived in the Garden of Eden, enjoying its beauty. When Adam wanted to take control over naming the animals, Lilith stood her ground, wanting to share the task. When neither would compromise, Lilith left Adam. Eve was then created and Adam called her the first woman, wanting to erase the memory of Lilith from his mind.

Review: The story of Lilith, the First Woman, is retold by Sasso in this collection of four stories from the Midrash. These Midrash stories paralleled traditional biblical texts, giving explanation or filling in the gaps that were left.

In God's Name   Ages: 5+
Author: Sandy E. Sasso   Illustrator: Phoebe Stone
Woodstock, Vermont: Jewish Lights Publishing, 1994
ISBN: 1879045265   Other Categories: Environment, Nature
Inclusive Language

Synopsis: All the beings of creation have a name. Plants, trees, animals, fish, and people all have names. The people then began to search for a name for God, and each insisted that their name was perfect. One day, the searching people sit by a still lake and look at the reflections of the other people and realize that all the names for God are good.

Review: This beautiful, multicultural book can be used in multifaith settings. It emphasizes the uniqueness of each person's relationship with God. The nature of God and the characteristics of God are evident in the various ways each person names God according to their own needs and understanding of God.

In Our Image: God's First Creatures   Ages: 5+
Author: Nancy S. Swartz   Illustrator: Melanie Hall
Woodstock, Vermont: Jewish Lights Publishing, 1998
ISBN: 1879045990   Other Categories: Environment, Animals
Inclusive Language

Synopsis: In this interpretation of Genesis 1:26–31, God is speaking to the animals of creation when saying, "Let us make humans in our image after our likeness." Each animal then suggests that God use their particular traits when people are created.

Review: This book stresses the connectedness of people with nature, showing how many traits and gifts we share with other animals. The illustrations use the "Black Magic" technique familiar to many children. This book may be used to open up discussion about who was present at creation, and what different people believe about the Trinity.

Stories Seldom Told:
Biblical Stories Retold for Children & Adults   Ages 8+
Author: Lois Miriam Wilson
Northstone Publishing, 1997   *Inclusive Language*
ISBN 1-896836-03-8   Other Categories: Environment, Humor

Synopsis: Wilson's retelling of the creation myth (pages 172–176), entitled "Mainly the male version," is based on a story by Phoebe Willetts ("Eve, Adam and Sneaky the Snake" in *Meet Mrs. Moses*. Gooday Publishers, 1992). In it, Adam and Eve argue about which of the two creation myths is true. Eve challenges Adam's image of God, "a mean tempered old man with a long, white beard and bushy eyebrows sitting on a cloud" (p. 176). The other stories in this collection are wonderful, giving names to unnamed women, voices to the voiceless.

Review: Lois Wilson, senator and former moderator of the United Church of Canada, presents a number of stories from the Bible with different interpretations and explanations. Each story is introduced and background is given to help the reader understand the context of the story. Wilson also provides suggestions for further reading on the subject area and age levels suitable for each story. A short rhyme introduces each story. Wilson's wonderful sense of humor and irony is present in the truth of these stories.

Old Turtle   Ages: 8+
Author: Douglas Wood   Illustrator: Cheng-Khee Chee
Duluth, MN: Pfeifer-Hamilton Publishers, 1992
ISBN 0-938586-48-3   *Inclusive Language*
Other Categories: Environment, Art, Nature of God

Awards: 1993 Book of the Year – American Booksellers Association and 1993 Children's Book Award – International Reading Association

Synopsis: All of nature begins to argue about the nature of God, each thinking that God has the characteristics of itself. Old Turtle settles the argument by affirming that God indeed is all that is good and positive in nature. People are described as "reminders of all that God is," but it is only when they stop arguing and harming the earth and each other that they begin to see God in others.

Review: This book, Wood's first, is a beautiful description of the nature of God. The beauty of Chee's watercolors adds a rich, yet soft element to the simple text. The Old Turtle, a female, is the one who shares her wisdom with the self-centered beings of creation. This can be used as an introduction to the apocryphal Book of Wisdom and the notion of Sophia and Shekinah.

9

Moving On
Novels & Books for
Older Readers

Trust in the Lord with all your heart,
and do not rely on your own insight.
In all your ways acknowledge God,
and God will make straight your paths.

PROVERBS 3:5–6

As children move into their teen years, the variety of books available for their spiritual development dries up. No longer do biblical retellings satisfy the needs of a confused, developing young person. The advice in the above passage from Proverbs seems downright naive when it comes to modern teens, with their everchanging needs and insights, which almost always seem beyond their years, or at least beyond what we are prepared to accept. As our children mature, their literature needs to mature with them. Unfortunately, with few exceptions, this is not the case. Teens are not a lost cause. They are wonderful, developing people who long to be challenged.

As the adults in a teen's life – teachers, ministers, youth leaders, parents – we need to be reading what they are reading if we are to understand what interests them. This will help us keep track of the literature that is influencing them, both positively and negatively. It will also tell our teens that we are interested in their lives. Most importantly, it will help us help them choose positive and challenging literature.

As children move from picture books to early chapter books to novels, we must remember that the content of their lives should be reflected in the content of their reading material. This means, that as children grow, their literature must also become more sophisticated and challenging. Teens know when a book (or a person) is too "preachy" or is talking down to them.

A good example of a book that bridges the gap between picture books and full-fledged novels is *Miriam's Well*, by Alice Bach and J. Cheryl Exum. This book of retellings about women in the Old Testament and Apocrypha uses information from the Midrash to enhance the stories. In doing this, Bach and Exum have created stories which are richly detailed and provide the character's point of view, giving us a glimpse into what they might have been thinking and feeling.

Values and Influences

Children hit puberty and suddenly their lives are turned upside down. The church is often the last place to affirm a teen's emerging sexuality. Christian books rarely treat sexuality in a healthy way. The same is true of other tough issues that face teens today.

But how do we find literature for teens that will reflect Christian values and still be relevant to them? One way is getting to know certain authors who write quality literature for young people. This is not always a guarantee, but it is a good guide. Speaking to children's librarians, bookstore owners, other parents, teachers, ministers, and youth leaders is another way to become knowledgeable and share your own insights. Reading reviews and writing and submitting reviews to magazines and newspapers can heighten awareness.

Teens need role models. We may not want to admit it, but peers are often the most important role models in a teen's life. As teens spend less and less time with parents and family, peers fill the gap. This is normal and usually healthy. But there are other role models, if minor ones. Sports heroes and celebrities are important to some teens. Teachers have a huge influence (both negative and positive), largely due to the amount of time they spend with their students.

Literature can also provide role models for teens. Characters that are well developed with vibrant personalities and strong convictions and beliefs can provide inspiration. Characters that always follow the rules are rarely interesting or worthy of our valuable reading time. It is the character who learns to face and overcome challenges that can move us forward and challenge us to face our own difficulties with courage.

Tough Topics

Some subjects lend themselves more easily to novel format. The Holocaust is one subject which has been dealt with in a number of novels, some of which are based on fact or compilations of facts from a variety of stories. This is an example of a topic which requires a maturity on the part of the reader, and perhaps some introduction by a caring adult.

I remember when I first read *The Diary of a Young Girl* by Anne Frank. I was about 12 and understood little of the Holocaust. I knew the basic facts, but not the full scope of the events which took place. Anne Frank's diary made the Holocaust real for me in a way that no other book could have at the time. I still remember reading the epilogue and learning that she died in Bergen-Belsen. I was shocked. I expected that after all she went through, she would have survived.

What that book did for me was teach me about life at that time for real people. It also taught me that I could never really understand the true extent of the atrocities that took place. Frank's diary planted the seed for me to read and understand more about the Holocaust, and as an adult, I have gone on to read the writings of Etty Hillesum, Hannah Arendt, Simone Weil, and others. The books we read as teens can affect us into adulthood. We must not underestimate them.

Choosing Literature

We know that children (and teens and adults) choose books based on recommendations from others. Giving teens time to share what they are reading is important if we are to encourage other teens to read. A shy teen may not come out and tell others what they are reading, but in a book talk where others are sharing, a shy teen may be encouraged to do so. It is very important to remember that it is always acceptable to choose not to share, too, and it is the role of the leader to make this known and comfortable.

For the teen who is reluctant to read, we must make it easier. We can take away any roadblocks to reading that may exist. By having books readily available, there is no excuse for a teen who does not have anything to read. Letting the teens choose books that interest and excite them can promote reading. Gift certificates are often better than books themselves, as you can give the reader the control of choice. If you wish, limit selections to Christian bookstores or stores that carry a quality selection of books. It is also important to eliminate or deal with any other barriers to reading such as learning disabilities, adequate quiet time, poor eyesight, and time constraints (limiting television, computers, or video games).

Literature does not have to be Christian to encourage us or help deepen our beliefs. Books of all types can challenge us to express and realize our faith. We must be open to quality literature of all types. This includes holy books from other faiths. The later teen years would be a good time to explore in depth the holy books of other faiths to compare them to the Bible. There is much truth to be found in many different places.

Using the Literature

I have made a number of suggestions for different ways to use the literature in church, youth group, or school settings. Some of these examples could also be used at home, especially if there is more than one teenager in the family. There is no guarantee that all or any of these suggestions will work. The best thing is to talk with your youth and get to know them. They will tell you what they like and do not like if they know the lines of communication are open and uncritical.

Above all, do not try anything that would be uncomfortable for you. Teens will sense it immediately. Do not be afraid to throw out an idea that is not working, or to extend an idea that I have not fully developed. Be open, especially to the ideas, opinions and feelings of the youth. Be open yourself, to the possibility of learning *from* them and *with* them.

Ways to Use the Literature

- Start a book club for teens. Agree to read a certain book and get together once a month for pizza and discussion. Do not tell teens what to read. Have a few suggestions and let them pick that interests them.

- Write to publishers to ask them for more books that deal specifically with the needs of Christian teens. Be specific about the types of topics you are interested in reading about.

- Talk to your librarians at school or the public library. Let them know what books you would like to read.

- Invite creative responses to literature. This may mean painting, improvisation, mime, debate, volunteerism, protest, dance, or letter writing.

- Read a book about a different faith. Invite some people from that faith to come and speak about their beliefs. Visit their places of worship, especially if they want you to share about your beliefs.

- Get together with a youth group from another faith tradition, or from a different Christian denomination. Read about each other's faiths before coming together.

- Take a book like *How I Celebrate: A Young Person's Guide to the Festivals of the World* by Pam Robson and create a similar book about how you worship. Send the book you create to a congregation somewhere else in the world, or use the book to explain the different parts of the liturgy to younger or new people.

- Books are expensive. Start a church library with books you have read that others might want to read. Encourage others to donate their books, or raise funds to buy new books for your library.

- Have a book talk. Bring in books you are currently reading and tell others about the books. Make it a fun evening of sharing, without pressure or expectations.

- Read a book about an issue of social justice; for example, child labor, homelessness, or fair trade. Find a way to get involved with the issue, such as volunteering, writing letters of protest, or encouraging your church/family/school to purchase goods which have been fairly traded.

- Read to younger people in your church. Some may not have a parent who reads to them on a regular basis.

- Read to older people in your church. Some may have difficulty reading due to failing eyesight.

- Read to people who may be mentally challenged. If there are none in your congregation, volunteer at a school or center that may need your help.

- Find out how to record books on tape for the blind, so they can enjoy the books you enjoy.

- Pick a topic that is not dealt with in Christian literature and write a book about it yourself. Send it to a publisher. You may even get it published!

- Write poetry and create an anthology of poems. Sell copies of it to raise money for your youth group or a cause you believe in.

- Find out which magazines accept unsolicited stories and poems and submit some of your best work. There may be a set of submission guidelines you can obtain from the magazine, which will help you with your submission.

- Read an historical novel and find out more about that period of time.

- Learn about reading itself. Many people in the world are illiterate. More women than men are illiterate, especially in certain countries. Find out why.

- Read an autobiography of a person who has made a difference. Write your own autobiography and emphasize how you have influenced or can positively influence others.

- Visit a Christian bookstore. Find books on the Internet. Look up books in the library. Go to garage sales. Borrow from your friends. Subscribe to a magazine. Rent videos.

- Make a video.

- Create a website for your church, school, or youth group.

- Pick a favorite author and read a number of books by that person. Some Christian authors also write books that do not necessarily have a Christian theme. See if you can pick out the Christian influences or references in "non-Christian" books.

- Write a letter to an author you like or dislike. You may receive a reply, even if it is a form letter. Be honest in your letter. You may even want to send a sample of your own writing.

- Adults, you can set an example for children and teens by letting them see you read and discuss books which have interested you. They may not admit it, but the people closest to them are huge influences.

Bibliography

Miriam's Well:
Stories about Women in the Bible   **Ages: 12+**
Authors: Alice Bach and J. Cheryl Exum
Illustrators: Leo and Diane Dillon
New York: Delacorte Press, 1991
ISBN: 0-385-30435-8   Other Categories: Teen Books, Women Retellings

Synopsis: Using biblical text and Jewish Midrash sources, this is a collection of stories about women in the Old Testament and Apocrypha.

Review: The stories are very well told, giving the reader the unique voice of each biblical character. Details are added to the stories through Midrashic sources, which amplify the basic biblical text. This is a good book for children who are growing out of picture book retellings.

A Wrinkle in Time   Ages: 10+
Author: Madeleine L'Engle
New York: Farrar, Straus and Giroux, 1962
ISBN: 0-374-38613-7   Other Categories: Science Fiction

Synopsis: The Murry children's father has been missing, and three odd strangers lead them through time to rescue him. In the process, Charles Wallace, the youngest Murry child is held captive by a controlling force which attempts to remove people's will and personality. Meg, his feisty sister, must go back and free him with her love, the only power that will overcome evil.

Review: This book is a Newbery Medal Award winner. L'Engle uses science fiction to illustrate the battle between good and evil. Her writing flows beautifully and the characters are passionately portrayed, with many faults and strengths. The religious references in the trilogy are subtle, but thread throughout the books as a base for the goodness which is always sought.

A Wind in the Door   Ages: 10+
Author: Madeleine L'Engle
New York: Farrar, Straus and Giroux, 1973
ISBN: 0-374-38443-6   Other Categories: Science Fiction

Synopsis: Charles Wallace is having difficulty fitting in at school, and is constantly beaten up by his peers. When he falls terribly ill, Meg must help save him with the help of a magical teacher and a "singular cherubim." Together, they fight the Echtroi, the forces of evil which would remove life from all beings.

Review: The second in the series, this book continues the imaginative work began in *A Wrinkle in Time*. L'Engle creates wonderful characters, and strong female characters who have deep intelligence and an incredible sense of adventure.

A Swiftly Tilting Planet   Ages: 10+
Author: Madeleine L'Engle
New York: Farrar, Straus and Giroux, 1978
ISBN: 0-374-37362-0   Other Categories: Science Fiction

Synopsis: An evil dictator has threatened nuclear war, and the American president calls Mr. Murry for help. When annihilation seems inevitable, Charles Wallace calls on "all Heaven with its power" for help. With the help of a unicorn, he travels through time and space to change the events that would lead to the destruction of the universe.

Review: This part of the trilogy is much more complicated than the first two books. The story moves back and forth through time. This book is fast-paced and very exciting.

His Banner over Me   Ages: 10+
Author: Jean Little
Toronto: Viking, 1995
ISBN: 0-670-85664-9   Other Categories: Family

Synopsis: In this semi-fictional biography of her mother, Jean Little describes the hardship of separation from missionary parents in the first half of the 1900s. Having grown up in Taiwan, Gorrie Gauld and her siblings are sent back to Canada to live with family whom they do not know. Eventually, Gauld became more at home in Canada and went on to medical school, only to return to Taiwan as a doctor.

Review: This book gives a good picture of how difficult life was for the children of missionaries in the last century. In addition to the physical separation, often for years at a time, correspondence was slow and children were often left to the care of virtual strangers. Jean Little is a true storyteller, giving an honesty and richness to her characters.

Little by Little: A Writer's Education   Ages: 12+
Author: Jean Little
Toronto: Puffin Books, 1987
ISBN: 0-14-032325-2   Other Categories: Autobiography, Abilities

Synopsis: The daughter of medical missionaries to China, Jean Little describes her early life in Taiwan and the family's move to Canada. Troubled with "bad eyes" since birth, Little writes about how she dealt with her poor eyesight and the taunts that she received.

Review: In this moving and honest autobiography, Jean Little describes the pain of being teased and the difficulty she had finding friends. It is almost impossible not to empathize with this lonely child who found solace in books, her family, and God.

Stars Come Out Within   Ages: 12+
Author: Jean Little
Markham: Viking, 1990
ISBN: 0-670-82965-X   Other Categories: Autobiography, Ability

Synopsis: This autobiography picks up where *Little by Little* leaves off. Jean is now a published author. She continues to deal with her failing eyesight with the help of her new companion, Zephyr, a Seeing Eye dog.

Review: The tone of this part of Jean Little's autobiography is more hopeful than *Little by Little*, but she still deals honestly with her depression and the many difficulties she faces as a visually impaired person. Little writes candidly and shares her struggles as a writer. Through her struggles, though, Little maintains her faith in God.

Jacob Have I Loved   **Ages: 12+**
Author: Katherine Paterson
New York: Scholastic, 1980
ISBN: 0-590-43498-5   Other Categories: World War II, Family

Synopsis: Sara Louise, the elder twin, resents her talented and beautiful sister, Caroline. Set on the island of Rass in Chesapeake Bay during World War II, Louise helps her father with his fishing. She meets a number of the island's characters along the way, always troubled by the attention and treatment paid to her sister. Louise struggles with the island's Methodist faith and practices.

Review: Paterson paints exquisite pictures with the words she uses to describe the scenery and events that take place in this Newbery Medal book. Using the story of Jacob and Esau, the elder twin loses her birthright to the younger. This is a lovely, rich novel with unforgettable characters.

Preacher's Boy   **Ages: 8+**
Author: Katherine Paterson
New York: Houghton Mifflin, 1999
ISBN: 0-395-83897-5   Other Categories: History, Family, Friendship

Synopsis: Robbie is the son of a preacher in Vermont in 1899, as the world awaits the new century and fears what it may bring. Robbie has a hard time living up to the expectations of the community and his family, especially when he decides to become an "apeist." After his temper gets away from him one day, he runs away and meets a girl and her father living rough in the woods. Robbie learns about friendship, the love of family, and standing up for what is right.

Review: Katherine Paterson has a wonderful sense of story. Her words paint pictures with rich, interesting characters and dramatic plot twists. This very readable book would be an excellent book to read aloud. I am sure every child of clergy will love reading this book.

Who Am I?   **Ages: 12+**
Author: Katherine Paterson   Illustrator: Stephanie Milanowski
Grand Rapids, MI: Wm. B. Eerdmans Publishing Company, 1992
ISBN: 0-08028-5072-3   Other Categories: Information, Beliefs, Teen Books

Synopsis: Written by the award-winning author of *Bridge to Terabithia* and *The Great Gilly Hopkins*, this book explores questions about God, our relationships with God and others, belonging, and purpose.

Review: Stories are woven throughout the book, but it is primarily an exploration of some basic questions about God. This would make an excellent book to use with young teens who are preparing for confirmation, or who are just wondering about where they fit with God and the church.

The Gospel According to the Simpsons: **Ages: 15+**
The Spiritual Life of the World's Most Animated Family
Author: Mark I. Pinsky
Louisville: Westminster John Knox Press, 2001
ISBN: 0-664-22419-9   Other Categories: Humor, Satire

Synopsis: *The Simpsons* television show is one of the most popular animated shows of all time. In this book, Pinsky looks critically at the way religion is portrayed through the show's characters and storylines.

Review: This is a book for adults and older teens. It is often difficult to see beyond the wisecracks on the television series, but this book delves into the rich religious (Christian, Jewish, and Hindu) themes depicted in the show. Pinsky also describes the opposition that some religious groups have presented.

The Gospel According to the Simpsons: **Ages: 15+**
Leader's Guide for Group Study
Authors: Mark I. Pinsky and Samuel F. (Skip) Parvin
Louisville, Kentucky: Westminster John Knox Press, 2002
ISBN: 066422590X   Other Categories: Humor, Satire, Activities

Synopsis: Written by a Jewish man and a Presbyterian minister, this Sunday school guide uses episodes of *The Simpsons* to engage youth and adults in discussion about the issues raised in the popular animated series.

Review: This is an excellent guide. Most of the episodes referred to are available in video stores. Each episode focuses on a main biblical principle, and includes a synopsis of the episode; readings from the Old and New Testaments; discussion questions, prayers, and activities.

Prayers on My Pillow: Ages: 12+
Inspirations for Girls on the Threshold of Change
Author: Celia Straus
Ballantine Books, 1999
ISBN: 0-345-42673-8   Other Categories: Teen Books, Prayer

Synopsis: A collection of prayers divided into 17 categories such as Self-Confidence and Pressures in School.

Review: Inspired by her daughter who asked her to write a prayer, Straus would place a prayer on her daughter's pillow each night. This collection speaks to the confusing experiences that girls face during puberty.

More Prayers on My Pillow: Words of Comfort & Hope
for Girls on the Journey to Self   Ages: 12+
Author: Celia Straus
Ballantine Books, 2000
ISBN: 0-345-44195-8   Other Categories: Teen Books, Prayer

Synopsis: A collection of prayers divided into 16 categories such as Boys, Finding God, and Courage from Within.

Review: See *Prayers on My Pillow: Inspirations for Girls on the Threshold of Change.*

Miriam Mary and Me   Ages: 8+
Author: Lois Miriam Wilson
Northstone Publishing Inc., 1996
ISBN: 1-55145-082-8   Other Categories: Retellings, Women

Synopsis: In this book, 62 stories of women in the Bible and in modern times around Canada and the world are told and retold. Some of the stories are legendary, while others are retold from the Bible.

Review: This book is meant to be read aloud and shared. The stories are short (1 or 2 pages each), and are introduced. Where applicable, the biblical reference is cited. Lois Wilson reclaims some of the stories that are often overlooked in the Bible, and gives respect to women who have been maligned. Modern stories which parallel biblical parables show how applicable these stories are to our lives today.

10

Fantastic Tales
The Narnia Chronicles

Do not weep. See, the Lion of the tribe of Judah,
the Root of David, has conquered...

REVELATION 5:5A

Clive Staples Lewis is one of the foremost Christian writers of the 1900s. While he wrote many books for adults, he wrote only seven children's books. The *Chronicles of Narnia* stand today as classics of Christian children's literature. They are a measure of beauty in language and imagination with no equal in the genre.

Lewis uses fantasy in a way that no other Christian children's writer has done. He makes magic a part of the Christian norm in his books. There is no need for Lewis to explain or justify his fantastic adventures. They must just be accepted on their merits.

The books in this series can be read alone by a mature eight-year-old, but younger children can enjoy them if an adult reads aloud. Children can process language they hear at an earlier age than language they read, because of the difficulty of decoding the words and making meaning at the same time. Some of the battle scenes may be scary for younger children, so it is best to pre-read and judge the suitability of each book for yourself. If you know your audience, you will be able to match the book to the children's readiness.

I have not provided ISBN numbers for the original series, but have done so for subsequent publications based on the series. A number of publishers have brought out copies of the original Narnia books, and there are a number of factors which may lead you to purchase from one publisher over another. The series is also available in one volume.

Of all the publications, one of the nicest is the 50th anniversary edition which has been brought out by HarperCollins. This edition is printed on white paper (rather than the cheaper newsprint we usually find in paperbacks), and the illustrations have been hand colored by the original artist, Pauline Baynes.

The characters in the Narnia chronicles flow from one book to the other. The books do stand on their own, but should be read in sequence, as each book builds on characters and events from the previous books. There is a reading order to the series, and it is different from the year of publication, so be sure to check the book for its number sequence.

Reading Order of the Narnia Books

1. *The Magician's Nephew*
2. *The Lion, the Witch and the Wardrobe*
3. *The Horse and His Boy*
4. *Prince Caspian*
5. *The Voyage of the "Dawn Treader"*
6. *The Silver Chair*
7. *The Last Battle*

Ways to Use the Literature

- Explore the genre of fantasy. Read other fantasy books and find the ways they are similar and different.

- C. S. Lewis uses many images in his books. Learn about the ways images are used in literature.

- The lion is one image of God used in the Bible. Make a list of other images of God. Many are from nature. Why?

- How does Aslan's character differ from the stereotypes of lions?

- Why is Aslan portrayed as a lamb in *The Voyage of the "Dawn Treader"* ?

- Take a favorite image of God and write a story using that image.

- In a number of the Narnia books, the land of Narnia must be renewed. How many ways does our land need renewal?

- There are many mythological creatures in the Narnia books. Read some Greek and Roman myths to find their origins.

- The Narnia books portray many strong female characters. Read some stories with female characters who are leaders.

- C. S. Lewis' books do not have positive parental figures. In fact, most of the "parents" are evil. Discuss why he has done this.

- The element of time in Narnia books is very distorted. Learn about the timelessness of *kairos*.

- Compare the murder of Aslan in *The Lion, the Witch and the Wardrobe* to the death of Jesus in the gospels. Look at the power of the resurrection of Aslan and Jesus. How did it affect those who believed in this power?

- An archetype is an original image which stands for patterns of future behaviors or models. What archetypes can you see in the Narnia books?

- The heroes in the Narnia books encounter many trials. Think about the ways you deal with the trials in your life. How is God present in those trials?

- Aslan is often not recognized immediately. Think about times when you have not recognized God in your experiences. When you have experienced God's goodness in your life, what helped you recognize it? How can you remember to find that presence in the future?

- The illustrations in the Narnia books are very detailed. Look at how Pauline Baynes has based her illustrations on the text. Take a part of the text and draw a picture based on the information in the text.

- In Chapter 11 of *Prince Caspian*, Lucy sees Aslan when the others cannot. How can you help others see and experience God?

- Aslan is a talking lion. How does God speak to you? What are the different ways we can listen to God?

- In *The Voyage of the "Dawn Treader,"* Aslan baptizes Eustace. Learn about the origins of baptism by reading about John the Baptizer in the gospels. Find out about different baptismal traditions (e.g., Anabaptists, Greek Orthodox, United Church of Canada, etc.).

- Ships are images which are used throughout the Narnia books. Read about the importance of ships and boats in the Bible (e.g., the boats of the disciples, Paul's journeys and shipwreck).

- In *The Silver Chair*, Jill is being bullied by her schoolmates. Make a list of ways you can stand up to bullies. What can you do when you see others being bullied? Act out some of these scenarios.

- In *The Last Battle*, a new Narnia is created. What does your church believe about heaven and life after death? What does the Bible say about it? How does the Bible describe heaven? What do you believe?

- Compare the Narnia Chronicles with the Harry Potter books by J. K. Rowling. How are they similar and different? How are the forces of good and evil represented in each series?

Bibliography

The Chronicles of Narnia

The Magician's Nephew   Ages: 8+
Author: C. S. Lewis   Illustrator: Pauline Baynes
1955   Other Categories: Fantasy

Synopsis: Digory and Polly enter Digory's Uncle Andrew's secret room and are given magical rings which transport them to other worlds. When they awaken Jadis, the witch, evil comes first to their world, then to the new world of Narnia. In Narnia, Polly and Digory meet Aslan, its creator, and are introduced to life and goodness in the face of evil.

Review: This is Book One of the Narnia series. While Book Two *(The Lion, the Witch and the Wardrobe)* is more popular and widely read, this book really sets up the events which take place in the rest of the series.

Lewis has created wonderful worlds and rich characters. Both male and female characters display positive and negative traits. These books are classics, and will remain so. Lewis is one of the best Christian writers of the last century.

The Lion, the Witch and the Wardrobe   Ages: 8+
Author: C. S. Lewis   Illustrator: Pauline Baynes
1950   Other Categories: Fantasy

Synopsis: Four siblings – Peter, Susan, Lucy, and Edmund – step through a wardrobe at their uncle's house and arrive in the land of Narnia. Edmund is taken by the witch, Jadis, but is released by Aslan's power. Battles with the witch ensue, but even death cannot overpower Aslan.

Review: This book is a classic depiction of the battles and archetypes of good and evil, life and death. A true storyteller, Lewis moves in and out of the fantastic narrative to connect with his readers. This book can be read on many levels, and it would be good to reread the story of the life of Jesus before examining the rich metaphors Lewis creates.

The Horse and His Boy   Ages: 8+

Author: C. S. Lewis   Illustrator: Pauline Baynes
1954   Other Categories: Fantasy

Synopsis: A young boy named Shasta escapes slavery after finding out that the man he thought was his father is not. With his talking horse, Bree, they leave for Narnia, Bree's homeland. Along the way, they encounter a girl named Aravis, who is escaping an arranged marriage that she does not agree with. As they travel to Narnia, they encounter many trials and even battles, but Aslan, the deliverer of Narnia is with them. Eventually, Shasta finds his birth father and learns that he is actually King Lune of Archenland, and that Shasta is a prince. Aravis is given a place of honor in their court.

Review: The style of this book is completely different from the previous two books in the series, and a more difficult read. The setting is similar to ancient Persia or Turkey. Shasta and Aravis are perfect foils to each other. Aravis is a girl with a strong will and courage. The four children from *The Lion, the Witch and the Wardrobe* are now grown, and are kings and queens in Narnia. They play minor roles in this book.

Prince Caspian   Ages: 8+

Author: C. S. Lewis   Illustrator: Pauline Baynes
1951   Other Categories: Fantasy

Synopsis: Peter, Susan, Lucy, and Edmund are magically brought back to Narnia. When they arrive, they find that civil war has disrupted the land and their former castle lies in ruins. They meet Prince Caspian, who has escaped from his evil uncle, King Miraz. With Aslan's help, the four children restore peace to the land, and Caspian is crowned as the new King.

Review: This book is much more readable than *The Horse and His Boy*. Again, the story revolves around the triumph of good over evil, and the need for God's help in life's troubles.

The Voyage of the *Dawn Treader*   Ages: 8+

Author: C. S. Lewis   Illustrator: Pauline Baynes
1952   Other Categories: Fantasy

Synopsis: While on holiday, Lucy and Edmund, together with their annoying cousin, Eustace, journey back to Narnia through a painting of a ship. There, they meet again with Caspian, who is trying to avenge the deaths of seven friends of his father. On board the *Dawn Treader*, they have many adventures, even to the end of the world as they know it.

Review: There is great humor in this book, especially in the character of Eustace, a whiny, spoiled, and uncooperative traveler. Eustace does repent, however, after he is turned into a dragon and then is baptized by Aslan back to human form. Peter and Susan do not accompany their siblings to Narnia, as Aslan has told them they are now too old to come back.

The Silver Chair   Ages: 8+
Author: C. S. Lewis   Illustrator: Pauline Baynes
1953   Other Categories: Fantasy

Synopsis: Eustace and his school friend, Jill, are called into Narnia to help rescue Prince Rillian, Caspian's son, who has fallen into the control of the Witch of the Underworld. Every night, Rillian is bound to a silver chair, raving in madness. Together, the children and Rillian kill the evil witch, and escape to Narnia, just before the death of Caspian. Rillian is crowned King of Narnia.

Review: The main focus of this book is overcoming bullying, both by the schoolchildren and the forces of evil. Jill finds that she has the strength to deal with adverse situations. We see in this book what happens when God's instructions to us are not followed, but that God's mercy prevails.

The Last Battle   Ages: 8+
Author: C. S. Lewis   Illustrator: Pauline Baynes
1956   Other Categories: Fantasy

Synopsis: Eustace and Jill are brought back to Narnia again, when an evil monkey convinces a donkey to don a lionskin and pretend to be Aslan. Narnia is overtaken by its enemies, and is no more. But the children enter a new Narnia, one that is all that is good in the old Narnia, together with their friends from previous Narnia adventures.

Review: With its sinister overtones, this is the darkest of the Narnia books; but it is also the brightest and most optimistic. Lewis' understanding of Heaven is one of true awe and wonder. It would be good to read the Book of Revelation in order to see the parallels to this book.

Books Based on the Chronicles of Narnia

Aslan's Triumph   **Ages: 8+**
Author: Adapted from C. S. Lewis – *The Chronicles of Narnia*
Illustrator: Deborah Maze
HarperCollins, 1998
ISBN: 0-06-027638-X   Other Categories: Fantasy

Synopsis: Four children step through a wardrobe into the land of Narnia, where they encounter the forces of good and evil.

Review: This simple adaptation of the C. S. Lewis classic is part of a series of World of Narnia Picture Books. It is an adequate introduction, but does not match the linguistic beauty of the original.

The Wood between the Worlds   **Ages: 8+**
Author: Adapted from C. S. Lewis – *The Chronicles of Narnia*
Illustrator: Deborah Maze
HarperCollins, 2000
ISBN: 0-06-443641-1   Other Categories: Fantasy

Synopsis: Two children come upon the study of Digory's Uncle Andrew. Suddenly, Polly disappears and Digory goes after her. They are lost in a world of fantasy until a magic ring leads them home.

Review: See review for *Aslan's Triumph*.

Lucy Steps through the Wardrobe   **Ages: 8+**
Author: Adapted from C. S. Lewis – *The Chronicles of Narnia*
Illustrator: Deborah Maze
HarperCollins, 1998
ISBN: 0-06-027450-6   Other Categories: Fantasy

Synopsis: Lucy decides to explore a wardrobe at Professor Kirke's house and finds herself in the wintry land of Narnia where she meets a faun.

Review: See review for *Aslan's Triumph*.

Aslan   **Ages: 8+**
Author: Adapted from C. S. Lewis – *The Chronicles of Narnia*
Illustrator: Deborah Maze
HarperCollins, 1998
ISBN: 0-06-443527-X   Other Categories: Fantasy

Synopsis: Four children step through a wardrobe into the land of Narnia. There, they meet Aslan who rescues Edmund from the White Witch.

Review: See review for *Aslan's Triumph*.

The Land of Narnia:
Brian Sibley Explores the World of C. S. Lewis   **Ages: 8+**
Author: Brian Sibley Illustrator: Pauline Baynes
London: Collins Lions, 1989
ISBN: 0-00-673591-6   Other Categories: Fantasy, Informational

Synopsis: This companion to the Narnia series of books gives biographical information about C. S. Lewis, Pauline Baynes, the illustrator of the Narnia tales, synopses of the books and other contextual information.

Review: It is clear that Brian Sibley is a big fan of the Narnia books. The information in this book gives a good understanding of the background to the books and especially the life of C. S. Lewis. Sibley also explores the Christian meaning behind the stories.

11

Beyond Comprehension
Literature about
the Holocaust

Out of depths I cry to you, O Lord.
Lord, hear my voice!
Let your ears be attentive
to the voice of my supplications!

Psalm 130:1–2

S ome topics are extremely difficult to approach. The Holocaust is one of those themes. How can we speak of such unspeakable horrors? How do we educate our children about cruelty beyond imagination? What price will we pay if this history is forgotten?

Most of the books reviewed for this chapter are about a small number of people who escaped or survived the Holocaust. Escape is a universal theme. Throughout history, oppression has always presented the need for escape. Wherever there is power, there is also powerlessness. None is immune, and in fact, it is those oppressors who are most in need of escape. Sadly, the stories of the majority of people have been lost forever.

Physical, spiritual, emotional, intellectual. Escape takes many forms. It looks and sounds different to each, according to the context. We believe that dependence on defenses is what we need to survive, but we recognize that those defenses only serve to keep us from change. Our stories frame the escapes we have chosen. For some, the stories may exist only within the heart's sanctuary, where they are safe from harm.

For many, however, there has been no escape. The stories are all we have – pieces strung together from writings, poems, songs, memories, letters, art, imagination. Such is the case with Holocaust stories. While there are a few stories written by people who were personally affected by the Holocaust, other stories are presented by people who are affected because those they know and love(d) were victims. So many of the first-person stories were lost.

But why include Holocaust stories in a book about Christian children's literature? Three main reasons come to mind. First, the Holocaust is everyone's history. It has affected everyone in the world because of the lost potential, the evils committed, the lives lost. Second, the Holocaust must never be repeated. It is necessary to know the history of the Holocaust and to be aware of the atrocities that have taken place in order to prevent further tragedies. Third, if we are to truly understand and appreciate other faiths, we must understand the horrors as well as the joys of those faiths.

Potential Outcomes

Books about the Holocaust can benefit those students who have had little experience with religious oppression or the need for escape. By examining the experiences of others, compassion can be fostered. We cannot hope to fully understand the experiences of others, but we can gain knowledge about their experiences, we can imagine ourselves in their place; and where we cannot even begin to understand, perhaps we can be empathetic or at least tolerant.

We can examine many aspects of the Holocaust through children's literature. Here is a partial list of concepts that could be studied through Holocaust literature: life before, during and after the war, concentration camps, work camps, death camps, transports, friendships, hiding, injustice, resistance, escape, freedom, death, life, forgiveness, survival, hope, hopelessness, change, need, power, anti-Semitism, propaganda, Kristallnacht, human rights, ghettos, confiscation of property, and genocide.

By telling the stories of the Holocaust, we face the evil head on. We take back control from those who have taken it away. To see the injustice that has taken place enables people to recognize and speak out about injustices that are happening now. It is leaving the safety of the familiar and facing the fear of the shadowed unknown. It is stepping towards healing and acquiring new lenses to view the world.

Can those who have been unjustly imprisoned or murdered because of their faith or race or belief in justice ever be free? Can we ever forgive our oppressors and in doing so, forgive ourselves? Should we? These are not easy questions to face, but they are necessary.

Cautions

Books about the Holocaust can potentially bring up some contentious issues. Some will not want to revisit painful memories even through story. Some may not be empathetic to the suffering of others. Parents may not want the stories of their survival brought out. Some still deny the Holocaust as an event. Others deny the need to keep the memory of it alive.

Many books have extremely graphic photographs and details about the Holocaust. While it is necessary to know and understand these events, we must also be aware that children are still developing, and they may not be ready for all the information at once. I have chosen to omit books which, because of their detail, I feel are not appropriate for children under the age of 15.

Teachers wear many hats – instructor, friend, counselor. A teacher must know his or her students, and must be aware of the life stories and of the students' potential reactions to sensitive issues. Constant monitoring and evaluation of the students' reactions to the theme is necessary. If a topic is not working for the students, it is the teacher's responsibility to see that and to make necessary changes.

An Author's View

Carol Matas is Canada's foremost author of children's books about the Holocaust. Her books open us to this part of history, and show us the strong example of many brave people who stood up to Hitler and the Nazis. Carol's writing is frank without being too frightening or gruesome. In her writing, Carol Matas keeps the history of the Holocaust alive for the present and future generations. I would like to thank Carol for her contribution to this book, and for her many contributions to children's literature. Below, Carol answers a number of questions about her writing, and the importance of using Holocaust literature with non-Jewish children.

1. **You have written a number of books about children's experiences during the Holocaust and its aftermath. Why do you feel it is important to write books about the Holocaust?**

    CM: I began writing about the Holocaust when I wrote *Lisa* about the Danish experience in World War II and what happened to the Jewish population. I wanted to write that book because the Danes managed to save almost all the Jews from the Nazis. I felt it was important to tell that story as an illustration of the difference people can make – had all countries behaved like Denmark, especially Poland – millions might have been saved, or the mass murders might never have happened.

As for the other Holocaust books, it's important that young people learn what can happen if you don't pay attention to the world around you. When you write about the experience of one child, like in *Daniel's Story*, suddenly children can relate to that one story and realize the full horror of what happened. They can relate it to the present as well as the past and see how destructive racism is. We must all recognize that we are brothers and sisters – all one human race.

2. **How have these books been used in classrooms?**

   CM: I believe that they are studied as a way to make the history come alive so that children can feel more closely the effects of these horrific acts.

3. **When you meet with children who have read your books, what is their response to them?**

   CM: Children are very thankful that someone has told them about this terrible time and often they vow to make sure nothing like that will ever happen again. They usually also tell me how much they enjoyed reading the story, which might seem odd, but it is history to them, and I feel my job as an author, no matter what the material, is to make sure it is a well-written book with compelling characters and a story that interests the reader.

4. **Do non-Jewish people respond to your books differently than Jewish people? Why do you feel it is important for people of other faiths to read Holocaust literature?**

   CM: The only difference I've noticed is the level of knowledge before reading the books. Jewish children already know about the Holocaust and will focus more on the particular story I am telling. Some non-Jewish children are also very knowledgeable, but the ones that aren't find it shocking and it makes them very sad. Of course it's important for people of other faiths to read it – more important than Jews – because it was anti-Semitism from other faiths that was the bedrock upon which Hitler built his exterminations.

5. **What is the value of using Holocaust literature in non-Jewish settings?**

   CM: It seems to me essential because it is the non-Jewish settings where children may be unaware of the history. Hopefully it will also prevent future anti-Semitism.

6. **How should a teacher prepare students when presenting Holocaust literature?**

CM: History lessons are very important to go along with the literature.

7. **At what age do you think it is appropriate to introduce the Holocaust to children?**

CM: I'd say 5th grade. Younger than that it is too difficult for children. And don't be afraid to let them read and learn about the Holocaust or any difficult subject. Knowledge is power. Children are not innocents who need to be protected from the truth. They see bullying and aggression every day. We must be honest with them.

Moving from Theory into Practice

When using these books in an educational setting, I would suggest extending the Holocaust theme to include other aspects such as war, peace, escape, and freedom. This will allow for a variety of approaches to the theme, and will enable readers to interact with literature that meets their maturity level. There is no need to force a child to read books that would be too upsetting or unsettling. Yes, many of these books will make us uncomfortable. They should. But no child should be pushed beyond their limits.

Alma Flor Ada says that "reading can also be understood as a highly creative act, a dialogue between reader and text, in which the reader not only brings to the text his or her experiences, values and beliefs but engages in an active – albeit internal and silent – dialogue with the text" (Flor Ada, 1988, p. 97).

Children who interact with the books in this theme will certainly bring their own life experiences, positive and negative, to the reading of the texts. As teachers, we must not only be aware of where our students are coming from, but must also be able to read the children – constantly look for their reactions and any possible discomfort that may arise from the theme. I believe a good teacher is a good kid-watcher. A teacher who is critical of his or her own practice will constantly adjust and readjust the curriculum to fit the needs of the students.

It is important, too, for each student to have ownership of this theme. This is vital if students are to engage in the theme, especially one as difficult as the Holocaust. Brian Cambourne (1988) describes engagement as the key to natural learning. Students can find books on the theme that are meaningful to them and add them to the class collection. They can bring in stories from their own lives, the lives of those around them, or from those who have gone before. Acceptance of the theme will be higher if the motivation comes from personal relevance.

Donna Norton describes the values gained from sharing multicultural literature and states that "Comparative activities encourage children to identify and to appreciate similarities and differences across cultures" (Norton, 1985, p. 105). The themes of war, peace, escape, and freedom are cross-cultural, even universal, in nature. They go beyond racial boundaries, because they are themes of all of humanity. These themes go back to biblical times (and beyond) with the exodus of the Hebrew people from Egypt, and they pervade the present and our dreams for the future. Freedom can be brought into Holocaust studies for more sensitive or younger readers. It can also be looked at as the outcome for the survivors – to the extent freedom was and is possible for those who have experienced such atrocities.

Lev Vygotsky encourages teachers to be aware of the gaps in our students' knowledge and the heights to which we can help them climb. He describes this as the "zone of proximal development." "For minority and immigrant children, these books mirror, reflecting and validating cultures and experiences. For mainstream children, these books can be a window, revealing a multicultural vista that juxtaposes the familiar and the less familiar" (Cox and Galda, 1990, p. 582).

Every theme we use in a class must have a purpose. We must be able to articulate that purpose to ourselves, and especially to the children. To invite those children to expand their knowledge about those who have known oppression is to help them move through that zone. To provide a community of learners who are free to critically question and probe is to trust the students to think for themselves and become constructivist learners.

Voice is extremely important in choosing books with a subject matter that is as delicate as this. I feel I have chosen books that have been written from an historical perspective which has been researched and stays within the framework of historical facts. This brings up the question of the child's voice in writing on these themes. If imagining ourselves in the shoes of another can bring about empathy and understanding, then I see potential gain and no harm from this. The danger lies in people who publish books under the guises of possessing unobtainable or unobtained understanding.

Finally, another important goal of using these themes is to help our children become critical thinkers. "The goal of the Creative Reading Method is not met with the awakening of the children's critical awareness as a mere intellectual exercise. Rather, process is completed only when the children can draw on it in order to make decisions regarding the world around them"

(Flor Ada, 1988, p. 105). Will they be able to stand up for themselves and the values we hope we pass on to them? Will they be able to make tough decisions about fairness and equity? When they can integrate the knowledge they have gained with decisions they will face in the reality of their lives, then our teaching and more importantly, their learning can be deemed a success.

Ways to Use the Literature

Because many of these books are historical fiction, it would be a good chance to explore this genre of writing. The richness of writing stories that would otherwise be forgotten cannot be overlooked. What a wonderful opportunity for students to explore anecdotes from their family tree, listen to an oral account of a fascinating event, or to visit a seniors' center and record a story of living history! These could be compiled into an anthology which could be copied and made into books to be shared with the storytellers.

The benefits of this type of writing are numerous. It links storytelling with writing. The stories are real, which gives personal relevance to the writing. The benefit of writing and publishing for an audience can be seen in the effort that goes into students' work. The pride that comes from sharing published material carries through to other areas of each student's life.

- Check the newspapers to see where religious oppression is still occurring. Do something about it. Sign a petition. Send letters to your government. Raise money to help fund aid workers in those countries.

- Interview a Holocaust survivor. If you cannot find one, talk to someone who lost their family in the Holocaust. With permission, write that person's story.

- Interview a war veteran. Learn about what she or he experienced during the Second World War and find out why that person fought during the war.

- Interview a Jewish family who lost relatives in the Holocaust.

- Visit a synagogue and learn about Jewish worship. How is it similar to or different from your worship traditions?

- Invite a Jewish youth group to visit your church.

- Learn more about the Holocaust. Find out which groups of people were taken into the camps. Jews were not the only people killed by the Nazis. Find out about different groups of people who were murdered in concentration camps.

- Learn about a concentration camp. Many still exist as memorials or museums.

- Find out about the different kinds of camps where Jewish people were sent – death camps, transit camps, labor camps, etc.

- Visit a Holocaust memorial. Most major cities have one. If you cannot get to one, visit one on the Internet.

- The children in the Terezin (Theresienstadt) Concentration Camp used art and music to help cope with their situation. List ways that you cope with adversity.

- Recognize Holocaust Awareness Week in your church. Sponsor special events to teach and remember.

- Designate Holocaust Remembrance Sunday if it is not already recognized in your church. Help plan the service around this theme. You may wish to work with a local synagogue on this.

- Learn a traditional Jewish folk song and sing it in church.

- Think about ways people are oppressed around you. It may be because of religion, gender, race, intellectual ability, place of birth, sexuality, looks, age, or socio-economic class. Role-play ways to stand up when you see this type of oppression taking place. By role-playing, you may find it is easier to really stand up to the oppressors when you need to.

- In *One Yellow Daffodil*, the sight of a flower gave a man hope to survive. What gives you hope? How can you give hope to others?

- Watch a video about the Holocaust. Be sure to watch with an adult. There is also a play about Anne Frank which you may be able to see at a local theatre.

- Find out about the work of Amnesty International, a group which fights for human rights around the world.

- A sad poem is called a "lament." There are many laments in the Bible, especially in the Psalms. Write a lament for those who did not survive the Holocaust.

- The Danish Resistance presented a strong force against Hitler. Find out what other resistance fighters have worked and are working against oppression.

Possible Subthemes

Holocaust Survivors	Gender Oppression	Escape
The Japanese Internment	Survival	Freedom
The Underground Railroad	Religious Freedom	Racism
War	Dreams	Anti-Semitism
Abuse	Resistance	Peace

References

Cambourne, Brian (1988). *The Whole Story – Natural Learning and the Acquisition of Literacy in the Classroom.* Auckland: Ashton Scholastic.

Cox, Susan and Galda, Lee (1990). "Multicultural Literature: Mirrors and Windows on a Global Community." *The Reading Teacher,* April.

Flor Ada, Alma (1988). "Creative Reading – A Relevant Methodology for Language Minority Children" in NABE/87. *Theory, Research and Application: Selected Papers* (Malave, L. M., Ed.). Buffalo: SUNY.

Moore, Opal and MacCann, Donnarae. "Cultural Pluralism" in Berman, S. and Danky, J. P. (Eds.). *Alternative Library Literature 1986–87 – A Biennial Anthology,* Jefferson, NC: McFarland & Co.

Norton, Donna E. (1985). "Language and Cognitive Development Through Multicultural Literature." *Childhood Education: Infancy through Early Adolescence,* November/December.

Rosenblatt, Louise M. (undated). "The Reading Transaction: What For?" *Writing and Reading.*

Taberski, Sharon (1987). "From Fake to Fiction: Young Children Learn about Writing Fiction." *Language Arts,* October.

Bibliography

Obviously, this is not a comprehensive list of all the possible books on this topic. I have chosen books that speak to me personally and have significant meaning to me and my students. I have chosen books at a variety of levels, because I know that my students come with varying abilities; both ability to read, and the ability to understand and make meaning with the texts. I am a firm believer that picture books can speak volumes to older students. The discussion that picture books can stimulate is invaluable, and the images that quality illustrations can evoke bring a sense of connection to the story. Novels can also be read to children who may find a chapter book too much. Often, children can understand a book which is read to them, even though they would not be able to read it alone.

There is a great range of description found in books about the Holocaust. Some books are very detailed and frank in their descriptions, while others merely allude to events without naming or describing specific events. Younger or more sensitive readers should start with books which have simpler descriptions. In all cases, there should be a caring adult ready to answer questions and offer comfort. Remember that "I don't know" is an acceptable answer, and that honesty is the best way to respond to such questions. Honesty does not mean giving more information than is necessary or desired. Stop once the curiosity or interest has been satisfied. When the child is ready for more information, he or she will ask for it.

Note that some of these books are not recent publications. Many Holocaust survivors are no longer living, but their stories are important, regardless of when they were published.

The Children We Remember   **Ages: 8+**
Author: Chana Byers Abells
New York: Greenwillow Books, 1983
ISBN: 0-688-06371 3   Other Categories: War, Children, History

Synopsis: Through moving photographs from the Yad Vashem Archives in Jerusalem, archivist Chana Byers Abells has created an unforgettable essay about the children who lived and died during the Holocaust.

Review: The simple words which accompany the photographs describe clearly the fate of the children of the Holocaust. This introduction can give children a real beginning understanding of the human cost of the Holocaust.

Hilde and Eli: Children of the Holocaust   **Ages: 8+**
Author: David A. Adler   Illustrator: Karen Ritz
New York: Holiday House, 1994
ISBN: 0-8234-1091-9   Other Categories: History, Death, Children

Synopsis: This book contains two separate stories of young children who died during the Holocaust. Hilde, a German Jew, was gassed during a transport; and Eli, a Czechoslovakian Jew was gassed at Auschwitz.

Review: This is a picture book. The language is very simple and straightforward, and the illustrations are well done and not too graphic. This provides a good introduction for children to see how others their age died at the hands of the Nazis.

A Picture Book of Anne Frank   **Ages: 5+**
Author: David A. Adler   Illustrator: Karen Ritz
New York: Holiday House, 1993
ISBN: 082341003X   Other Categories: Biographies, War

Synopsis: A book tracing the life of the young Jewish girl whose diary chronicles the years she and her family hid from the Nazis in an Amsterdam attic. The pictures are vividly drawn and painted with detailed depictions of the characters.

Review: This is a simple introduction to the facts surrounding the Frank family and their years in hiding in Amsterdam. This biography is one of a series examining the lives of famous people such as Helen Keller, Harriet Tubman, and Martin Luther King, Jr.

One Yellow Daffodil: A Hanukkah Story   **Ages: 5+**
Author: David A. Adler   Illustrator: Lloyd Boom
San Diego: Gulliver Books, 1995
ISBN: 0-15-200537-4   Other Categories: War, Family, Friendship

Synopsis: Morris Kaplan owns a flower shop and generously serves his beloved customers. When two children invite him to share Hanukkah with them, he reluctantly accepts, and finds the memories of his past. As a young man in Auschwitz, Morris saw a daffodil in the mud and decided if the flower could survive, so could he.

Review: There is little information about the Nazis and Auschwitz, so this book would need a bit of explanation for a child with scant knowledge of the Holocaust. This lovely book introduces the Holocaust in a gentle way for young readers.

Child of the Warsaw Ghetto   **Ages: 8+**
Author: David A. Adler   Illustrator: Karen Ritz
New York: Holiday House, 1995
ISBN: 0-8234-1160-5   Other Categories: War, Biographies

Synopsis: Froim Baum, a Jewish boy, lived in Warsaw, Poland. When his father died, his family struggled, and Froim went to live in an orphanage. The family was eventually moved to the Warsaw ghetto with thousands of other Jews until they were sent to Auschwitz. Froim was sent from death camp to death camp until he was liberated at Dachau.

Review: The pastel illustrations are very dark, set on gray pages with black text. This shows the mood of the story – the tragedy of so many. While this true story is not graphic, it is dark and realistically sad.

Hiding from the Nazis   Ages: 8+
Author: David A. Adler   Illustrator: Karen Ritz
New York: Holiday House, 1997
ISBN: 0-8234-1288-1   Other Categories: Family, Friendship, War

Synopsis: Ernst Baer flees to Amsterdam in 1933 to escape the Nazis. He starts a new life there, but soon, his family must hide. Lore, their daughter is sent away with friends who become her new family.

Review: This true story of unlikely survival is presented in a factual manner. There are many details, and a chronology of the events of World War II.

We Remember the Holocaust   Ages: 8+
Author: David A. Adler
New York: Holt, 1989
ISBN: 0613144171   Other Categories: War, Biographies

Synopsis: Survivors tell their personal stories of the Holocaust.

Review: Accompanied by photographs, these memories and stories come alive.

Twenty and Ten   Ages: 8+
Author: Claire H. Bishop
New York: Viking, 1952
ISBN: 0140310762   Other Categories: Resistance, War, Escape

Synopsis: The story of a French convent school for orphans that takes in ten Jewish children in addition to the 20 they already have. A story of sharing and interdependence.

Review: Based on a true story, this short book is accessible for younger readers with adult support. It is not gory or too descriptive.

Tunes for Bears to Dance To   Ages: 12+
Author: Robert Cormier
New York: Dell, 1992
ISBN: 0-440-21903-5
Other Categories: Mental Health, Compassion, Life after the War

Synopsis: This is a story about a young boy who works part-time for a racist and is attempting to help his family support themselves. The boy also meets an older gentleman who has a very specific talent. The boy must make a major decision, but the outcome could be devastating.

Review: This is not historical fiction, but is based on the reality of post-war racist attitudes, and the enduring realities of wartime memories. This book deals with issues such as mental health, confronting racism, and equality.

Sleeping Boy   Ages: 5+
Author: Sonia Craddock   Illustrator: Leonid Gore
New York: Atheneum Books for Young Readers, 1999
ISBN: 0-589-81763-0   Other Categories: Poetry, Family, Folk Tales

Synopsis: A child is born to the Rosen family, but before he can be blessed, Major Krieg curses him. Only his aunt's blessing helps him avoid that curse, and, like Sleeping Beauty, he and his family sleep through war until peace comes to Berlin.

Review: This is more a poem than prose. This multi-leveled story is haunting in its text and acrylic illustrations.

Jacob's Rescue: A Holocaust Story   Ages: 10+
Author: Malka Drucker and Michael Halperin
New York: Bantam Books, 1993
ISBN: 0-533-08976-5   Other Categories: War, History

Synopsis: Jacob, a 10-year-old Jewish boy, is taken in by a non-Jewish family in Poland. There, the Roslan family changes his name and hides him, then his brother. The family risks capture for helping the boys, and sacrifices much to care for them. The boys are later reunited with their father in Palestine.

Review: Based on a true story (there are photographs at the end of the book), this book shows the courage of those who resisted the Nazis by aiding Jewish people. We are told little about the Roslan family in the book, but the afterword states that they were awarded a medal in 1981 for their courage.

Anne Frank   Ages: 10+
Author: Rachel Epstein
New York: Franklin Watts, 1997
ISBN: 0-531-20298-4   Other Categories: Biographies, Family

Synopsis: A synopsis of the short life of Anne Frank, with photographs of her and her family, as well as general photos of life during World War II.

Review: This would be a good book to accompany the reading of *Anne Frank: The Diary of a Young Girl – The Definitive Edition*, as it gives information, photographs, and explanations which are not in the diary. On its own, it is not as good as the diary itself.

Remember Not to Forget: A Memory of the Holocaust Ages: 10+
Author: Norman H. Finkelstein   Illustrators: Lois and Lars Hokanson
New York: Franklin Watts, 1985
ISBN: 0-531-04892-6   Other Categories: War, History, Art

Synopsis: A German man enters a shop in Jerusalem to buy a menorah, and encounters a shopkeeper who survived the Holocaust. What follows is a synopsis of the Holocaust and explanations of the events that took place.

Review: The simple and straightforward text makes this story very approachable without being graphic. The woodcuts by the Hokansons are outstanding.

Memories of My Life in a Polish Village 1930–1949   Ages: 8+
Author and Illustrator: Toby Knobel Fluek
New York: Alfred A. Knopf, 1990
ISBN: 0-394-58617-4   Other Categories: Autobiography, War, Family

Synopsis: Ninety-four paintings and drawings illustrate the life of the author in Czernica, Poland. The family survives the Russian occupation; but when Germans occupy the village, the Jews are taken to a ghetto, concentration camps, or work camps. Only Toby and her mother survive by hiding in the woods and with the help of peasants.

Review: The illustrations bring this story to life and give the reader a very good visual understanding of life in Eastern Europe during the war. The accompanying text is simple and straightforward, written with honesty.

Anne Frank:
The Diary of a Young Girl – The Definitive Edition Ages: 10+
Author: Anne Frank
New York: Doubleday, Reissue 1997
ISBN: 0553577123   Other Categories: Biography, War

Synopsis: The diary of Anne Frank, a Jewish girl hiding from the Nazis in Amsterdam. Anne, her family, and other friends hid in a secret annex, aided by Christian friends, until they were discovered shortly before the war ended. Anne's father was the only one to survive.

Review: This edition has many details that were left out of the first edition, which was edited by her father. It reflects a more honest account of what happened in the secret annex. In her diary, Anne recalls the humor and sadness of living in hiding with the help of their friends.

I Am David   **Ages: 8+**
Author: Anne Holm
London: Mammoth, 1963
ISBN: 0772510857   Other Categories: Adventure, Escape

Synopsis: A boy searches for freedom and information about his own background after he escapes from a concentration camp.

Review: This is not a true Holocaust story, but an adventure story set in this place and time. The book contains many inaccuracies and should not be read as historical fiction.

Anne Frank: Life in Hiding   **Ages: 10+**
Author: Johanna Hurwitz
New York: Avon Books, Inc., 1988
ISBN: 0-380-73254-8   Other Categories: War, History, Information

Synopsis: This is a short synopsis of the life of Anne Frank and the historical events that were taking place during World War II.

Review: Anne Frank's diary is much more compelling, but this biography gives a simple introduction to her life. There is a chronology of events and an index.

Torn Thread   **Ages: 10+**
Author: Anne Isaacs
New York: Scholastic, 2000
ISBN: 0-590-60364-7   Other Categories: Biographies, War, Family

Synopsis: Eva and her sister, Rachel, have been taken away from their father to a work camp in Czechoslovakia. While working in a textile mill, they experience many illnesses and hardships.

Review: This is a very believable book, probably because it was based on the story of the author's mother-in-law, Eva. The story moves quickly, and the reader will easily imagine what life was like in the work camp. Unfortunately, the epilogue does not tell what happened to Rachel after she emigrated to Canada.

The Secret of Gabi's Dresser   Ages: 8+
Author: Kathy Kacer
Toronto: Second Story Press, 1999
ISBN: 1-896764-15-0   Other Categories: Biographies, Family, War

Synopsis: When the Nazis invade Czechoslovakia, Gabi's life changes. Her friends can no longer associate with her because she is Jewish. Gabi is not allowed to go to school anymore, and must stay at home. When the Nazis start to search for young girls, Gabi hides in a dresser.

Review: This book is based on the real-life experiences of the author's mother. The writing is straightforward and not too graphic.

Clara's War   Ages: 10+
Author: Kathy Kacer
Toronto: Second Story Press, 2001
ISBN: 1-896764-42-8   Other Categories: Music, War

Synopsis: Clara and her family are sent to the Jewish ghetto of Terezin (Theresienstadt), outside Prague. There, Clara slowly adjusts to life in the ghetto and participates in the opera *Brundibar*, even performing for the visiting representatives of the Red Cross.

Review: This story is based on the concentration camp at Terezin, which was unique in that cultural activities were allowed to continue during the imprisonment of the Jews. Kacer's writing is very readable, and the descriptions are not frightening.

When Hitler Stole Pink Rabbit   Ages: 8+
Author: Judith Kerr
New York: Dell, 1971
ISBN: 0698115899   Other Categories: Family, War, Escape

Synopsis: The true story of a secular Jewish family living in Berlin during the time of the Nazi occupation, told through the eyes of young Anna. The family is temporarily separated, but is reunited in Switzerland where they learn new languages, visit new places, and learn the skills to survive as refugees. They eventually travel to France, then England in search of a new home.

Review: The simple language of this novel is riveting. The family struggles to survive in Switzerland and France after having led a very comfortable life in Berlin. There is a lot of information about the confiscation of Jewish-owned property that took place, but little about the other atrocities.

The Big Lie: A True Story   Ages: 10+
Author: Isabella Leitner with Irving A. Leitner
Illustrator: Judy Pedersen
New York: Scholastic, 1992
ISBN: 0-590-45570-2
Other Categories: War, History, Family, Autobiography

Synopsis: This tells the true story of the amazing survival of three Jewish Hungarian sisters who were able to remain together in Auschwitz and eventually escape a death march by hiding in a doghouse. The sisters lived in an abandoned house until the Russian liberation. Eventually, with the aid of a sympathetic American soldier, the sisters were able to rejoin their father in America.

Review: The story is told in a very matter-of-fact, almost detached way, which does not match the amazing and unlikely events which took place. Simple, charcoal sketches are scattered throughout the story.

Number the Stars   Ages: 10+
Author: Lois Lowry
Boston: Houghton Mifflin, 1989
ISBN: 0-395-51060-0   Other Categories: Resistance, Friendship
Awards: Newbery Medal

Synopsis: A family takes in their daughter's Jewish friend and pretends she is one of their own to keep her safe in spite of the Nazis' skepticism. A story of the Danish Resistance, and how almost 7,000 Danish Jews were relocated to neutral Sweden.

Review: This award-winning book is a story of love and dedication. It is based on true stories told to the author by a friend. Almost more fascinating than the book itself is the afterword.

Daniel's Story   Ages: 12+
Author: Carol Matas
New York: Scholastic, 1993
ISBN: 0-590-46588-0   Other Categories: Resistance, Escape, War

Synopsis: Daniel, whose family suffers as the Nazis rise to power in Germany, describes his life in concentration camps. Slowly, his memories of life in Frankfurt fade.

Review: Based on real experiences, this fictional book is very frank in the descriptions of the horrors that took place. It requires a mature reader and adult support should be close by. It includes a glossary and chronology.

After the War   Ages: 12+
Author: Carol Matas
Richmond Hill: Scholastic Canada, 1996
ISBN: 0-590-12384-X
Other Categories: Life after the War, Escape, Freedom

Synopsis: Life does not return to normal when the war is over and the prisoners of the concentration camps are freed. Ruth and her new friends set out for Eretz Israel, and encounter many difficulties along the way.

Review: The research which has gone into this book is evident in the details of the survivors' struggle for freedom. Matas presents a history which is often overlooked – that pogroms, racism, murders, etc., continued long after the war was officially over.

The Garden   Ages: 12+
Author: Carol Matas
New York: Aladdin Paperbacks, 1997
ISBN: 0-689-80723-6   Other Categories: War, Resistance, Racism

Synopsis: In this sequel to *After the War*, Ruth settles in Palestine and joins the Pulmach, troops who were working to defend their rights to the land which would become Israel. Ruth and her friends face many dangers and moral dilemmas.

Review: This book requires a mature reader. It would be necessary to have an understanding of the Holocaust and the events that led up to the establishment of the State of Israel. In the main character, we see a deep belief in what she is fighting for, as well as a true compassion for the innocent individuals who are caught in the middle. This book can help people understand some of the pain behind the ongoing crises in the Middle East.

Lisa   Ages: 10+
Author: Carol Matas
Toronto: Lester & Orpen Dennys, 1987
ISBN: 0-590-24189-3   Other Categories: War, Resistance, Escape

Synopsis: The story of a family living in Denmark who have refused to perish despite the attempts of the Nazis. The daughter joins the Resistance and the son joins the anti-Nazi movement.

Review: This exciting book is a real page-turner and highlights the commitment of the Danish people who resisted the Nazi regime. It is refreshing and encouraging that the female character is a strong heroine.

Jesper   Ages: 12+
Author: Carol Matas
Toronto: Lester & Orpen Dennys, 1989
ISBN: 0-88619-109-2

Synopsis: In the sequel to *Lisa*, a young member of the Danish Resistance goes underground to protect his family. When Jesper is arrested for his work on an underground newspaper, he must hide and use a new identity. Jesper fights the Nazis who have taken over Copenhagen.

Review: Learning about various resistance movements makes up an important part of understanding the Holocaust. The bravery of people who stood up to Hitler serve as an example for us, when we must face injustice in our own lives. This book requires a very mature reader, as there is violence and language that may upset a younger reader. This is an exciting, fast paced novel.

Anne Frank   Ages: 10+
Author: Yona Zeldis McDonough   Illustrator: Malach Zeldis
New York: Henry Colt and Company, 1997
ISBN: 0-8050-4924-X   Other Categories: Biography

Synopsis: A short biography of the life of Anne Frank.

Review: This biography is written in simple language, with bright, naive-style illustrations done in gouache. This is a good introduction to Anne Frank's life and her experiences during World War II.

The Cage   Ages: 12+
Author: Ruth Sender Minsky
Toronto: Macmillan, 1988
ISBN: 068981321X   Other Categories: Survival, War, Family

Synopsis: A true story detailing the life in Lodz, Poland within the confines of a Jewish ghetto, and the deportation of family members to Auschwitz. A 16-year-old attempts to protect her family members and survive the camp's horror and degradation. The story is told by a survivor to her daughter, so she will never forget.

Review: The straightforward writing gives a matter-of-fact tone to the book, but the details are clear. This book requires a mature reader with background knowledge. The book is not too graphic, but the story is told honestly and frankly.

To Life   Ages: 12+
Author: Ruth Sender Minsky
New York: Penguin, 1988
ISBN: 0-689-83282-6   Other Categories: War, Family, Survival, Escape

Synopsis: A Holocaust survivor recounts her liberation from a Nazi concentration camp, her search for surviving family members and the long and difficult ordeal of trying to emigrate to America. Through the difficulties, she never gives up hope of a new life.

Review: This sequel to *The Cage* picks up the story after the survivors' release from the concentration camps. There were many hardships endured following the war, and for many, starting over was extremely difficult. It would be good to read *The Cage* first, to give some knowledge of the prior events in this story.

The Holocaust Lady   Ages: 10+
Author: Ruth Sender Minsky
Toronto: Macmillan, 1992
ISBN: 0-02-781832-2
Other Categories: Autobiography, Teaching, Survival

Synopsis: In an effort to teach children about the Holocaust, the author describes the impact of this horrifying event on her life and the lives of other survivors. She teaches school groups about her experiences, and the importance of remembering the events of the war.

Review: This book picks up where *To Life* left off. Now known as Ruth, she finally makes it to America. After many years of struggle, she reconnects with the surviving members of her family. Once in a new home, though, there are still many difficulties that face the family. This story helps provide insight into the ongoing problems faced by new immigrants and the difficulties they face in putting the past behind them.

The Lily Cupboard   Ages: 5+
Author: Shulamith Levey Oppenheim
New York: HarperCollins, 1992

ISBN: 0064433935   Other Categories: Interfaith Relations, Family

Synopsis: A young Jewish girl is forced to leave her parents and hide with strangers in the countryside during the German occupation of Holland. When soldiers come to search the house, this Christian family takes Miriam in and hides her in a cupboard with lilies on the front.

Review: Courage is the main theme of this book; the courage of Miriam's parents who sent her away to be safe, and the courage of the Christians who took her in and kept her safe. While this book is fictional, it represents the selfless acts performed by many courageous Christians who hid or helped Jews during the war.

The Butterfly   **Ages: 8+**
Author and Illustrator: Patricia Polacco
New York: Philomel Books, 2000
ISBN: 0-399-23170-6   Other Categories: Resistance, Friendship

Synopsis: Nazis occupy a small village in France and terrorize the people. Monique's mother hides Jewish families in their cellar. One day, they are discovered and must leave to find safety.

Review: Based on the story of her aunt Monique and her mother, this tells of the French underground, which helped many Jewish families during the war. This is a touching, well-told story.

Anne Frank –
Beyond the Diary – A Photographic Remembrance   **Ages: 8+**
Author: Anna Quindlen
New York: Penguin Books, 1992
ISBN: 0-14-036926-0   Other Categories: Information, War, History

Synopsis: A compilation of articles and photographs depicting the life of Anne Frank and her family. There are photos of historical artifacts from the time of the Holocaust in Europe and people who were affected by the war.

Review: This collection provides fascinating details that are not available in the diary. The book acts as an archive of documents and photographs which have detailed captions.

Fireflies in the Dark   **Ages: 10+**
Author: Susan Goldman Rubin
Illustrators: Children of the Terezin Concentration Camp
New York: Holiday House, 2000
ISBN: 0-8234-1461-2   Other Categories: Resistance, Art

Synopsis: This biography of Friedl Dicker-Brandeis, an artist who was a prisoner in the Terezin (Theresienstadt) Concentration Camp, shows how she worked with children in the camp, teaching them art and drama to keep their spirits up.

Review: This is a fascinating biography of a woman who used art as her way to resist the Nazis. The children's illustrations show a wide variety of experiences in the camps, from hope to despair. Sadly, Friedl died 6 months before the war ended, but she left a legacy of students who survived, as well as 5,000 drawings which were found after the camp was liberated.

The Upstairs Room   Ages: 10+
Author: Johanna Reiss
New York: Harper and Row, 1972
ISBN: 006440370X   Other Categories: War, Family

Synopsis: The story of two sisters forced to leave their family in Holland and go and live with a generous Gentile family in a remote farmhouse. The girls live hidden away in a small, cramped room for more than two years.

Review: Many brave Dutch families hid Jews during the war. This true story tells of the sacrifices made by one such family. There is some swearing in this book, but it fits in the context of the story.

Journey Back   Ages: 10+
Author: Johanna Reiss
New York: HarperCollins Children's Books, 1976
ISBN: 0-06-447042-3

Synopsis: Annie and Sin move back home, but not all is well with the family or in the community, where anti-Semitism still exists. Their older sister, Rachel, has become a Christian, and the father is unhappy about it. When their father remarries, Annie is constantly criticized by the woman she now calls "Mother." Slowly, they rebuild their lives.

Review: This is the continuation of *The Upstairs Room*. This sequel emphasizes that freedom did not necessarily mean a return to normal life. This sad book shows how difficult it was to start over again.

Best Friends   Ages: 8+
Author: Elisabeth Reuter
New York: Yellow Brick Road Press, 1988
ISBN: 0-943706-18-1   Other Categories: Friendship, Justice, War, Racism

Synopsis: Two girls who are best friends become separated by the hatred that one is taught about Jewish people. When Judith disappears on Kristallnacht, Lisa feels deep remorse, and searches futilely for her friend whenever she sees a girl wearing a yellow star.

Review: This simple picture book with straightforward language introduces some of the realities leading up to the Holocaust. At first, the racism is subtle, but it becomes more pronounced and directed at individuals as time progresses. This book would provide some answers to younger children who are just learning about the Holocaust.

Anna Is Still Here   Ages: 10+
Author: Ida Vos
New York: Puffin Books, 1986
ISBN: 0140369090   Other Categories: Survival, Friendship

Synopsis: Thirteen-year-old Anna, who was a "hidden child" in Nazi-occupied Holland during World War II, gradually learns to deal with the realities of being a survivor after meeting another woman who is awaiting the return of her daughter, long after the war has ended.

Review: Anna and Mrs. Neumann exchange stories throughout this book. The stories could be read alone, as each is based in historical fact. This book can be a bit grim, but it is not explicit.

Good-Bye Marianne   Ages: 10+
Author: Irene N. Watts
Toronto: Tundra Books, 1998
ISBN: 0-88776-445-2   Other Categories: War, History

Synopsis: The world starts to change for Marianne in 1938 in Berlin. Her father goes underground, school is closed, shops are damaged, and Marianne begins to experience anti-Semitism firsthand. When there is an opportunity for her to leave on a Kindertransport, she must leave her family, friends, and everything she knows.

Review: This book is based on the actual events of the Kindertransport, which removed 10,000 Jewish children and sent them to safety. The author, herself, was one of these children.

A Time for Toys   Ages: 5+
Author: Margaret Wild   Illustrator: Julie Vivas
Toronto: Kids Can Press, 1991
ISBN: 0-531-05937-5   Other Categories: War, Community, Giving

Synopsis: A girl remembers a time when she had toys of her own. The women in a concentration camp make toys out of scraps for the children as the war draws to an end. The inmates know that the soldiers are coming to liberate them, and plan a wonderful party.

Review: This beautiful story of giving and celebration shines in contrast to the harshness of the concentration camps. The illustrations show the thin, bald truth of life in the camps. This book, one of the few picture books about concentration camps, was also published under the title *Let the Celebrations Begin*.

The Devil's Arithmetic   Ages: 12+
Author: Jane Yolen
New York: Scholastic, 1988
ISBN: 0-59096578-6   Other Categories: Fantasy, War, Family

Synopsis: A Jewish girl tires of the stories at her family's Passover Seder, but plays along with the rituals in spite of her boredom. When she is asked to open the door to welcome the prophet Elijah, she travels through time to a Polish shtetl in 1942. With her family, Chaya is "relocated" to a concentration camp, where she is the only one who fully understands the scope of what is happening.

Review: Like many Holocaust stories, this book is a compilation of stories told to the author and taken from the author's family history. The subject matter in this book is frankly presented, and should only be read by a mature reader, who has an understanding of the history of the Holocaust.

12

All God's Children
Books from Many Cultures & Faiths

Praise the Lord, all you nations!
Extol God, all you peoples!
For great is God's steadfast love toward us,
and the faithfulness of the Lord endures forever.
Praise the Lord!

PSALM 117

Some people are so used to hearing their own voices that they hardly hear
anything else, while others have been silenced or unheard for so long that they
either never learned to speak or have forgotten how.

(McELROY-JOHNSON, 1993, P. 85).

There are some important things to keep in mind when presenting books from a variety of faiths and cultures. It is important that children see themselves and others reflected in the literature that they are reading. It is also important for children who live in more homogeneous settings, where one culture is highly dominant, to be exposed to children from other cultures. If these children do not have any exposure to other cultures in real life, then reading can provide a small way to foster some understanding of other people, their beliefs, and practices.

Defining Multicultural Children's Literature

Many questions influenced my own definition of multicultural children's literature and what I would include when completing my observations and when recording the books being selected and used. Where is the line between authentic and non-authentic representation? Should I consider a book that has stereotypical images, words, or illustrations to be a valid part of multicultural literature? Is it enough to just show people of parallel cultures (a term which attempts to "denote equality in value and respect for the contributions of cultures co-existing within an area" [Walker-Dalhouse, 1992, p. 416]), without referring to or examining the culture in question? Is a book to be considered multicultural if the main character comes from a parallel culture even if the theme or setting is not about that culture? How much culture is required to call a book "multicultural"? Do I include folk tales because they show an important side of the storytelling aspect of a culture or should I only consider contemporary and realistic works?

In the end, based on the definitions found in the literature, discussions with people, and my own feelings as a teacher working with a multicultural population, I decided that for me, identity is what defines a piece of literature as multicultural. Can a reader see himself or herself reflected in the book? Does the book connect to the history of the reader; either recent personal experiences or those of the reader's ancestors? Does the book provide some emotional or spiritual connection for a reader to his or her own culture or another culture? Do the illustrations provide a familiar and accurate connection to traditional, cultural artistic styles? For a reader interacting with a book that is not about the reader's culture, does that book provide a window through which to obtain an understanding of or information about the culture being presented? Does it provide a positive personal experience for the reader?

Definition of culture, therefore, boils down to self-identification. There will be variance and dissent about how groups and individuals identify themselves – who they include or exclude. This cannot be resolved easily. This identification carries through to the definition of what is and is not multicultural. In the end, each definition is accepted because to do so is to value the informant and their own personal cultural identity. Such is the case in this chapter. "Multicultural literature is a literature of inclusion: stories from and stories about all our children" (Harriet Rohmer, quoted in Madigan, 1993). It is a literature that speaks of "struggles, myths, movement, beauty, rituals, religion and holidays of our people" (Henderson, 1991).

I would like to propose the following definition of multicultural children's literature: Multicultural Children's Literature is literature about groups of people who find or gather themselves into community through a common bond of self-identification such as race, religion, belief, sexual orientation, ability, or color.

The following questions and answers speak to what is included and excluded from the above definition.

1. **Does this definition include authors who write outside their culture?**

   Rarely. While I believe it is possible to write with a certain degree of success outside one's culture, I believe that it is important and essential to the authenticity of a piece of writing (or illustration) that the creator know the nuances of the culture.

2. **What about illustrations?**

   The same rules apply for authentic illustration and authentic text.

3. **Does this definition include folk and fairy tales?**

   Sometimes. When a folk or fairy tale gives insight into the culture in question, then it can be a valuable tool in multicultural education. Cross-cultural examinations of similar tales can also provide insight into a culture. However, when a tale has become unidentifiable with the culture from which it originated (e.g., the Brothers Grimm), it can no longer find a place in the category of multicultural literature.

4. **Does the definition include historical fiction?**

   Yes, as long as it is a history that comes from the perspective of the people who are involved. Many cultures have suffered because their histories have not been told in a consistent manner.

5. **Can this definition include books about mainstream culture?**

   Yes. If a book is about a specific culture within the dominant group (e.g., a book about Celtic culture), then it is identifiable as a self-standing culture.

6. **Why include sexual orientation and ability?**

   Both of these groups are populations that are becoming more visible within society, but they are also groups that have been overlooked and shunned in the past, similar to many other cultural groups. In both cases, the members of the groups have no choice about their membership within the group, which points to a need for acceptance and understanding – both on the part of the group members and of those who will interact with them.

7. **What is meant by those who "find or gather themselves into community"?**

   Some people become members of a culture by birth (e.g., being born Chinese). Others join by choice (e.g., those who join a religion). In each case, there is a community of people who have a bond of similar cultural membership.

8. **What is considered to be "literature" within this definition?**

   I consider literature to be books; either written for or by children, videos, film, plays, drama, dance, computer programs, magazines, music, and storytelling.

Using Multicultural Children's Literature

Martinez and Nash (1990, p. 599) quote Violet Harris in an interview about the importance of multicultural children's literature. Harris states the following reasons for using this literature for non-mainstream children:

1. to affirm and empower the children and their cultures

2. to see that people in their culture contribute and have contributed to human life

3. for pleasure and pride, and to hear about people like themselves and see illustrations of themselves and their communities

4. to offer hope and encouragement

5. to read material with inventive and memorable language, and multidimensional characters; and to engage in a holistic literary experience.

There are, however, potential problems with the way multicultural children's literature is used. When we read these books only during Black History Month, for example, or on anti-racism day, we may be doing more harm than good by relegating (segregating?) them to an isolated pocket of the curriculum. This can lead to what Derman-Sparks (1989) calls a "tourist curriculum," comprising a tokenistic treatment of culture by only experiencing superficial aspects such as food, holidays, and heroic figures. In the tourist curriculum, the students visit a culture for a short period of time, only to return "home" when they are finished.

Mascha Rudman (1984, p. 160) raises a number of excellent questions regarding issues in multicultural children's literature: "What criteria do we consider when we build a library? How do we handle racist attitudes in books? How aware are we of the connotations and innuendoes in the books our children read? How do we manage the classics? What of the popular fantasies and novels and even works of so-called nonfiction that are rife with racist ideas? How do we manage to keep progressing with our own sense of openness and world-mindedness, and at the same time influence children who are, perhaps, not at the same level of awareness that we are? How can we recognize our acts of omission?"

Ways to Use the Literature

- Discuss different ways racism still exists in your community.

- Discuss why racism still exists in your community.

- Discuss how your children have been personally affected by racism. Brainstorm solutions for dealing with this when it arises, both for the victim and those who see the racism happening. Role-play these situations, so children have the words to use when they need them. Whenever racism occurs, we all suffer, whether we are the intended target or if we are bystanders.

- Ask people what specific changes can be made at your school/church to help include others. Make plans for implementing these changes. Work slowly. Change cannot happen at once.

- Examine the ways your community is inclusive. What is your community doing well? Why do those things work? What else could be done?

- Brainstorm ways to make others aware of racist views and practices.

- Collect books for your library or classroom written by and about people from other cultures. Make an effort to represent people from your school/church, as well as those in the wider community.

- Visit places of worship from other cultures, denominations, or faiths. Invite groups from those places to worship with you.

- Write a story about your own family's background.

- Interview someone from another culture, perhaps someone who lives at a seniors' residence. Write their biography and present it to that person.

- Find out how many people in your school or congregation were born in a different country. Find those places on a map.

- Learn about the people who helped North America in history – the black pioneers, the Chinese railroad workers, etc.

- Celebrate Worldwide Communion Sunday. This occurs on the first Sunday in October. Invite members to bring bread from their culture to share during the service. Ask the people to talk about the bread and its significance in their culture. Learn about how other Christian denominations celebrate Communion.

- Try different foods. After the service on Worldwide Communion Sunday, have a potluck dinner with foods from different cultures. Be sure to label each item, carefully explaining the ingredients.

- Learn about different types of families. This may include blended and blending families, separated families, chosen families, adoptive families, foster families, children with gay/lesbian parents, etc.

- Learn about refugees in your country. Volunteer at an agency that helps refugees. Find out why people must leave their homes, and what your government can provide for these people.

- Learn songs from other cultures or faiths. Sing a song during a service. You may even try to sing in another language.

- Learn about people who are differently abled. Is your church/school accessible? What can you do to make it more accessible? Some ideas: raise money to build ramps, refurbish washrooms, purchase hymnbooks in Braille or with large print, or provide an amplified hearing system.

- Learn a prayer in another language and read it during a service.

- Find out about the different clothing people from other cultures wear. Some items are used for comfort (e.g., long flowing material in hot weather), and others are used for religious practices (e.g., head coverings or shawls for prayer). Invite people to talk about their clothing.

- Recognize the significant holy days from other religious traditions. The Multifaith Calendar makes a wonderful resource that can point you to these days and explain a bit about the traditions. How does that day celebrate or further their understanding of God?

- Make a list of the different names for God. There are many in the Bible, and there are others that are used in worship. Different cultures have names for God, too.

References

Derman-Sparks, L. (1989). *Anti-Bias Curriculum: Tools for Empowering Young Children*. Washington, DC: National Association for the Education of Young Children.

Henderson, V. M. (1991). "The Development of Self-Esteem in Children of Color." *The Multicolored Mirror: Cultural Substance in Literature for Children and Young Adults* (M. Lindgren, Ed.). Fort Atkinson: Highsmith Press.

Madigan, D. (1993). "The politics of multicultural literature for children and adolescents: Combining perspectives and conversations." *Language Arts*, vol 70 March.

Martinez, M. and Nash, M. (1990). "Bookalogues: Talking about children's literature." *Language Arts*, vol 67 October.

McElroy-Johnson, B. (1993). "Giving Voice to the Voiceless." *Harvard Educational Review*, Spring.

Rudman, M. (1984). *Children's Literature – An Issues Approach*. White Plains, NY: Heath.

Walker-Dalhouse, D. (1992). "Using African-American Literature to Increase Ethnic Understanding." *The Reading Teacher*, vol 45 no 6.

Bibliography

African American

Celebration Song   Ages 3+
Author: James Berry   Illustrator: Louise Brierley
London, UK: Hamish Hamilton, 1994
ISBN: 0-241-00209-5   Other Categories: Life of Christ

Synopsis: On Jesus' first birthday, Mary tells him the story of his birth in song.

Review: The illustrations are set in the Caribbean and picture the Holy family as black. The words are written on ribbons, which wind through the story. This is a wonderful book to use with all children to show how people portray Jesus in ways that they can relate to him.

Celebrating Kwanzaa   Ages: 5+
Author: Diane Hoyt-Goldsmith   Illustrator: Lawrence Migdale
New York: Holiday House, 1993
ISBN: 0-8234-1048-X   Other Categories: Information, Activities

Synopsis: This is a photo-essay of Andiey, a 13-year-old girl living in Chicago with her parents and 5-year-old brother, Max. It shows how they celebrate Kwanzaa, the African American festival which takes place over seven days starting on December 26.

Review: The photos are very good and clear. This book contains information about the history of Kwanzaa, the seven principles (unity, self-determination, collective work and responsibility, co-operative economics, purpose, creativity, and faith). The book is filled with explanations, definitions, and quotations.

Lift Ev'ry Voice and Sing   Ages 5+
Author: James Weldon Johnson
New York: Scholastic, 1995
ISBN: 0-590-46982-7   Other Categories: Song

Synopsis: An illustrated version of the hymn of the same name.

Review: This hymn is described as the "African American National Anthem." The words to this hymn are richly illustrated. This would make a good introduction to the history of African people in North America.

Let My People Go   Ages: 8+
Authors: Patricia and Fredrick McKissack
Illustrator: James E. Ransome
New York: Atheneum Books for Young Readers, 1998
ISBN: 0-689-80856-9   Other Categories: Retellings

Synopsis: A freeman in the American state of South Carolina in the early 1800s retells 13 stories from the Old Testament to his daughter, Charlotte. Each Bible story is introduced by a story of the family's history as free black people during the time of slavery, how they bought their freedom, and how they survived.

Review: This exceptional book mixes African American history and Bible stories and the retellings flow beautifully. The introductions, told in Charlotte's voice, contrast with the stories of her father, which are told in his southern dialect.

Amish

An Amish Year   Ages: 8+
Author: by Richard Ammon   Illustrator: Pamela Patrick
New York: Atheneum, 2000
ISBN: 0-689-82622-2   Other Categories: Family

Synopsis: A young Amish girl describes her life, chores, joys, and fears throughout the year.

Review: This contains notes about modern Amish life and translations of Pennsylvania Dutch words. Note that neither the author nor illustrator is Amish, but the book appears to be well researched.

Just Plain Fancy   **Ages: 5+**
Author and Illustrator: Patricia Polacco
New York: Bantam, 1990
ISBN: 0-553-05884-3   Other Categories: Animals, Family

Synopsis: Two Amish girls learn about beauty in nature when they find out that the newly hatched chick from the egg they found is not a chicken but a peacock! They worry at first, because the Amish culture eschews fancy dress and behavior, but soon learn that God's beauty is found in nature.

Review: A lovely coming-of-age story. There is humor in the misunderstanding, without poking fun at the Amish traditions of simple living. The language reflects the vernacular used by the Amish people.

Buddhist

Buddha Stories   **Ages: 8+**
Author and Illustrator: Demi
New York: Henry Holt and Company, 1997
ISBN: 0-8050-4886-3   Other Categories: Art, Morals

Synopsis: A collection of ten stories used by the Buddha to explain morals.

Review: Demi illustrates this collection with beautiful gold and indigo paintings using traditional Chinese inks on vellum. These give the book a wonderful, rich feeling, which fits with the spirit of the text.

Hinduism

Lights for Gita   **Ages: 5+**
Author: Rachna Gilmore   Illustrator: Alice Priestley
Toronto, ON: Second Story Press, 1994
ISBN: 0-929-00563-5   Other Categories: Friendship

Synopsis: Gita is excited to share the joyful celebration of Divali with her friends until a winter storm interrupts her plans.

Review: This lovely story shows the desire of a young girl in Canada to share her celebration with friends from school who are not Hindu. Predictably, the Canadian weather does not cooperate, and Gita must find joy in disappointment. Any child who has ever felt disappointment will relate to this wonderful story.

Hindu Festivals   **Ages: 5+**
Author: Kerena Marchant   Illustrator: Rebecca Gryspeerdt
Austin, Texas: Raintree Steck-Vaughn Publishers, 2001
ISBN: 0-7398-2734-2-0   Other Categories: Information, Song, Poetry

Synopsis: This is a collection of stories, poems, plays, and songs about some of the Hindu festivals. There is a Hindu lunar calendar in the Appendix.

Review: This book includes information about the festivals as well as a glossary of terms. The illustrations are colorful, and the stories are easy to understand.

Japanese

Sadako   **Ages: 8+**
Author: Eleanor Coerr   Illustrator: Ed Young
Puffin Books, 1993
ISBN: 0-698-11588-0
Other Categories: War, Peace, Celebrations (Peace Day)

Awards: ALA Notable Book, IRA (International Reading Association) Teacher's Choice Book, A Booklist Editor's Choice

Synopsis: Sadako Sasaki falls ill with leukemia following the dropping of the atomic bomb on Hiroshima. She dies before she can make the 1,000 paper cranes necessary for the gods to grant her wish and make her well.

Review: This beautiful, sensitive retelling of the true story of Sadako Sasaki is based on the book *Sadako and the Thousand Paper Cranes*. Young's watercolors are lovely. Children could learn how to make origami cranes to celebrate Peace Day.

Hiroshima No Pika   **Ages: 12+**
Author and Illustrator: Toshi Maruki
New York: Lothrop, Lee and Shepard Books, 1980
ISBN: 0-688-01297-3   Other Categories: War, Peace

Awards: Ehon Nippon Prize (Japan)

Synopsis: A child has breakfast with her family on August 6, 1945, when the atomic bomb is dropped on Hiroshima. They escape to safety at the river, but many around them do not survive.

Review: This book is based on a true story. The pictures and text are frank, and should only be used by mature readers with guidance.

Judaism

Hanukkah Fun: Great Things to Make and Do   Ages: 8+
Authors: Judy Bastyra and Catherine Ward
New York: Kingfisher, 1996
ISBN: 0-7534-5011-9   Other Categories: Activities

Synopsis: Instructions for 15 different Hanukkah crafts and recipes.

Review: This excellent beginning resource for classroom teachers has simple instructions with good illustrations. Most of the activities require some adult help.

The Story of Shabbat   Ages 3+
Author: Molly Cone   Illustrator: Emily Lisker
HarperCollins, 2000
0-06-027944-3   Other Categories: Information, Activities

Synopsis: This informational book explains history of Shabbat (Sabbath) and gives examples of how it is kept in modern times. The book compares Jewish, Christian, and Muslim days of rest. There is a recipe for Challah and instructions for making a Challah Cover.

Review: This excellent introduction to the Jewish day of rest has beautiful, bright pictures and clear explanations. The illustrations show Jews from a variety of cultural backgrounds.

The Family Treasury of Jewish Holidays   Ages: 8+
Author: Malka Drucker   Illustrator: Nancy Patz
New York: Little, Brown and Company, 1994
ISBN: 0-316-19343-7
Other Categories: Information, Song, Poetry, Activities

Synopsis: This is a collection of stories, poems, activities, and recipes which go with various Jewish holidays and celebrations.

Review: This collection contains lots of information about Jewish holidays and the activities which accompany them. A very good introduction explains the holidays and their origins. The book has a glossary of terms at the back.

On Rosh Hashanah and Yom Kippur   Ages: 5+
Author: Cathy Goldberg Fishman   Illustrator: Melanie W. Hall
New York: Aladdin Paperbacks, 1997
ISBN: 0-689-83892-1   Other Categories: Information

Synopsis: A Jewish girl learns about Rosh Hashanah, the day God created the world, and awaits Yom Kippur, the Day of Atonement.

Review: The information in this book is presented in a simple story with dark illustrations. There is a glossary at the back.

On Purim   Ages: 5+
Author: Cathy Goldberg Fishman   Illustrator: Melanie W. Hall
New York: Atheneum Books for Young Readers, 2000
ISBN: 0-689-82392-4   Other Categories: Retellings, Information

Synopsis: This is a retelling of the story of Esther. A girl prepares for Purim, the celebration of how Esther saved the Jewish people.

Review: This provides a good introduction to Purim with adequate illustrations. The reasons behind the traditions are explained. There is a glossary of terms.

101 Jewish Read Aloud Stories: 10-Minute Readings   Ages: 5+
from the World's Best-Loved Jewish Literature
Edited and Retold by: Barbara Diamond Goldin
New York: Black Dog and Lementhal Publishers, 2001
ISBN: 1-57912-212-4   Other Categories: Retellings

Synopsis: A collection of 101 stories from the Bible, Talmud and Midrash, Kabbalah and Hasidim; Jewish tales from around the world, Israeli stories, and holiday tales.

Review: The simple and short retellings could be used for storytelling with children. Each category has a wide variety of topics.

The Passover Journey: A Seder Companion   Ages: 8+
Author: Barbara Diamond Goldin   Illustrator: Neil Waldman
New York: Puffin Books, 1994
ISBN: 0-14-056131-5   Other Categories: Retellings, Information

Synopsis: This is a retelling of the Israelites' journey (the Exodus) and how it relates to the Passover Seder. There is information about the 14 steps of the Seder.

Review: This book explains Jewish customs from many lands. The watercolor illustrations are gorgeous. There is a glossary at the back.

Celebrate: A Book of Jewish Holidays   **Ages: 3+**
Author: Judith Gross   Illustrator: Bari Weissman
New York: Platt and Munk, 1992
ISBN: 0-448-40302-1   Other Categories: Holidays, Information

Synopsis: This introductory book goes through a variety of Jewish celebrations – Shabbat, Rosh Hashanah, Yom Kippur, Sukkot, Simhat Torah, Hanukkah, Tu Bishvat, Purim, Passover, and Shavuot.

Review: The celebrations are explained in simple terms and have pronunciations for the Hebrew words. The cartoon-like illustrations show only white characters.

A Window into the Jewish Culture   **Ages: 8+**
Author: Betty Hunt
Torrance, CA: Good Apple, 1999
ISBN: 0-7682-0214-0   Other Categories: Information, Activities

Synopsis: This teaching tool has reproducible pages which can be used to introduce children to Judaism (history, culture, practices, traditions, and holidays).

Review: This is good for people who have little background on Judaism. There are some critical thinking questions, as well as information on the Holocaust. Many of the references are to the United States.

The Uninvited Guest and Other Jewish Holiday Tales Ages: 8+
Author: Nina Jaffe   Illustrator: Elivia
New York: Scholastic, 1993
ISBN: 0-590-44654-1   Other Categories: Legend, Information

Awards: Sydney Taylor Award

Synopsis: This collection of seven stories from Jewish folklore and legend tells about the important holidays in the Jewish year.

Review: Each story is preceded by a short explanation of the holiday it pertains to. The book also contains a description of the Jewish calendar, a glossary of terms, a list of sources, and a bibliography.

Gershon's Monster: A Story for the New Year   Ages: 8+
Author: Eric A. Kimmel   Illustrator: Jon J. Muth
New York: Scholastic, 2000
ISBN: 0-439-10839-X   Other Categories: Repentance, Forgiveness

Synopsis: Gershon is a man who does not care about others or the consequences of his actions. He tosses his mistakes like monsters into the cellar and takes them to the sea on Rosh Hashanah. When Gershon and his wife want a child, the tzaddik promises twins, but with a strange prophecy. On their fifth birthday, a sea monster threatens the children, and when Gershon finally begs forgiveness, the monster disappears.

Review: The story is a bit scary and complicated for younger children, but the watercolor illustrations are lovely. This is a wonderful story about repentance, even for adults.

When Mindy Saved Hanukkah   Ages: 8+
Author: Eric A. Kimmel   Illustrator: Barbara McClintock
New York: Scholastic, 1998
ISBN: 0-590-37136-3
Other Categories: Family, Heroines, Information

Synopsis: The Klein family (who are miniature people) need a Hanukkah candle, but the Synagogue has a terrifying cat which threatens their existence, like Antiochus threatened the Jews. Mindy is not afraid and faces the cat to save Hanukkah.

Review: The gorgeous, old-fashioned illustrations enhance the story. The girl is the hero of the story, when all others fail. There is a glossary and a latke recipe.

Dance, Sing, Remember: A Celebration of Jewish HolidaysAges: 5+
Author: Leslie Kimmelman   Illustrator: Ora Eitan
HarperCollins, 2000
ISBN: 0060277254   Other Categories: Information, Song, Activities

Synopsis: This is a collection of stories, recipes, songs, activities, games, and a glossary about Jewish Holidays.

Review: This gives a wonderful introduction to Jewish celebrations, with simple, joyful illustrations. The book explains the history of each holiday, and shows how it is celebrated today. There is also a section dedicated to the Shoah (Holocaust).

Let's Celebrate Our Jewish Holidays   Ages: 8+
Author: Alfred J. Kolatch   Illustrator: Alex Bloch
Middle Village, NY: Jonathan David Publishers, Inc., 1997
ISBN: 0-8246-0394-X   Other Categories: Information

Synopsis: Brief introductions to a variety of Jewish festivals.

Review: This picture book has simple introductions to Jewish holidays. The illustrations are bland, but show people from a variety of cultures.

How I Saved Hanukkah   Ages: 8+
Author: Amy Goldman Koss   Illustrator: Diane deGroat
New York: Scholastic, 1998
ISBN: 0-439-35644-X   Other Categories: Chapter Books, Friendship

Synopsis: Marla is disappointed in her secular Jewish family. They go through the motions of some of the Hanukkah traditions, but do not follow through with the meaning of Hanukkah. Marla, with her Christian friend Lucy, sets out to find out what Hanukkah really is, learns the traditions, and brings the celebration home to her family.

Review: This simple chapter book introduces the history and traditions of Hanukkah. It shows with honesty the frustration of not understanding a holiday and not connecting with a faith tradition.

Hanukkah Lights   Ages: 3+
Author and Illustrator: Ben Lakner
New York: Random House, 2001
ISBN: 0-375-80289-4   Other Categories: Information

Synopsis: A family celebrates Hanukkah.

Review: This board book has 25 flaps to open. The illustrations are bright and fun, and the text provides a good introduction to Hanukkah.

Hooray for Hanukkah!   Ages: 0+
Author: Fran Manushkin   Illustrator: Carolyn Croll
New York: Random House, 2001
ISBN: 0-375-81043-9   Other Categories: Holidays, Family, Counting

Synopsis: Told from the point of view of the menorah, each night of Hanukkah is described with its different observances and rituals.

Review: The joy of Hanukkah is described by the menorah, as it talks about the different happenings in the household during the holiday of Hanukkah. This is a simple story for young children, and a good introduction to Hanukkah.

Latkes and Applesauce: A Hanukkah Story   **Ages: 5+**
Author: Fran Manushkin   Illustrator: Robin Spowart
New York: Scholastic
ISBN: 0-590-42265-0   Other Categories: Cooperation, Information

Synopsis: There are no potatoes or apples during Hanukkah because of a storm. When the Menashe family takes in a stray cat and then a stray dog, their meager food supplies dwindle; until one night, the dog digs and finds potatoes, and the cat climbs a tree and finds apples.

Review: This lovely story would be wonderful to act out or use for storytelling. There is information about Hanukkah, a latke recipe, and rules for playing dreidel.

The Matzah that Papa Brought Home   **Ages: 5+**
Author: Fran Manushkin   Illustrator: Ned Bittinger
New York: Scholastic, 1995
ISBN: 0-590-47147-3   Other Categories: Predictable Books, Poetry

Synopsis: The rhyme is patterned after "The House that Jack Built."

Review: This book also has the story of Passover with a glossary of terms. It is a fun way to introduce children to the various parts of the Passover Seder. The illustrations are oil paint on linen.

Chanukah Lights   **Ages: 0+**
Author and Illustrator: Judith Moffatt
New York: Little Simon, 2001
ISBN: 0-689-84389-5   Other Categories: Poetry

Synopsis: This poem about Chanukah introduces menorahs, dreidels and latkes.

Review: This fun, simple board book glows in the dark.

Why on This Night?
A Passover Haggadah for Family Celebration   **Ages: 5+**
Author: Rahel Musleah   Illustrator: Louise August
Simon and Schuster Juvenile, 2000
ISBN: 0-689-83313-X   Other Categories: Judaism, Celebrations

Synopsis: This Haggadah enables children to play an active role in all parts of the Passover Seder. It has recipes, songs, text to recite, stories, and instructions for the preparation of the Seder, as well as the Seder itself.

Review: This Haggadah is very detailed and easy to follow and uses gender-neutral language. The Hebrew, English, and English transliteration allow all to follow the text. The illustrations are linocuts printed in oil.

By the Hanukkah Light   Ages: 8+
Author: Sheldon Oberman   Illustrator: Neil Waldman
Honesdale, PA: Boyds Mills Press, 1977
ISBN: 1-56397-658-7   Other Categories: War, Family

Synopsis: Rachel helps her grandfather shine the Hanukkiah to prepare for Hanukkah. He tells Rachel of a time when they could not light the Hanukkiah for fear of persecution, and the joy of finding it again after the war.

Review: This is a beautiful story, told in a sensitive manner. The watercolor marbled papers provide the background for acrylic paintings which accompany the story.

The Always Prayer Shawl   Ages: 5+
Author: Sheldon Oberman   Illustrator: Ted Lewin
Honesdale, PA: Boyds Mills Press, 1994
ISBN: 1-878093-22-3   Other Categories: Family

Synopsis: A young Russian boy leaves for North America with two special and enduring things – his name, Adam, and his Always Prayer Shawl, a gift from his grandfather. The shawl remains a part of his life until he gives it to his grandson, Adam.

Review: This book is as timeless as the shawl in the story. As Adam grows, the watercolor illustrations move from black and white to color. This is a book to be cherished.

Jewish Festivals: Stories, Poems, Plays, Songs   Ages: 5+
Author: Saviour Pirotta   Illustrator: Anne Marie Kelly
Austin, Texas: Raintree Steck-Vaughn Publishers, 2001
ISBN: 0-7398-2733-2   Other Categories: Activities, Song, Poetry

Synopsis: This is a collection of stories, poems, plays, and songs about the Jewish festivals. Some of the stories are legend, and some are biblical. There is a Jewish calendar in the Appendix, as well as information about the festivals.

Review: This book includes information about the festivals as well as a glossary of terms. The illustrations are colorful, and the stories are easy to understand.

The Keeping Quilt   Ages 5+
Author and Illustrator: Patricia Polacco
New York: Simon and Schuster Books for Young Readers, 1988
ISBN: 0-671-64963-9   Other Categories: Family

Synopsis: Polacco presents the true story of a quilt that has been passed down through her family. She tells how it has been used as a wedding *huppa* (ritual canopy), a receiving blanket to welcome babies; and for play and comfort. The quilt is made from the only two pieces Anna brings with her from Russia – her dress and her babushka.

Review: This book is similar to *The Always Prayer Shawl* by Sheldon Oberman, where the cloth holds ties to the past. Patricia Polacco's stories are always rich and moving, usually drawing on her own family and community experiences.

Our Eight Nights of Hanukkah   Ages: 8+
Author: Michael J. Rosen   Illustrator: DyAnne DiSalvo-Ryan
New York: Holiday House, 2000
ISBN: 0-8234-1476-0   Other Categories: Sharing

Synopsis: A young boy talks about all the different traditions in his family on the eight nights of Hanukkah. It also describes how they share celebrations with people from other religions.

Review: This book presents an introduction to Hanukkah in a picture book/ story format. It is lovely to see how the characters share with non-Jewish friends.

Uncle Eli's Special-for-Kids, Most Fun Ever, Under-the-Table Passover Haggadah   Ages: 5+
Author: Eliezer Segal   Illustrator: Bonnie Gordon-Lucas
San Francisco: No Starch Press, 1999
ISBN: 1-886411-26-3   Other Categories: Information

Synopsis: A children's Haggadah, which is recited to relive the experiences of slavery and freedom of the Jewish people.

Review: This offers a good way to bring children into the Passover Seder celebrations. The rhymes are fun and the illustrations are bright. There is a glossary of terms.

Festival of Lights: The Story of Hanukkah   Ages: 5+
Author: Maida Silverman   Illustrator: Carolyn S. Ewing
New York: Little Simon, 1987
ISBN: 0-671-65663-5   Other Categories: Retellings

Synopsis: King Antiochus rules Judea, and wants the Jews to worship idols of Greek gods. He desecrates the temple and attacks the Maccabees, who stand up to him and win, in spite of their small numbers. When the temple is rededicated, there is only enough oil for one day, but by a miracle, it lasts for eight days.

Review: The illustrations are not well done, but the story is easy to follow and understand. This book gives the history of the story of Hanukkah, rather than focusing on the celebration of lights, as so many Hanukkah stories do.

Hanukkah:
A Counting Book in English, Hebrew and Yiddish   Ages: 3+
Author and Illustrator: Emily Sper
New York: Scholastic, 2001
ISBN: 0-439-28291-8
Other Categories: Counting, Information, Languages

Synopsis: A counting book with die-cuts of the eight candles of Hanukkah.

Review: This book has a pronunciation key and explanation of the different items in the book. The glossy black pages provide a dramatic background for the bright candles and text.

Golem   Ages: 8+
Author and Illustrator: David Wisniewski
New York: Clarion Books, 1996
ISBN: 0-395-72618-2   Other Categories: Information, Legend

Synopsis: A rabbi creates a golem (a creature made of clay), and brings it to life in order to protect the Jews and guard the ghetto of Prague. The golem turns into a monster and must be destroyed.

Review: The cut-paper illustrations in this book are amazingly intricate. This is a story about fantasy, but it may have too many supernatural and frightening qualities for young children. There is a section which gives historical information.

The Magic Menorah: A Modern Chanukah Tale   Ages: 8+
Author: Jane Breskin Zalben   Illustrator: Donna Diamond
New York: Simon and Schuster Books for Young Readers, 2001
ISBN: 0-689-82606-0   Other Categories: Family, Magic

Synopsis: Stanley uncovers an old menorah in the attic. When he polishes it, a genie named Fischel appears. As expected, Fischel promises to grant Stanley three wishes, and Stanley finds out that fame and fortune are not what he expected. In the end, Stanley learns how blessed he really is in his family.

Review: This is an early chapter book. The story is a bit predictable, but enjoyable nonetheless. The small illustrations fit into the text of the story.

Muslim

Ramadan   Ages: 8+
Author: Suhaib Hamid Ghazi   Illustrator: Omar Rayyan
New York: Holiday House, 1996
ISBN: 0-8234-1275-X   Other Categories: Information

Synopsis: A boy and his family participate in the fasting month of Ramadan. This book presents information in a picture book format.

Review: The watercolor illustrations are beautifully detailed with intricate borders. This is a wonderful blend of fiction and information, making this book accessible for a wide range of readers.

Muslim Child   Ages: 8+
Author: Rukhsana Khan   Illustrator: Patty Gallinger
Toronto: Napoleon Publishing, 1999
ISBN: 0-929141-61-X
Other Categories: Information, Poetry, Activities

Synopsis: This is a collection of poems, stories, glossaries, recipes, crafts, and information about the Muslim religion. There are also some stories from the Holy Qur'an.

Review: This book has excellent information about the Muslim faith and traditions, with stories woven throughout. There is information in the sidebars to help in understanding the stories, as well as a glossary of terms. The pencil sketch illustrations are very good. This makes a wonderful introduction and reference book.

Muslim Festivals: Stories, Poems, Plays, Songs   Ages: 5+
Author: Kerena Marchant   Illustrator: Tina Barber
Austin, Texas: Raintree Steck-Vaughn Publishers, 2001
ISBN: 0-7398-2735-9   Other Categories: Information, Song, Poetry

Synopsis: This is a collection of stories, poems, plays, and songs about the Muslim festivals. There is a hegira, the Muslim calendar, in the Appendix as well as information about the festivals.

Review: This book includes information about the festivals as well as a glossary of terms. The illustrations are colorful, and the stories are easy to understand.

Id-ul-Fitr   Ages: 5+
Author: Kerena Marchant
Brookfield, Connecticut: Millbrook Press, 1996
ISBN: 0-7613-0963-2   Other Categories: Information

Synopsis: An informational book about the celebration of Id-ul-Fitr around the world.

Review: Photographs show the various celebrations and rituals of Id-ul-Fitr, the Muslim celebration that follows the month of fasting during Ramadan. The photographs show how Muslim people in different countries share and celebrate. The book has many interesting facts about Muslim customs and the different requirements of Islam.

Magid Fasts for Ramadan   Ages: 8+
Author: Mary Matthews   Illustrator: E. B. Lewis
New York: Clarion Books, 1996
ISBN: 0-395-66589-2   Other Categories: Information

Synopsis: Magid, an Egyptian boy, wants to fast for Ramadan like everyone else in his family. He does so without telling them, and learns a lesson in obedience.

Review: This is a nice story about the Muslim Ramadan fast and how children are introduced to it, even though it is not required of them. It is not clear from the biography whether the author is Muslim herself, but she has studied Religion and Arabic languages. The watercolors are lovely, but are unrealistic of modern Cairo.

And the Earth Trembled: The Creation of Adam & Eve   **Ages: 5+**
Author: Shulamith Levey Oppenheim   Illustrator: Neil Waldman
San Diego: Harcourt Brace and Company, 1996
ISBN: 0-15-200025-9   Other Categories: Other Faiths

Synopsis: God has created the world, but is lonely and decides to create humans. The angels and the earth protest, knowing that murders, hatred, jealousy, greed, and war will follow. Even Soul is reluctant to enter Adam, but God persists.

Review: This is an Islamic version of the creation of Adam and Eve, based on the work of an Islamic scholar Abou-Djafar al Tabari, who lived in the 9th century. The illustrations are beautiful, painted in an impressionistic style, but portray God as an old man with white hair and a white beard. This goes against the Islamic rule about depicting images of animals and people. The author and the illustrator do not identify themselves as Muslim.

Eid ul-Fitr   **Ages: 5+**
Author: Susheila Stone
Photographs by: Prodeepta Das
London: A & C Black, 1988
ISBN: 0-7136-3054-X   Other Categories: Information

Synopsis: A young English girl named Fozia experiences the joys of Eid ul-Fitr with her family and in her school.

Review: This story is told in the first person. Real photographs of Fozia and her friends and family show how she visits a mosque with her schoolmates and how she celebrates Eid at home. It is wonderful to see a school taking such an interest in these celebrations.

Native Spirituality

The Elders Are Watching   **Ages: 8+**
Author: by David Bouchard   Illustrator: Roy Henry Vickers
Grasshopper Books Pub, 1998
ISBN: 1-55192-110-3
Other Categories: Respect for Creation, Poetry, Wisdom, Environment

Synopsis: Native Elders share their wisdom about people who mistreat the land. This poem is presented in collaboration with the paintings of Roy Henry Vickers.

Review: The rich paintings enhance the beauty of this poem. In spite of the mistreatment of the land, there is a positive message of hope in this book that some slow progress has been made and that continued progress is possible.

ABC's of Our Spiritual Connection   **Ages: 5+**
Author and Illustrator: Kim Soo Goodtrack
Penticton: Theytus Books, 1993/94
ISBN: 0-919441-44-0   Other Categories: Alphabet Books, Information
Inclusive Language

Synopsis: This alphabet book gives explanations for various items and concepts in Native spirituality.

Review: This is a wonderful introduction to Native spirituality and can serve as a resource book. There is a list of items in the illustrations, but the items are not labeled individually. The book describes traditions in different nations.

SkySisters   **Ages: 5+**
Author: Jan Bourdeau Waboose   Illustrator: Brian Deines
Toronto: Kids Can Press, 2000
ISBN: 1-55074-697-9   Other Categories: Family

Synopsis: Two girls explore the nature around their home as they await the SkySpirits dance (the Northern Lights).

Review: Written by a Nishinawbe Ojibway, this book shows a number of Native values, which are exemplified in the two sisters – respect for nature, elders, family, and patience. The illustrations are as hauntingly beautiful as the aurora borealis.

Sikhism

The Sikh Canadians   **Ages: 8+**
Author: Manmohan Singh (Moni) Minhas
Edmonton, Alberta: Reidmore Books, Inc., 1994
ISBN: 1-895073-44-8   Other Categories:

Synopsis: The history, religion, culture, and success of Sikh Canadians is highlighted in this informational book.

Review: The research presented in this book is factual and interesting with a variety of maps, tables, and photographs. There is much information about how Sikhs have adapted to life in Canada and kept their own traditions.

Other

Creation: Read-Aloud Stories from Many Lands   Ages: 8+

Author: Anne Alling   Illustrator: Michael Foreman
Cambridge: Candlewick Press, 1997
ISBN: 1-56402-888-7   Other Categories: Multiculturalism

Synopsis: A collection of 16 creation stories from around the world.

Review: There is a good representation of stories from China, Scandinavia, Sri Lanka, Africa; Greek mythology; and Inuit, Australian Aborigine, and Native American and Canadian cultures. The stories are accompanied by lovely watercolor illustrations.

Whoever You Are   Ages: 5+

Author: Mem Fox
San Diego, CA: Harcourt Brace and Company, 1997
ISBN: 0-15-200787-3   Other Categories: Multiculturalism

Synopsis: This simple book emphasizes the uniqueness and similarities of children around the world.

Review: The message of this book is that there are no essential differences between races and classes that cannot be overcome. The illustrations are bold, but lack the specificity that would identify and distinguish the particular cultures.

Chicken Sunday   Ages: 5+

Author and Illustrator: Patricia Polacco
New York: Philomel, 1992
ISBN: 0-399-22133-6   Other Categories: Friendship, Sharing

Synopsis: Neighborhood children work together to try to help Miss Eula purchase a special hat for Easter. This is a delightful book about sharing each other's gifts and faith traditions.

Review: Patricia Polacco has the unique ability to write books about interfaith relationships without being preachy or didactic. This is likely due to the fact that her stories are based on her own experiences. This is a beautiful and moving story.

13

Informational Texts
People, Places, & Things

At that time the disciples came to Jesus and asked,
"Who is the greatest in the kingdom of heaven?" He called a child, whom he
put among them, and said, "Truly I tell you, unless you change and become
like children, you will never enter the kingdom of heaven. Whoever becomes
humble like this child is the greatest in the kingdom of heaven. Whoever
welcomes one such child in my name welcomes me."

MATTHEW 18:1–5

People

There are many good books written about famous people in the Bible, as well as inspirational leaders throughout the different ages. Jesus, of course, is one obvious subject of biographical information, both biblically based, and legendary information and story. Often, it is the story that is central, such as Noah's Ark, rather than the life of the character. In other stories, such as Jonah, we have insight into who Jonah was as a person, his character flaws, and eventual strength through God.

The biographies of modern heroes often show their work against injustice and adversity. Martin Luther King Jr., Mother Teresa, Mahatma Gandhi are all examples of people who tried to overcome the inequality of people's conditions. Their words and actions are solidly based in the teachings of their faith, yet they were all very real, human beings with faults, doubts, and flaws.

Every faith has leaders who have been examples to the people of that faith. No matter what our beliefs, we can all learn from the character and acts of those leaders. Gandhi had as much to say to Christians as he did to Jains. Like Jesus, his life exemplified self-sacrifice, desire for justice for all peoples, and a deep love for every person, regardless of their place in society. We must not be afraid to move beyond the boundaries of our own faith to find people who can be real-life examples for us.

The stories of the saints can also provide interesting insight into the lives and works of ordinary people who did extraordinary things. Because their stories seem to grow with their legends, the stories of the saints are often a mixture of biography, legend, and supposition. Not every faith recognizes saints as holy people, but we can all learn from people whose lives were lived to help others and point to the love of God.

Places

Some books have been written to look at the important places in the Bible, as well as other holy places around the world. One of the very best is *Sacred Places* by Philemon Sturges. Through magnificent paper sculpture, illustrator Giles Laroche depicts sacred buildings and cities of different faiths throughout the world.

Other books, such as *The Golden City: Jerusalem's 3000 Years*, by Neil Waldman, look at places and their centrality to certain faiths, such as the importance of Jerusalem to the Jewish, Christian, and Muslim peoples of the world. These books can help us understand and see the places we read about in scripture, bringing them to life and creating visual recognition.

Things

Informational books can appeal to some children and not others. Many children will spend hours poring over non-fictional books, but show little interest in stories. For others, the opposite is true. While a balance is optimal, it is not always achievable. It is important that children read and talk about what they are learning, whether it be from fiction or non-fiction.

There are some informational texts written about religious things, such as the Bible itself, maps, artwork, and religious artifacts. Many of these books, such as *Eyewitness Books: Religion*, by Myrtle Langly, have high-quality photographs and illustrations accompanying the text. They are often written in bite-sized pieces so a child can glean information without being overwhelmed by large quantities of text. This type of book is especially good for more reluctant readers, who may like to pick a book up and put it down, often in no particular order, rather than working all the way through a book at once.

We often take for granted the things we use in worship, or the various festivals of the Christian year. Rarely is the significance of these items and celebrations adequately explained to children or newcomers. I sometimes wonder if they have lost some of their meaning, when we use them without question or value. By looking at religious artifacts and symbols, we can find a way to talk about the meaning and history behind them, and hopefully help people understand more about their place in worship.

Ways to Use the Literature

- Take a Bible character and write a biography of that person. You may want to fictionalize the story a bit to add more detail and interest.

- Many women in the Bible do not have names, but have important roles. Learn about the stories of some of these nameless women. Using a baby name book, find a name that has a meaning that suits the character of the woman you are researching.

- Learn about a famous person in history or modern times and write a biography of that person.

- Interview an older person in your congregation and write their biography. Ask that person to bring photographs of when they were younger. You may want to photocopy the pictures or scan them into your computer.

- Write your own autobiography. Illustrate it with photographs and drawings.

- If your church is having a new-members service, invite the new members to submit biographies of themselves to be shared in the bulletin so others can get to know a bit about them. Take pictures of the new members and put them up on a bulletin board along with their biographies so people can recognize them and learn their names.

- Some churches recognize saints, while others do not. Find out what your church believes about saints and the reasons for those beliefs.

- Each saint has a special feast day assigned to him or her. Match your birthday with the saint whose feast day is the same day. You can use *The Treasury of Saints and Martyrs* by Margaret Mulvihill to do this, or check to see if your name is also a saint's name and find out which day is that saint's feast day.

- Many saints died terrible deaths for their faith. What would you be willing to do for your faith? How do you profess your beliefs and show God's love to others? How do others see God's love in you?

- Collect biographies of famous people and compare their stories. What made that person special? What did each of them do? What were they fighting against? What were they fighting for? How did they achieve their goals? What is still left to be done?

- Find a special place in your life and write about it. What makes a place sacred? Why is that place special to you? What makes that place interesting? Does it have an interesting history you could research?

- Write about your church, its worship times, special events, etc., and develop your findings into a brochure you could give to visitors or friends.

- Are there things that are used during worship that you do not understand, like the colors of the seasons of the Christian year, or the candles of the Advent wreath? Make a list of the different symbols used in worship and what they mean.

- In many churches, the worship service itself often has a special structure that is followed. Learn about the structure of your service, what comes where and why. Visit a church that follows a completely different structure, and compare the two types of worship.

Bibliography

Biographies

The Life of Saint Francis   **Ages: 8+**
Author: Rachel Billington   Illustrator: James Mahew
Hodder and Stoughton, 1999
ISBN: 0340714271   Other Categories: Saints

Synopsis: The life of Saint Francis is retold in detail.

Review: The life of Saint Francis of Assisi is retold in story format. The drawings are lovely pastels. This text is more detailed than Brian Wildsmith's book about St. Francis.

Gandhi
Ages: 5+

Author and Illustrator: Demi

New York: Margaret K. McElderry Books, 2001

ISBN: 0-689-84149-3   Other Categories: Other Faiths

Synopsis: A fascinating biography of Mohandas Karamchand Gandhi.

Review: This is an outstanding book! Demi's gorgeous illustrations and text merge to create a wonderful biography of an extraordinary and inspirational man. This book is not to be missed.

The Barefoot Book of Heroic Children
Ages: 8+

Author: Rebecca Hazell   Illustrator: Helen Cann

New York: Barefoot Books, 2000

ISBN: 1-902283-23-6   Other Categories: History

Synopsis: Twelve stories of heroic children from around the world are retold in this collection. The characters range from David to Pocahontas to Anne Frank and Sadako Sasaki.

Review: This is a wonderful collection of stories about boys and girls who find themselves in extraordinary circumstances. The stories are well-written, and the watercolors are beautiful.

The Good Man of Assisi
Ages: 5+

Author: Mary Joslin   Illustrator: Alison Wisenfeld

Nashville: Lion Publishing, 1997

ISBN: 0-8499-5821-0   Other Categories: Saints

Synopsis: Francis sets out to be a knight, but has a dream that tells him to serve God instead.

Review: This is a simple retelling of the life of Saint Francis and includes the prayer of St. Francis of Assisi. The lovely, soft watercolors and bordered illustrations complement the text.

The Story of St. Francis
Ages: 8+

Author: Margaret Mayo   Illustrator: Peter Malone

London: Dolphin, 2000

ISBN: 1-85881-770-6   Other Categories: Saints

Synopsis: A biography of St. Francis of Assisi with a collection of his writings.

Review: This is an in-depth book about St. Francis. The collections of his writings gives insight into his person.

The Treasury of Saints and Martyrs   Ages: 8+
Author: Margaret Mulvihill
New York: Viking, 1999
ISBN: 0-670-88789-7   Other Categories: Saints

Synopsis: Contains 1- or 2-page biographies of saints from the early days, the Roman Empire, the Middle Ages, the Reformation, and modern times.

Review: More than 50 biographies are accompanied by classical paintings of each saint or martyr, with quotations from each. The endpages section has a calendar of saints days. This is a beautifully designed book.

The Holy Twins: Benedict and Scholastica   Ages: 5+
Author: Kathleen Norris   Illustrator: Tomie dePaola
New York: G. P. Putnam's Sons, 2001
ISBN: 0-399-23424-1   Other Categories: Saints

Synopsis: Twins Benedict and Scholastica are sad at being separated when she is sent to a convent and he goes to Rome to be trained as a nobleman. In Rome, Benedict is disturbed by the injustice he sees, and starts a monastery at Monte Cassino. The brother and sister visit yearly until her death.

Review: This endearing story of sibling love is complemented by dePaola's typical naive style.

Brother Wolf of Gubbio: A Legend of Saint Francis   Ages: 5+
Author and Illustrator: Colony Elliott Santangelo
New York: Handprint Books, 2000
ISBN: 1-929766-07-6   Other Categories: Saints, Legends

Synopsis: A wolf strikes fear into the townsfolk of Gubbio. Saint Francis befriends the wolf, understanding that it did not mean harm, but just needed to eat. Saint Francis convinces the townsfolk that the wolf is not really to be feared.

Review: This is a lovely tale. The illustrations are dark, but have beautiful gold decorations – a metaphor for the light and dark in the story. The book, Santangelo's first, is well researched.

The Children's Book of Saints   Ages: 8+
Author: Louis M. Savary S.T.D.   Illustrator: Sheilah Beckett
New York: Regina Press, 1986
ISBN: 0-88271-130-X   Other Categories: Saints

Synopsis: The lives of more than 50 saints are depicted, with a short biography, illustration, prayer, and date of the feast day for each.

Review: This collection talks about the good words of the saints and their often early demises (but without the gory details). Both male and female saints are discussed.

Saint Francis   Ages: 5+
Author and Illustrator: Brian Wildsmith
Grand Rapids, MI: Wm. B. Eerdmans Publishing Co., 1996
ISBN: 0802851231   Other Categories: Saints, History

Synopsis: The life of St. Francis of Assisi is told in the first-person. One day, St. Francis heard the voice of God. From then on, Francis traveled and preached God's word, caring for the poor and ill.

Review: This is a simple, beautiful book about the life of a man who turned his back on wealth and lived a life devoted to love and respect for all of God's creation. Wildsmith's exquisite watercolors are enhanced with gold borders.

Celebrations and Festivals

Seasons to Celebrate:
God's Children Celebrate the Church Year   Ages: 5+
Author: Mary E. F. Albing
Minneapolis: Augsburg Fortress, 1994
ISBN: 0-8066-2722-0   Other Categories: Liturgy, Activities

Synopsis: There is a detailed calendar of the church year. Each season has a description, a symbol for a craft, a sign in American Sign Language, songs, activities, worship ideas, and ideas for learning about the church year in the home.

Review: This is a good resource for teaching the church year to children and adults who often take the church year for granted. The ideas are supported with background information and detailed instructions.

Come Worship with Me:
A Journey through the Church Year   Ages: 5+
Author: Ruth Boling Illustrator: Tracey Dahle Carrier
Louisville, Kentucky: Geneva Press, 2001
ISBN: 0-664-50045-5   Other Categories: Church Year, Beliefs

Synopsis: The invitation to worship comes from a young mouse who leads the reader through the Christian year and its symbols.

Review: This excellent resource should be a part of every Sunday school, whether they follow the Christian year or not. Each entry has an explanation of the worship, the reason for the celebration, and the symbols which belong to that season.

A Calendar of Festivals   Ages: 8+
Author: Cherry Gilchrist   Illustrator: Helen Cann
Barefoot Books, 2000
ISBN: 1841482447   Other Categories: Multiculturalism

Synopsis: Eight festivals from different countries (Russia, China, Japan, Ireland, etc.) and faith traditions are told in story and information.

Review: Each tale is prefaced by background information with a history of each festival. The stories are succinct, with bright, bold illustrations.

Celebrations of Light:
A Year of Holidays around the World   Ages: 8+
Author: Nancy Luenn   Illustrator: Mark Bender
New York: Atheneum Books for Young Readers, 1998
ISBN: 0-689-31986-X   Other Categories: Other Faiths, Multiculturalism

Synopsis: Short introductions to light festivals in different countries and faiths.

Review: This presents a very brief treatment of different festivals. The bold illustrations are airbrushed. This does not contain an exhaustive list of festivals, but is an enjoyable way to see that there are light festivals in almost every faith and culture.

Seasons of Celebrations:
Prayers, Plays and Projects for the Church Year   Ages: 3+
Author: Patricia Mathson
Notre Dame, Indiana: Ave Maria Press, 1995
ISBN: 0-8793-566-1   Other Categories: Liturgy

Synopsis: A large collection of activities for all the seasons of the church year.

Review: This is a very good resource for those churches that follow the church year. Some of the activities are extremely simple, while others are more intricate for older children. There are explanations of the different liturgical seasons.

Christian Festivals: Stories, Poems, Plays, Songs   **Ages: 5+**
Author: Saviour Pirotta   Illustrator: Helen Cann
Austin, Texas: Raintree Steck-Vaughn Publishers, 2001
ISBN: 0-7398-2733-2   Other Categories: Songs, Poetry, Activities

Synopsis: This is a collection of stories, poems, plays, and songs about the Christian festivals. Some of the stories are legend, and some are biblical.

Review: This book includes information about the festivals as well as a glossary of terms. The illustrations are colorful, and the stories are easy to understand.

How I Celebrate:
A Young Person's Guide to the Festivals of the World Ages: 5+
Author: Pam Robson
Oxford: Transedition Limited, 2001
ISBN: 1-898250-76-6   Other Categories: Celebrations, Other Faiths

Synopsis: Seven fictional children from different faiths tell their stories, which are surrounded by photos and information about different religions.

Review: This combines fiction and non-fiction. There is more information about the celebrations – including birth celebrations, weddings, special days, national days, religious celebrations – but little explanation of how each festival came to be. There is a glossary and incomplete charts of saints' days, etc.

Places

Exploring Ancient Cities of the Bible   **Ages: 8+**
Authors and Illustrators: Michael and Caroline Carroll
Colorado Springs: Faith Kids, 2001
ISBN: 0-78143-695-8   Other Categories: History, Archeology

Synopsis: A look at archeology with a biblical view. The authors are careful to distinguish between faith and the science of archaeology.

Review: This informational book relates biblical places to archeological discoveries. There are "fun facts" and sidebars with extra information.

The Children's Illustrated Encyclopedia of Heaven   **Ages: 8+**
Author: Anita Ganeri
Boston: Element Children's Books, 1999
ISBN: 1-90261812-2   Other Categories: Information, Death, New Life
Inclusive Language

Synopsis: Ganeri states in her introduction that this book "tries to make you think – about life and death, and the hope of Heaven." She looks at a variety of beliefs about heaven and hell from different faiths and traditions.

Review: This excellent book brings together many myths, stories, traditions, and beliefs about heaven, the afterlife, reincarnation, hell, angels, etc. from different faiths. The book includes stories, quotations from famous and ordinary people, a glossary, and many photographs and illustrations.

The Golden City: Jerusalem's 3000 Years   Ages: 8+
Author and Illustrator: Neil Waldman
Honesdale, PA: Boyd's Mills Press, 1995
ISBN: 1-56397-918-7   Other Categories: Other Faiths

Synopsis: This book shows the history of Jerusalem from the time of David to the present.

Review: Jewish, Christian, and Muslim history is presented in this book. Places of significance and important historical events are explained and illustrated.

Sacred Places   Ages: 5+
Author: Philemon Sturges   Illustrator: Giles Laroche
New York: G. P. Putnam, 2000
ISBN: 0-399-23317-2   Other Categories: Other Faiths

Synopsis: Illustrations and information of sacred places from different countries and religions around the world are presented.

Review: This is a fabulous book mainly because of the paper relief illustrations showing the intricate detail of each building. A map of all the different places shows that they are mainly from the northern hemisphere, but represent Hindu, Buddhist, Jewish, Christian, and Muslim faiths.

Religions

What I Believe: Kids Talk about Faith   Ages: 8+
Author: Debbie Holsclaw Birdseye   Contributor: Tom Birdseye
Photographer: Robert Crum
New York: Holiday House, 1996
ISBN: 0-8234-1268-7
Other Categories: Children's Writings, Beliefs, Other Faiths
Inclusive Language

Synopsis: Six children talk about their faith. The religions represented are Hinduism, Buddhism, Judaism, Christianity, Islam, and Native American Spirituality.

Review: Real children speak in an open, down-to-earth manner about their faith. There are photographs of the children in their faith communities as well as doing everyday things at home. This provides a good introduction to different faiths as they are lived out, rather than factual information out of context.

Religions Explained: A Beginner's Guide to World Faiths Ages: 8+
Author: Anita Ganeri   Consultant: Marcus Braybrooke
New York: Henry Holt and Company, 1997
ISBN: 0-8050-4874-X   Other Categories: Other Faiths, Multiculturalism

Synopsis: In this informational book about different religions, Ganeri looks at ancient religions, people of the book (Jews, Christians, and Muslims), religions of India, Chinese and Japanese religions, Spirit religions, and new religions.

Review: Symbols, illustrations, and photographs are used to provide this overview of world religions. The information covers the beliefs and practices of the religions, but does not go into much detail about their differences.

Oxford Children's A–Z of World Religions   Ages: 8+
Author: Anita Ganeri
Oxford: Oxford University Press, 1999
ISBN: 0199104670   Other Categories: Multiculturalism, Other Faiths

Synopsis: Photos, illustrations, and definitions help explain the important rituals, artifacts, and places that make up the major religions of the world.

Review: This is a good reference book, with short, succinct definitions. This would not be adequate for a research project on any particular religion, but it is a good starting point to look at other religions.

Eyewitness Books: Religion   Ages: 8+
Author: Myrtle Langly
Toronto: Stoddart, 1996
ISBN: 0-7737-2946-1   Other Categories: Multiculturalism, Other Faiths

Synopsis: Information and photographs about a variety of religions and traditions are presented in a factual manner.

Review: The series of Eyewitness Books contains high-quality information and photographs on a wide variety of topics. This makes an excellent book for those interested in the historical backgrounds of religions and how those religions are practiced today.

The Story of Religion   Ages: 8+
Author: Betsy Maestro   Illustrator: Biulio Maestro
New York: Mulberry Books, 1996
ISBN: 0-395-62364-2   Other Categories: Information, Other Faiths

Synopsis: An eclectic collection of information about the world's major religions.

Review: This book touches on aspects of different religions, but does not go into depth, nor does it organize the information around topics or themes.

World Religions: Christianity   Ages: 8+
Author: Katherine Prior
New York: Franklin Watts, 1999
ISBN: 0-7496-3377-8   Other Categories: Art, Christian Traditions

Synopsis: This book has basic information on Christianity, along with photos, maps, illustrations, and classical paintings.

Review: While this book has an overview of information, there is much generalization about Christianity, rather than showing a variety of ways in which the faith is expressed. The photos show many cultures, but not cultural variation on traditions. One photo shows two women Anglican bishops, but does not go into the controversy about the ordination of women. There is a glossary and a list of important dates.

Other Informational Books

I Dream of Peace   Ages: 10+
Images of War by the Children of Former Yugoslavia
Authors: Children of the Former Yugoslavia
Preface by Maurice Sendak   Illustrators: The Children
New York: HarperCollins, 1994
ISBN: 0-06-251128-9
Other Categories: War, Peace, Children's Writings

Synopsis: This is a collection of illustrations and quotations by children of the former Yugoslavia. There are four chapters – Cruel war, The day they killed my house, My nightmare, and When I close my eyes I dream of peace.

Review: Most of the book is focused on war rather than peace. The children are very frank in their illustrations and quotations. This is a moving book, but one which should be read with an adult.

A Child's Book of Angels   Ages: 8+
Author: Joanne Crosse   Illustrator: Olwyn Whelan
Barefoot Books, 2000
ISBN: 1841480827   Other Categories: Angels

Synopsis: A boy's guardian angel explains about the various types of angels. This book is a mixture of story, history, and information about angels.

Review: The illustrations show angels of different colors. The book is a good mixture of poetry, prose and scripture about angels, including Angels of the Zodiac (the circle of life), the Elements of Life, Planetary Angels, and the Angelic Hierarchy.

Christianity: The Way of Goodness and Mercy   Ages: 12+
– Religions of the World Series
VIDEO   28 Minutes
Delphi Productions, United Learning, Inc., 1994

Synopsis: This live-action video introduces the basic tenets of the Christian faith, and shows how the rituals of Christianity are observed in different parts of the Christian church.

Review: Starting with the Sermon on the Mount, this video talks about the various beliefs of the Christian faith and also discusses the differences of beliefs within the Christian faith. This video presents the information in a factual manner, rather than an evangelical one. This is an excellent documentary of the Christian faith. The video comes with a Study Guide.

Sun, Moon and Stars   Ages: 8+
Author: Mary Hoffman   Illustrator: Jane Ray
New York: Dutton Children's Books, 1998
ISBN: 0-525-46004-7
Other Categories: Other Faiths, Multiculturalism, Legends

Synopsis: This is a collection of Norse, Egyptian, First Nations, Latvian, Korean, Chinese, Mayan, Japanese, Greek, Afro-Caribbean, English, Hindu, Australian and Japanese myths, legends, and folk tales. Topics include the sky, the sun, the moon, and the stars.

Review: The myths, legends, and folk tales are short retellings (one to two pages each) taken from a variety of sources, which are listed at the back of the book. Jane Ray's paintings are, as always, richly detailed and beautiful, trying to convey the spirit of their cultural source.

If You'd Been There in Bible Times   **Ages: 8+**
Author: Stephanie Jeffs   Illustrator: Jacqui Thomas
Nashville: Abingdon Press, 2000
ISBN: 0-687-01507-3   Other Categories: Retellings

Synopsis: Very short retellings with explanations and biblical references are combined with information about life in biblical times from Creation to the resurrection of Jesus.

Review: This book talks about the lifestyles, customs, and rituals of biblical times, and discusses what certain items referred to in the Bible may have looked like.

Cathedral: The Story of Its Construction   **Ages: 8+**
Author and Illustrator: David Macaulay
New York: Scholastic, 1973
ISBN: 0-590-95511-1   Other Categories: Architecture, Art

Awards: Caldecott Honor Book, Jugendbuchpreis (Germany), New York Times Best Illustrated Book of the Year, ALA Notable Book.

Synopsis: Workers in 13th-century France build a Gothic cathedral. People from many different trades contribute to this enormous project.

Review: This is a fictional story, but it is really an amazing informational book about the architecture of cathedrals and the work that went into their building. Macaulay's line drawings are detailed and accurate. Although it was written more than 25 years ago, this book withstands the test of time.

Crafts for Christian Values   **Ages: 5+**
Author: Kathy Ross   Illustrator: Sharon Lane Holm
Brookfield, Conn: Millbrook Press, 2000
ISBN: 0-7613-1284-6   Other Categories: Activities

Synopsis: Each of the 28 crafts has a moral, illustrated instructions, and a reference to a Bible verse about each value.

Review: There is a materials list and instructions/illustrations for each craft. These simple crafts can be easily made with everyday materials.

For Every Child: Ages: 5+
The UN Convention on the Rights of the Child –
The Rights of the Child in Words and Pictures
Foreword by Archbishop Desmond Tutu
Phyllis Fogelman Books, 2001
ISBN: 0-09-176815-2   Other Categories: Art, Human Rights

Synopsis: Fourteen of the 54 principles that make up the UN Convention on the Rights of the Child are interpreted by well-known children's illustrators.

Review: All the royalties from this book go to Unicef. A wide variety of illustrative techniques are used to interpret the principles. There is information about each illustrator and the media they use. The rights featured in the book are listed in detail.

Let's Explore inside the Bible   Ages: 5+
Author: Fiona Walton
Illustrators: Tony Morris and Linda Kelsey
London: Augsburg, 1994
ISBN: 0-8066-2745-X

Synopsis: This is a collection of retellings of Old and New Testament stories together with activities, recipes, and quizzes.
Review: The activities are simple, using everyday items. This is a great way to connect activities and Bible stories.

The Big Book of Bible People   Ages: 5+
Author: Mark Water   Illustrator: Graham Round
Nashville: Thomas Nelson, 1996
ISBN: 0-7852-7893-1   Other Categories: Biography, Information

Synopsis: An alphabetical listing of 30 biblical figures (with sublists of related characters), highlighting their stories.

Review: Each entry has a number of short synopses about significant events in the life of the character. Unfortunately, the cartoon character illustrations depict white people.

Title Index

Author Index

Illustrator Index